ALMS: A Budget Based Library Management System

by BETTY JO MITCHELL
Associate Director
California State University
Library, Northridge

JAI PRESS INC.

Greenwich, Connecticut *London, England*

Foundations in
LIBRARY AND INFORMATION SCIENCE

A Series of Monographs, Texts and Treatises

Series Editor: **Robert D. Stueart**
Dean Graduate School of Library and Information Science
Simmons College, Boston

Volume 1. **THE MEXICAN AMERICAN: A Critical Guide to Research Aids**
Barbara J. Robinson, *University of California Library, Riverside and J.* Cordell Robinson, California State College, San Bernardino

Volume 2. **A PRACTICAL APPROACH TO SERIALS CATALOGING**
Lynn S. Smith, *University of California Library, Riverside*

Volume 3. **THE MICROFORM REVOLUTION IN LIBRARIES**
Michael R. Gabriel, *Mankato State University Library and* Dorothy P. Ladd, *Boston University Libraries.*

Volume 4. **CHINA IN BOOKS: A Basic Bibliography in Western Language**
Norman E. Tanis, David L. Perkins and Justine Pinto, *California State University Library, Northridge*

Volume 5. **BUDGETARY CONTROL IN ACADEMIC LIBRARIES**
Murray S. Martin, *Pennsylvania State University Libraries*

Volume 6. **COST ANALYSIS OF LIBRARY FUNCTIONS: A Total System Approach**
Betty Jo Mitchell, Norman E. Tanis and Jack Jaffe, *California State University Library, Northridge*

Volume 7. **A GUIDE TO LIBRARY ACADEMIC INSTRUCTION**
Hannelore B. Rader, *Eastern Michigan University Library*

Volume 8. **MANAGEMENT OF A PUBLIC LIBRARY**
Harold R. Jenkins, *Kansas City Public Library*

Volume 9. **DEVELOPMENT AND ORGANIZATION OF A HEALTH SCIENCE LIBRARY**
Katherine Cveljo, *School of Library Science, North Texas State University*

Volume 10. **COLLECTION DEVELOPMENT IN LIBRARIES: A Treatise**
Edited by Robert D. Stueart, *Graduate School of Library and Information Science, Simmons College and* George B. Miller, Jr., *University of New Mexico*

Volume 11. **INTRODUCTION TO SERIALS MANAGEMENT**
Marcia Tuttle, *University of North Carolina Library, Chapel Hill*

Volume 12. **DEVELOPING COLLECTIONS OF U.S. GOVERNMENT PUBLICATIONS**
Peter Hernon, *Graduate School of Library and Information Science, Simmons College and* Gary Purcell, *University of Tennessee Library*

Volume 13. **LIBRARY MANAGEMENT WITHOUT BIAS**
Ching-Chih Chen, *Graduate School of Library and Information Science, Simmons College*

Volume 14. **ISSUES IN PERSONNEL MANAGEMENT IN ACADEMIC LIBRARIES**
Murray S. Martin, *Pennsylvania State University Libraries*

Volume 15. **INFORMATION NEEDS OF THE 80's: Libraries and Information Services Role in "Bringing Information to People"** *Edited by* Robert D. Stueart, *Graduate School of Library and Information Science, Simmons College*

Volume 16. **ALMS: A Budget Based Library Management System**
Betty Jo Mitchell, *California State University Library, Northridge*

Volume 17. **OPTIONS FOR THE 80's**
Proceeding of the Second National Conference of the Association of College and Research Libraries
Edited by Michael D. Kathman, *College of St. Benedict and St. Johns University and* Virgil F. Massman, *James J. Hill Reference Library*

ALMS: A Budget Based Library Management System

FOUNDATIONS IN LIBRARY AND INFORMATION SCIENCE, VOLUME 16

Editor: Robert D. Stueart, *Dean, Graduate School of Library and Information Science, Simmons College*

Library of Congress Cataloging in Publication Data

Mitchell, Betty Jo.
ALMS, a budget based library management system.

(Foundations in library and information science;
v. 16)
Bibliography: p.
Includes index.
1. ALMS (Library management system) 2. California
State University, Northridge. Libraries. I. Title.
II. Title: A.L.M.S., a budget based library management
system. III. Series.
Z678.M52 1983 025.1 82-81208
ISBN 0-89232-246-2

36 Sherwood Place
Greenwich, Connecticut 06836

JAI PRESS INC.
3 Henrietta Street
London WC2E 8LU
England

ISBN NUMBER: 0-89232-246-2
Library of Congress Catalog Card Number: 82-81208
Manufactured in the United States of America

CONTENTS

List of Examples

Chapter 2

Chapter 3

Chapter 4

Chapter 5

List of Tables

Appendix 3

Foreword

In 1980, Charles R. McClure stated:

> Of late, Library managers have fallen on hard times. Library staffs demand more autonomy and benefits; patrons ask for improved or increased kinds of services; governing bodies require justification for expenditures and accountability for actions; and various forms of governmental subsidies are substantially reduced. In short, the needs and requirements of various constituencies are surpassing the responses of library managers.[1]

Although oft remaining unsaid, this statement describes a situation that is recognized by most library managers.

B. J. Mitchell has been grappling with this phenomenon for many years, as have many of us at California State University—Northridge. While we cannot match the cloistered atmosphere of a library school or the leisure for study and research afforded by grants and fellowships, Northridge nevertheless has produced the stimulus required for several members of the library faculty and staff to conduct research and write. This book by B. J. Mitchell is just such an effort. It answers the problems posed by McClure and develops ingenious examples of how library administrators can understand operations and share data with librarians and staff. Her volume even answers McClure's second assertion:

> The most frequent managerial responses to these and other demands have been input or resource oriented—more money, extra staff, better equipment, larger facilities, or obtaining a larger slice of the federal pie. In the current environment the "more is better" mentality will no longer be accepted or supported to improve the performance of our libraries. The focus now is on organizing and managing our extensive information and physical resources to meet society's growing and changing information needs. The dominant concept for library and information professionals as we enter the next hundred years is that of management.

Mitchell explains her scheme of Functional Cost Analysis and adds important insights which must be joined to quantitative data—professional judgments about levels of library service. Academia compares FTEs to "body counts," deplores discussion of "cost effectiveness," and states that management techniques cannot be applied to the university which is, after all, essentially a European, medieval institution. They assert that no one knows how to measure the right elements, or that those who attempt such measurement employ erroneous techniques. All of the same points have been made with reference to the university library, or indeed, all libraries. Mitchell and some of us at Northridge disagree. Measurement *is* possible, data about library operations *can* be collected, and outputs *can* be described in quantitative terms.

This volume describes a system of data collection, and how that quantitative data, coupled with professional judgment, may be utilized in the various facets of library management—budget, personnel, and goal setting. How well the book accomplishes this task is left to the reader's discretion. The writer of this foreword has been too closely associated with the techniques described to make objective claims, but through practical experience with these procedures, he can affirm their serviceability during the "hard times" that library managers have fallen upon. This volume provides the best system of data collection that I have encountered for gaining an understanding of costs for library resource management. The concepts and procedures form the basis upon which libraries must build to survive and prosper.

Having said all that, I must join the author in pointing out that not all aspects of these programs were an unqualified success. We did encounter resistance on the part of library staff, pressures from unions and magnificent and unqualified indifference from the administration of the university. People screamed bloody murder, shouted that we had not validated our instruments, pleaded for an understanding of their unique contribution, and groaned when the Chancellor's Office of our system adopted the study, modified it slightly, and applied it to the whole system of libraries—nineteen libraries, as a matter of fact. Further, the Chancellor's Office has planned a second, lengthy study in 1984 using the techniques explained in this book. So. . . read on and see what Mitchell has done.

Norman E. Tanis
Director of University Libraries

NOTE

1. Charles R. McClure (1980), "Library Managers: Can They Manage? Will They Lead?" *Library Journal* 105(20): 2388.

Acknowledgments

The author gratefully thanks Gayle Goldberg for her special editorial assistance, and all the librarians and staff at California State University—Northridge who provided assistance and advice.

Chapter 1

Introduction

Today's library is a complex system of information distribution, far from the timeworn image of the one-room building with a single librarian, a system where individuals perform specific, interrelated tasks designed to provide the most efficient service possible for library patrons. The efficient integration and management of these tasks is the responsibility of the library's administrative team, who must respond to service needs as defined by (1) the user community, (2) the librarians, and (3) the funding agency (or agencies) involved. These needs may conflict with each other, although all may be valid. The administrator, attempting to respond to all three, is faced with the delicate task of balancing user needs, the librarians' conceptions of user needs, and the financial limitations set by the funding agency.

There are three spheres of influence which appear to be characteristic of most, if not all, human service organizations. These have been defined as the Policy Domain, the Management Domain, and the Service Domain.[1] Each operates on the basis of different and sometimes conflicting governing principles. The Policy Domain is occupied by those responsible for establishing governing policies who are usually elected or appointed representatives of the community which provides financial support. Those within the Management Domain are charged by the policy makers with the responsibility for assuring that their policies are applied, while those in the Service Domain are expected to translate those policies into the satisfaction of client needs. It all appears to be very logical and orderly until the working realities are examined. The Policy Domain operates democratically, accepting the wishes of the community as valid and binding. The Service Domain, made up of well-trained professionals who see themselves as capable of self-governance and who believe they are best prepared to determine the needs of their clients, operates on the basis of individual professional judgment. The Management Domain, expected by the Policy Domain (which is made up primarily of individuals with a business/ industry orientation) to operate on the model of business and industrial management, must accept cost efficiency and effectiveness as measures of success, while at the same time responding to the expectations of the Service Domain that professional judgment and expertise will provide the primary input for decision making. Fortunately, many librarians are beginning to accept accountability as a requirement of the Policy Domain and cost efficiency as a necessary component of accountability. This book attempts to recognize the needs of all three domains and is directed toward cost efficiency and accountability for the benefit of the Policy Domain and collegial decision making for the benefit of the Service Domain.

Recent literature of the profession is filled with statements of the need for accountability, the need for managers to manage. Some typical examples follow:

> There is a misapprehension on the part of some librarians, although admittedly fewer these days, that cost accounting has no application to library administration. All organizations that receive and expend money are governed by fundamental accounting laws. The fact that some of those organizations may be profit-seeking while others are intentionally philanthropic is quite unimportant. While the fact that a library does not operate for profit may affect the forms of its bookkeeping, it does not affect the fundamental principles. Just as every business has, so every library has assets and liabilities, operating receipts and expenditures, labor costs and overhead costs, depreciation losses, and in interest on investment burden.[2]

> It is undoubtedly true that interest in management techniques has quickened in the library world in the past few years. Without attempting to distinguish between those developments which have some chance for success (that is, to result in increased and improved services), one can readily refer to the flurry of articles about budgeting techniques (mostly about the very most complex and therefore least likely to be applied), and the interest of the ARL expressed through its Management Review and Analysis Program. The pressures of diminishing resources, one might assume, will lead to even greater interest, especially when accompanied by gradually increasing "professionalization" of local government and increasing involvement of state governments in all levels of education. Surely, in self-protection, librarians will want increasingly to turn more mature management techniques than they have traditionally used.[3]

> In the current environment the "more is better" mentality will no longer be accepted or supported to improve the performance of our libraries. The focus now is on organizing and managing our extensive information and physical resources to meet society's growing and changing information needs. The dominant concept for library and information professionals as we enter the next hundred years is that of management.[4]

But what type of management system is available to the library administrator, to any administrator for that matter, who deals in an output of services rather than saleable units, and with organizations such as those in libraries in which the Service Domain dominates daily decision making? Such a system must be able to respond to management's needs to:

1. judge the quality of services to users;
2. set meaningful, service-oriented goals for the future;
3. utilize personnel to the best of their capabilities; and
4. defend the present budget or justify additional funds.

ALMS (A Library Management System), a system based upon the library budget and designed to satisfy the above needs, provides a base for administrative decisions. The system recognizes and addresses the accountability requirements of the Policy Domain while at the same time utilizing the professional expertise of the Service Domain. ALMS includes (1) an analysis of the use of personnel hours provided by the current budget; (2) an analysis of the quality of service currently provided with those personnel hours; and (3) the use of those analyses as bases for the preparation and justification of personnel and operating expense budgets, the assignment and reassignment of personnel, and the establishment of service-based goals and objectives. Although this system was designed for use in an academic library, I believe that ALMS is adaptable to and valid in any type of nonprofit organization which must measure its service to clients in something other than profit dollars. Every nonprofit organization must be concerned with profits, but profits take the form of more and better service to the clients/patrons, rather than dividend checks to stockholders as in the case of business and industry. Taking the view that improved service is in fact an increase in profit to the institution allows us to view the pursuit of increased profits in a positive way and the use of administrative efficiency/effectiveness tools from the private sector as necessary and desirable for the improvement of service in the public sector.

It is my firm conviction that far too much of the librarian's time, both the administrative librarian and the nonadministrative librarian, is devoted to attempting to make necessary operational decisions without adequate data. In order for such operational decisions to assume their proper status as low-level "background noise" rather than as a librarian's *raison d'être*, management systems must be developed which will produce a steady stream of operational data, providing bases for both an historical perspective and forecasting. These data must become routine management tools, as routine as book fund accounting reports. A decision regarding the purchase of an expensive book without benefit of accounting records indicating the expenditures for the year and the balance, and without an overall collection strategy (or plan for library growth), would be viewed as fiscally irresponsible. Yet, literally millions of dollars in personnel are allocated without the knowledge of the total cost of the service provided or a clear understanding of its level of adequacy. Unlike the book budgeting process, we do not know the cost of each individual service, nor do we have a long-range strategy as to the services and the level of those services to be provided. Management data for personnel in a nonprofit organization should be at least equivalent to the data collected for other operating expenses. Only after this kind of management data is routinely produced will we be able to devote more time and attention to the important issues and to reduce the necessity for crisis management. Once our services have been analyzed for quality and quantity, and once the amount and type of personnel necessary to produce a specified quantity and quality of service have been identified, both budget defense and goal setting become simplified.

The purpose of this book is to outline a methodology for (1) analyzing the personnel hours utilized in a given library, relative to each specific service provided; (2) analyzing the quality of the service provided; and (3) relating the analysis of personnel hours expended and the quality of service provided to (a) the defense and justification of future personnel and operating expenses budgets, (b) the internal allocation of personnel resources and (c) the development of a formal planning process for the library.

ALMS is in reality a simplified version of a Planning-Programming-Budgeting System (PPBS)[5] for libraries, which can be used as the basis for a sophisticated PPBS, complete with mathematical models and the techniques of applied economics. Or, ALMS can be utilized as a complete, relatively uncomplicated system which can be improved upon and fine-tuned with experience. The importance of the PPBS approach lies not in its degree of sophistication of method, but rather in its linking of the planning and budgeting processes. The following definition of PPBS by James Cutt most nearly approximates my own view:

> The term PPBS is taken to refer to the collection of concepts and techniques which aids the educational planner in evaluating the present allocation of resources in education, and in choosing among alternative ways of allocating these resources in the future. The fundamental premise of PPBS is that policy and budgets are inseparable and that the relationship between the structure and implementation of budgets and the determination and achievement of policy objectives should be made explicit. The concepts and techniques which constitute PPBS effect a union between overall planning and the translation of planning objectives into programs, on the one hand, and budget procedures on the other, the union intended to obviate the

detachment which budgetary authorities traditionally have from content of plans and programs, and planners have from the constraints imposed by scarce resources.[6]

The concepts of PPBS were first developed at Rand Corporation by Charles J. Hitch, former president of the University of California, who in 1961, at the request of the Kennedy Administration, initiated it into the U.S. Department of Defense.[7] It was so successful that President Johnson ordered its adoption by all federal agencies in 1965. Only six years later, the Office of Management and Budget acknowledged the failure of PPBS through the distribution of a memorandum stating that federal agencies no longer would be required to submit multiyear programs and financing plans.[8]

Reasons for the failure are not clear, but probably relate to the sheer size of the program and the possible lack of sufficient planning in advance of its adoption. Congresswoman Patricia Schroeder has remarked that "Past productivity efforts have produced, in addition to reams of consultant's reports, a lifetime supply of excuses by federal managers of why productivity efforts cannot work."[9] She believes the excuses can be grouped into six basic ones:[10]

Excuse No. 1. "We don't have the resources to do it."
Excuse No. 2. "You can't measure productivity. Sure you can measure productivity of a factory worker making widgets, but you can't for research and development. Besides, for jobs without tangible outputs, measuring productivity is a matter of subjectivity. Even if you can measure efficiency, you surely can't measure effectiveness."
Excuse No. 3. "We're already doing it."
Excuse No. 4. "There's no incentive to increase productivity."
Excuse No. 5. "You can't hold an employee accountable for things beyond his or her control".
Excuse No. 6. "There are all sorts of disincentives to measuring productivity, such as loss of budget and loss of status for increasing efficiency."

She concludes that the real reason for the lack of success in improving productivity at the federal level is the absence of "sustained and strong interest from the top." This may also speak to the rise and fall of PPBS in the literature of library science. Articles began appearing in 1968 as a result of the Institute on PPBS for Libraries at Wayne State University. Interest peaked in 1971 and 1972, with more than a dozen offerings appearing in the literature, and began a steady decline to zero in 1979. In both cases, libraries and the federal bureaucracy, PPBS began with a bang and ended with a whimper. However, in spite of such failure, the basic intent of PPBS remains sound. Robert Goldberg, following a discussion of the federal failure in his *A Systems Approach to Library Program Development*, concluded:

> My own view of PPBS is that it is the single most important planning approach embracing all aspects of programming and evaluation that has yet been conceptualized and tried. It is a successful adaptation of the systems approach, sound in inception and certain to improve good planning, implementation, and evaluation if carefully and painstakingly pursued. But it is fraught with many problems as, indeed, is any kind of open system approach. For the approach declares that there are nonfinite variables and these cannot be absolutely controlled.[11]

To say that implementation of any form of PPBS in libraries is fraught with problems is an understatement. Perhaps the two major problems of implementing such a program are the difficulty of collecting sufficient data to determine the current utilization of human resources, and the ability to develop a management team that is committed to and supportive of the program. Richard Hall puts it this way:

> To function properly a program budget system requires a substantial quantity of refined input data. This forces the management team to overcome a tendency to plan superficially and avoid decisions which may be difficult, but not impossible, to quantify. It forces management to plan on a comprehensive basis, including all phases of the operation, because programs usually transcend jurisdictional and organizational lines. In short, program budgeting requires the involvement of the total management organization in the planning process.[12]

The above statement characterizes the basic difficulties of this type of program. They are not insurmountable problems, but tedious and frustrating. If even one key member of the management team consistently declares that "it won't work," "it costs too much," "my staff is too busy," or "no one 'up there' cares about service—just statistics," then your program, however well-intentioned or badly needed, will encounter many problems, at best. There are those who sincerely believe that extensive planning of this nature is a waste of time; that crisis management is less costly and equally as effective in the long run. At the beginning of this chapter, three categories of people who define library service needs were identified: (1) the user community, (2) the librarians, and (3) the funding agency (or agencies) involved. The user community will probably never be aware of the management style used, will not be able to judge whether the budget is being effectively applied to service needs. The librarians will likely find themselves divided in philosophy, some opting for crisis management and some preferring careful planning. It is the third category, the funding agency, that will always choose analysis and planning whenever there is a choice. The funding agents are the people who must weigh the services of the library against the services provided by all the organizations under their jurisdiction. It is clear that an understanding of both the value and cost of services assists in the prioritization of budget allocations.

Although I suspect the absence of teamwork to be one of the root causes of the failure of the PPBS approach to management, I must assume that management teams do exist who want more than an intuitive approach to organizational planning. For those teams, ALMS can represent a beginning.

It will require experience and trial and error to develop, refine, and fine-tune the system to a specific organization, but ALMS contains the basic framework necessary to develop a management system to provide input for administrative decisions. Such fine-tuning of the data-gathering portion of ALMS has already begun through the use of the California State University, Northridge (CSUN) cost analysis program[13] by the California State University and Colleges (CSUC) system. A description of the adaptation of the CSUN program for statewide application can be found in Appendix 4. Data collected in that study has been utilized in the development of a staffing formula (see Appendix 3) while the service analysis portion remains in its initial stages of development.

It should be noted that CSUC library budgets are formula-driven and while the ultimate goal is to make the formulas more representative of actual service needs, the current focus of ALMS is maximum utilization of what the formulas currently produce. Its use as an open budget exercise should prove to be even more effective than in the allocation of a formula-driven budget. In the chapters that follow, the elements of the ALMS process will be described in more detail.

NOTES AND REFERENCES

1. James M. Kouzes and Paul R. Mico (1979), "Domain Theory: An Introduction to Organizational Behavior in Human Service Organizations," *The Journal of Applied Behavioral Science* 15: 449-469.
2. Eleanor Frances Brown (1979), *Cutting Library Costs: Increasing Productivity and Raising Revenues*. Metuchen, N.J.: Scarecrow, p. 15.
3. Robert L. Goldberg (1976), *A Systems Approach to Library Program Development*. Metuchen, N.J.: Scarecrow, p. viii.
4. Charles R. McClure (1980), "Library Managers: Can They Manage? Will They Lead?" *Library Journal* 105(20): 2388.
5. A discussion of the more scientific approach to PPBS can be found in Willard Fazar (1969), "Program Planning and Budgeting Theory: Improved Library Effectiveness by Use of the Planning-Programming Budgeting System," *Special Libraries* 60: 423-433.

I consider ALMS to be a simplified PPBS because it utilizes professional judgment in the determination of planning objectives rather than requiring detailed analysis of all viable alternatives. It is assumed that over a period of years such professional judgment will be tested in various ways for validity, but it allows planning to begin with the resources and talents at hand rather than waiting until the budget can support the hiring of an individual skilled in statistical analysis. Additionally, ALMS allows for varying levels of sophistication in the analysis of service standards. Human beings are equipped with a wide variety of talents and ability. The results of the application of their talents can also be expected to vary in both depth and accuracy of analysis.

6. James Cutt (1972), *Program Budgeting and Higher Education, A Review of the "State-of-the-Art."* Canberra: The Australian National University, p. 3.
7. Charles J. Hitch (1968), "Program Budgeting in a University Setting," *The Tax Digest*, Second Quarter: 13.
8. Goldberg (1976), p. 69.
9. Patricia Schroeder (1980), "The Politics of Productivity," *Public Personnel Management Journal* 9:238.
10. *Ibid.*, pp. 238-239.
11. Goldberg (1976), pp. 73-74.
12. Richard W. Hall (1973), "Program Budgeting—Why?" In Sul H. Lee (ed.), *Planning-Programming Budgeting System (PPBS): Implications for Library Management.* Ann Arbor, Mich.: Pierian, p. 6.
13. For a full description of the CSUN cost analysis program see, Betty Jo Mitchell, Norman E. Tanis, and Jack Jaffe (1978), *Cost Analysis of Library Functions: A Total System Approach.* Greenwich, Conn.: JAI Press.

Chapter 2

Strategy for Development of a Management System

Before the question can be answered as to whether or not library personnel funds are being expended judiciously, it is only logical to first determine the cost and level of present services—you must know what has been purchased and at what price. In a library setting, we may ask "How much money must be expended to staff the reference desk(s)?" or "What is the actual cost in personnel funds of operating the interlibrary loan process?" To answer these questions, both the level of staffing and number of hours contributed to the particular task must be examined. In addition, the quality and quantity of the service produced with a given number of personnel hours must be established. A combination of these two analyses, the labor analysis and the service analysis, along with the operating expenses which relate to each service produced by the various tasks, provide the data bank for this management system. From these analyses, the operating budgets are both developed and defended, personnel assignments are created and revised, goals are established, and progress is measured. The labor analysis provides historical expenditure data which indicate the labor shifts that occur in response to environmental changes such as the application of new technology or newly emerging user demands. The service analysis defines and describes that changing environment and develops and justifies the organization's responses to it.

ALMS is based upon both the total library budget for salaries/wages and the budget for operating expenses and is designed to provide management control of allocated resources through the use of historical expenditure data and projections of service needs.

ALMS consists of three basic processes that encompass the two major budget categories (salaries/wages and operating expenses):

1. an analysis of the personnel hours required to perform each task within the organization;
2. an analysis of the service provided by each task with an accompanying evaluation of service adequacy; and
3. the application of both analyses to the preparation of future personnel and operating expense budgets, the assignment of personnel, and goal setting.

LABOR ANALYSIS

The first process—analysis of the personnel hours required to perform each task within the organization—requires the development of a program to account for the number of personnel hours expended for each particular service, a time-consuming but essential element in adequate budget utilization. The American Management Associations' Extension Institute offers a course in Human Resource Development that emphasizes the importance of paying proper attention to the utilization of personnel:

> How important are a company's human resources? Total dollar cost, as a percentage of operating expense alone, makes the purchase of human time the key to financial results. Typically the total company expense for human time and presence on the job amounts to 70 percent of the total cost of operation. This figure includes the direct cost of payroll and employee benefits but does not include the accompanying costs of employment, training and the like. . . . The relative size of this expenditure would certainly justify management's giving human resources its top priority in planning and commitment. The company can go all out to control expenses in production, freight, paper flow, utilities, and so on but still achieve only limited results unless it concentrates on the largest, most flexible element of operating cost—human time.[1]

The analysis process requires careful definition of each task by a systems analyst or other administrator in cooperation with the various organizational units within the library and a statement of production units, if in fact identifiable units are produced. One-third of the tasks are likely to be non-unit-producing tasks, such as training, administration, vacation/sick leave, and personnel activities. In general, a systems analyst is the best qualified to manage such an assignment and to work with the various organizational units within the library to establish task definitions. However, if a systems analyst is not on the staff, department administrators should assume this responsibility, with coordination of the project being assumed by the library director's office.

The process begins with a complete listing of activities within a functioning unit and a grouping of related activities into tasks. It is essential that tasks be carefully and clearly defined so that staff members can easily recognize their activities and correlating task name. For example, within a library the following activities could be grouped into a task called "receiving library materials":

open packages
check materials received against invoice for accuracy
check materials received against order slip for accuracy
return incorrectly shipped materials to vendor
write vendor for correction of invoice errors
forward correct invoices to accounting section for payment
forward correctly shipped materials to catalog department

A task entitled "pre-order checking and verification" might be defined as follows:

establish entry to appear on the purchase order
check library holdings
record call number on duplicates and return to requestor
supply all bibliographic data needed for ordering and cataloging
establish price of material
establish availability of material
type order request card

Another example, much broader in scope but which must also be similarly defined, is "library administration." This task might be defined as:

plan and review operations throughout the library
plan for physical facilities (building, space, etc.)
direct activities of staff working within the administrative office
plan and monitor the library budget
develop management tools and policy manuals
investigate patron and staff complaints

Such a task could also include committee work, or a separate task for committees may be established.

Since *all* personnel time will need to be reported, a separate task will be required for authorized time-off, possibly defined as follows:

all nonproduction activities for which the funding agency provides payment, for example, vacation, sick leave, compensating time-off, holidays, coffee breaks, jury duty, Christmas parties.

Let me again emphasize that the intent here is to account for *all* budgeted time. A true management system must account for all personnel expenditures so that (1) accuracy checks may be developed for the reporting mechanism, and (2) judgments can be made as to whether maximum value is derived from the allocated resources. Therefore, tasks must be defined in such a way as to encompass all activities, both unit-producing and non-unit-producing. It is this very significant amount of non-unit-producing time that most isolated effectiveness studies fail to take into account. It should be noted that non-unit-producing time is not the same as nonproductive time. Non-unit-producing time includes nonproductive time (i.e., authorized time-off) along with other productive time during which no easily recognizable units are produced (such as training and administration). In the California State University and Colleges system, authorized time-off alone, on the average, accounts for 10-15% of the total library personnel hours. If other non-unit-producing tasks, such as training, administration, personnel hiring, and professional activities are included, this percentage will increase to approximately 25-40% of the total time recorded by all staff. The point is that these costs are just as real as the costs of actually providing such services as cataloging a book or serving at a reference desk, and if not accounted for, budget justifications and planning documents will be incomplete. In an academic library, some tasks may be performed by student assistants who do not have the same benefits, such as vacation time or sick leave, as do the regular clerical staff. Therefore, tasks primarily utilizing student assistant hours will exhibit an overhead figure much less than for tasks performed by librarians or regular staff.

In addition to the grouping of activities into tasks, it may prove useful to group tasks into broader functions. For example, the task of "pre-order checking and verification" cited above could be combined with other tasks which are functionally related such as (1) general selection: books, nonbooks, serials; (2) selection from approval programs; and (3) selection of gifts; and a combined cost for the broader based "selection" function can be obtained. While such a larger grouping may not be as important for in-house management purposes, as for drawing comparisons between libraries, a broader categorization by function does provide certain advantages:

1. While libraries perform essentially the same functions, there is wide divergence in the specific tasks composing these functions. Examples 1

and 2 illustrate two different sets of function/task relationships for the same library with different levels of breakdown of tasks within the functions. Example 1 resembles the early CSUN function/task relationships while Example 2 represents a finer breakdown of tasks to accommodate the needs of other CSUC libraries. There are, of course, many possible arrangements. You will note that some functions report only one task. Functional categorization provides a base for multiorganizational comparisons and is essential if these data are to be used for system-wide formula development.

2. Grouping tasks into larger functions assures that costs for tasks which may be performed by more than one organizational unit are grouped together. For example, all cataloging costs will be charged to the cataloging function regardless of whether the task is physically performed within the catalog department or another organizational unit. The cost for cataloging will not be limited to the costs incurred by the specific cataloging unit or department, but will be accumulated for all units involved in that process. While the same information may be obtained by reviewing the whole process task by task, the level of detail may be confusing and time-consuming. The grouping of tasks into functions reveals the major operating categories of the library in more concise and understandable format.

In addition to recording the number of personnel hours devoted to a specific task, it is also important to record hours on the basis of type of employee. At the very least, a breakdown should be made by professional and clerical hours. In an academic library, it is also important to show student assistant hours separately. Another category of personnel which should be isolated is subsidized employees and/or volunteers; that is, personnel from federally funded programs such as CETA and student work-study, as well as volunteers. Federal programs are designed primarily to provide training for unskilled workers, and, in the case of student work-study programs, to assist students with their educational expenses. However, state, county, and city agencies frequently become dependent on these employees to provide needed services for which authorized funding has been eliminated. Precise recording of the hours logged by these federally subsidized employees may illustrate dramatically—in a manner that councilors, trustees, and legislators can understand—the possible impact of their loss.

In the beginning of this chapter, I stated that tasks should be defined by a systems analyst or other administrator in cooperation with the various organizational units. However, "organizational units" may not refer, necessarily, to a library department, rather, as with our study at CSUN, subunits within the departments may be treated as organizational units.

For example, instead of an organizational unit called "reference service," you may wish to identify some of the larger reference service areas, such as government documents or the instructional materials laboratory (curriculum center), and define them as organizational units so that costs may be maintained separately. Separation of personnel hours by organizational unit, as well as by type of employee, thus allows for the collection of data in such a manner that service costs may be derived for individual units, as well as for departments or for the library as a whole. For example, such tasks as training, administration, and authorized time-off could be determined for the entire library, but, in addition, comparisons could be drawn between the various organizational units and/or departments.

Examples 3 and 4 illustrate both sides of a data collection form which may be used for the recording of personnel hours. Examples 5 through 16 are monthly labor reports and illustrate the kinds of task overlap that can occur between organizational units, that is, tasks that are performed by more than one organizational unit. Note that there are six categories of personnel for which hours are recorded: librarian, staff, student assistant, subsidized librarian, subsidized staff, and work-study student assistant.

From the collection of personnel hours, it is possible to calculate a defensible cost figure for each task by assigning an average hourly wage for each personnel category. For more precision in costing, the actual hourly wage for each employee may be recorded on the data collection sheet. This process is certainly more time-consuming, but quite rewarding in its accuracy. All subsidized personnel categories are considered as if the library were paying full cost for their services, although when drafting a cost report, these personnel costs can easily be subtracted, leaving actual library costs, if desired. However, cost data for subsidized personnel provides, at a glance, information as to which tasks are most heavily dependent upon subsidization. A more thorough discussion of the CSUN tasks, functions and organizational units can be found in *Cost Analysis of Library Functions: A Total System Approach.*[2]

(***Text continues on page 31***)

Example 1. Function and Task Relationships

Functions	*Tasks*
Administration	Administration
Personnel	Personnel
Administrative Support	Administrative Support
Training	Training
Professional Activities	Professional Activities
Problem Solving	Problem Solving
Miscellaneous	Miscellaneous
Systems Analysis	Systems Analysis
Programming Group	Programming Reprogramming Program maintenance
Building & Machine Maintenance	Building and copy machine maintenance Equipment maintenance and repair
Selection Group	General selection Approval selection Gifts selection Reference selection Special Collections selection
Preliminary Cataloging	Bibliographic checking Card procurement Card typing
Ordering	Ordering library materials
Receiving	Gifts receiving Receiving ordered materials Approval receiving Book distribution
Accounting	Book fund accounting Claims preparation Operating expense accounting
Cataloging	Adaptive cataloging Original cataloging Recataloging
Physical Preparation	Pam and togic binding Bindery preparation Mending Final processing (labels and book pockets, etc.)
Inventory Processes	Deselection Withdrawing Missing issues Search-hold

(*continued*)

(Example 1. Continued)

Functions	*Tasks*
File Maintenance	Serial record processing Periodical record processing Card preparation Public catalog maintenance Automated shelflist maintenance IML catalog maintenance Reference catalog maintenance Special Collections catalog maintenance
Circulation System	Circulation Fines and billing Exit control Stack maintenance Reserve Book Room
Desk Services	Reference desks Microform desk Periodical Reading Room desk General Information desk Special Collections patron services Automated data base service
Library Instruction	Class lectures Bibliographies/Instructional handouts Library tours
Interlibrary Loan	Interlibrary loan
Exhibit Preparation	Exhibit preparation

Example 2. More Function and Task Relationships

Function	*Task*
Administration	Library administration, general
	Library administration, advisory committees
	Department administration
	Campus administration
	Exhibits
	Chancellor Office administration
	Regional cooperation groups
Library Personnel	Personnel hiring and evaluation
Administrative Support	Typing and other clerical support: Departmental
	Typing and other clerical support: All others
	Support of professional associations and research
	Opening, sorting and distributing mail
Library Personnel Training	Required training
	Optional training
Professional Tasks	Professional development
	Professional associations
	Research
Special Assistance	Nonroutine assistance to other departments or units
Authorized Time Off	Vacation, sick leave, coffee breaks, jury duty
Systems Analysis	Systems analysis
Computer Programming	New programming
	Reprogramming
	Program maintenance
Maintenance	Building maintenance and security
	Revenue-producing machines maintenance
	Non-revenue-producing machines maintenance
Deselection	Deselection
	Withdrawing
Selection	General selection
	Approval selection
	Gifts selection
	Pre-order checking and verification (manual)
	Pre-order checking and verification (OCLC)
Ordering	Ordering library materials
Receiving	Receiving: general
	Receiving: gifts
	Receiving: approval
	Periodical check-in
	Serial check-in
	Government docs processing
Accounting	Library materials accounting
	Fiscal claims

(*continued*)

(*Example 2.—Continued*)

Functions	*Tasks*
	Payroll Operating expense accounting
Cataloging	Bibliographic checking Adaptive cataloging Original cataloging Recataloging Add holdings (manual) OCLC copy cataloging/checking OCLC adaptive cataloging OCLC orginal cataloging OCLC recataloging Card preparation OCLC inputting
Physical Processing	In-house binding Bindery preparations and returns Mending Final processing/labels and pockets, etc.
Inventory Processes	General inventory
Major or Public File Maintenance	Public periodical record creation and maintenance Public serial rcord creation and maintenance Catalog maintenance Automated shelflist maintenance Authority file maintenance Union lists maintenance
General Circulation	Circulation control and desk Fines and billing Exit control Stack maintenance Stack reading Reserve Book Room Search/holds
Reference and Information Services	Reference desks General reference Photocopy service Information desk Thesis consultations Automated data base searches Microform desk
Library Instruction	Informal library instruction Bibliographies, lecture handouts, patron instruction
Interlibrary Loan	Borrowing Lending
Special Projects	Restrospective conversion Other

Example 3. Data Collection Form—Personnel—Hours—Front

CSUC LIBRARY FUNCTIONAL ANALYSIS STUDY FORM (please see instructions on reverse side)

CAMPUS ______________________

Organizational Unit # _____ Organizational Unit Name __________ Name ___________ Employee Number ___________ Month/Year _____

PLEASE! 1) Use a separate form for each different organizational unit you charge time to.
2) Write legibly.
3) Enter in full, half and quarter hour increments only—e.g., 3½.

TASK NAME	TASK NO.	1	2	3	4	5	6	7	8	9	10	11	12	13	14	15	16	17	18	19	20	21	22	23	24	25	26	27	28	29	30	31
DAILY TOTALS																																

Example 4. Data Collection Form—Personnel Hours—Back

1. Enter time in full and quarter hour increments only: ¼, ½, ¾, 1, 2, etc.
2. Enter only one value per box (do not enter morning and afternoon activities separately).
3. At the end of the work day please add hours giving daily total at the bottom of the sheet. Full time staff members' hours should total 8; half time staff, 4; librarians on the 4-C workweek may work more or less than 8 hours on any given work day. Student assistants daily work totals should match the number of hours worked as entered to pay voucher (timesheet).
4. CTO, holidays, vacation, sick leave and breaks are entered under Authorized Time Off, Task #056.
5. Use a separate sheet for each organizational unit you work for, if more than one.
6. Use a separate sheet if you have two pay rates, e.g., clerk and student assistant. There should be a different employee number for each sheet.
7. Check that you are using task numbers allowed for your organizational unit.
8. If you have more task numbers than spaces on the sheet, please use a second sheet.

ORGANIZATIONAL UNITS

01 Admin.	04 Circ-Oviatt	12 Microform	19 Coll. Devel. Bibliography	☐ ______
02 Acq/Ser	05 Reference-Ov.	13 Archives (CSUN) Spec. Coll.	27 Circ-South	☐ ______
03 Cataloging	10 I.M.L.	15 Sci/Tech Ref	28 Ref-Fine Arts	☐ ______

TASK NAMES AND NUMBERS

Task #	
001	Library administration; general
002	Library administration; advisory cmtes
003	Department administration
004	Campus administration
005	Assigned library representation
006	Exhibits
007	Chancellor's Office administration
008	Regional cooperation groups
016	Faculty promotion, tenure, and review
017	Faculty and staff personnel, general
021	Administration, departmental
022	Administration; library and all others
023	Support of prof. associations/ research

Task #	
027	Opening/sorting/distributing mail
031	Required training
032	Optional training
041	Professional development
042	Professional associations
043	Research
051	Special assistance and consultation
056	Authorized time off
066	Systems analysis
076	New programming
077	Reprogramming
078	Program maintenance
081	Building maintenance and security
082	Revenue-producing machines
084	Non-revenue-producing machines
101	Deselection: Weeding
102	Deselection to storage

(*Example 4.—Continued*)

Task #	
103	Withdrawing
104	Withdrawing records via on-line data base
111	General selection
112	Approval selection
113	Gifts selection
118	Pre-order checking and verification
119	Pre-order checking and verification: OCLC
131	Ordering; library materials
141	Receiving; general
142	Receiving; gifts
144	Receiving approval
145	Periodical processing; check-in
146	Serial processing; check-in
147	Government documents processing
151	Library accounting system
152	Preparation of claims schedules (FISCAL)
153	Payroll
154	Equipment and operating expense
160	Bibliographic checking
161	Adaptive cataloging
162	Original cataloging
163	Recataloging
164	Add holdings—manual
165	OCLC copy cataloging/checking
166	OCLC adaptive cataloging
167	OCLC original cataloging; new
168	OCLC original cataloging; revised
169	OCLC recataloging
170	Card preparation
171	OCLC inputting
172	Add holdings—OCLC

Task #	
201	In-house binding
202	Bindery preparation and returns
203	Mending
204	End processing (all materials)
220	General inventory
242	Pub. period. record creation & maint.
244	Pub. serial records creation & maint.
250	Catalog maintenance
251	Machine shelflist maintenance
252	Authority file maintenance
257	Union lists
271	Circulation control and desk
272	Fines and billing
273	Exit control
274	Stack maintenance; general
275	Stack reading; general
276	Reserve book room; operation
277	Search holds
310	Reference desk
311	General reference
312	Photocopy service
314	Information desk
316	Thesis consultations
318	Automated data base searches
319	Slide collection desk
320	Microform desk
331	Informal instruction by library staff
333	Bibs, handouts, patron instructions
334	Formal instruction by library staff
351	Interlibrary loan: Borrowing
352	Interlibrary loan: Lending
450	Retrospective conversion
451	Campus designated special project

Example 5. CSUN Labor Report—Administration

REPORT 1. HOURS AND COSTS BY ORGANIZATIONAL UNITS FOR 3/31/79NO, ORGANIZATIONAL UNIT NO. 01 ADMINISTRATION

		HOURS BY EMPLOYEE TYPE						COST BY EMPLOYEE TYPE									
TASK	TASK NAME	LIBRN.	STAFF	STUD.	SUBLIB	SUBSTAFF	W.S.	LIBRN.	STAFF	STUD.	SUBLIB	SUBSTAFF	W.S.	HOURS TOTAL	COST TOTAL	% ORG. TOT.HRS.	% ORG. TOT.COST
1	LIB.ADMN.GEN	370						4883						370	4883	14	25
2	LIB.ADMN-COM	44						505						44	505	2	3
3	DEPT. ADMIN.	1	15					11	70					16	81	1	0
4	CAMPUS ADMIN	35						466						35	466	1	2
5	LIB.REPRSNTN	5						78						5	78	0	0
7	C.O. ADMIN.	202						1945						202	1945	8	10
8	REGIONAL COO	5						76						5	76	0	0
16	FACLTY P,T,&	46						737						46	737	2	4
17	PERSNL. GENL	32	6					337	40					38	377	1	2
21	ADMN.SUP.DEP		2						9					2	9	0	0
22	ADMN.SUP.OTH	143	380	96			195	869	2310	336			583	814	4098	31	21
23	SUP.PROF&RES	6						45						6	45	0	0
27	US&CAMPUSMAI	4		68				26		211				72	237	3	1
31	REQ. TRAININ	2	4	1			4	10	24	1			12	11	47	0	0
32	OPT. TRAININ	7						82						7	82	0	0
41	PROF.DEVLPMN	7						74						7	74	0	0
42	PROF. ASSOC.	1						17						1	17	0	0
51	SPECL.ASSIST	12	16					143	68					28	211	1	1
56	AUTHORD. T/C	161	158	6			9	1876	1003	15			28	334	2922	13	15
66	SYS.ANALYSIS	83						779						83	779	3	4
77	RE+PROGRAMNG	6						45						6	45	0	0
78	PROGRAM MAIN	52						454						52	454	2	2
81	BLDG. MAINT.	2	17					16	95					19	111	1	1
82	REV.MCH.MAIN		50	64			248		367	185			768	362	1320	14	7
84	NON-REV.MAIN		2						10					2	10	0	0
153	PAYROLL		50						218					50	218	2	1
154	O. AND E.		9						48					9	48	0	0
		-----	-----	-----	-----	-----	-----	-----	-----	-----	-----	-----	-----	------	------	--	--
		1226	709	235			456	13474	4262	748			1391	2626	19875		

Example 6. CSUN Labor Report—Acquisitions

REPORT 1. HOURS AND COSTS BY ORGANIZATIONAL UNITS FOR 3/31/79NO, ORGANIZATIONAL UNIT NO. 02 ACQUISITIONS

		HOURS BY EMPLOYEE TYPE						COST BY EMPLOYEE TYPE									
TASK	TASK NAME	LIBRN.	STAFF	STUD.	SUBLIB	SUBSTAFF	W.S.	LIBRN.	STAFF	STUD.	SUBLIB	SUBSTAFF	W.S.	HOURS TOTAL	COST TOTAL	% ORG. TOT.HRS.	% ORG. TOT.COST
3	DEPT. ADMIN.	30	8					346	41					38	387	1	2
4	CAMPUS ADMIN		3						19					3	19	0	0
17	PERSNL. GENL	8	5					92	26					13	118	0	1
21	ADMN.SUP.DEP		83				13		455				36	96	491	2	2
27	US&CAMPUSMAI		22	14			63		124	40			183	99	347	2	2
31	REQ. TRAININ		248	221		83	96		1305	638		347	279	648	2569	14	12
32	OPT. TRAININ		16						111					16	111	0	1
51	SPECL.ASSIST		5						30					5	30	0	0
56	AUTHORD. T/O		387	16		14	16		2148	48		57	46	433	2299	9	11
84	NON-REV.MAIN		2						8					2	8	0	0
131	ORDER.LIB.MA		377	17			2		2077	51			5	396	2133	9	10
141	RECVNG.GENL.		133				65		800				189	198	989	4	5
144	RECVNG.APPRV		70	57					387	168				127	555	3	3
145	PERIOD.PROCS		193	91			44		1105	271			128	333	1504	7	7
146	SERIAL PROCS		376	15			110		2021	44			322	501	2387	11	11
151	LIBRY.ACCOUN		101						601					101	601	2	3
152	FISCAL CLAIM		146	5			9		870	14			27	160	911	4	4
201	IN-HOUSE BIN			73			92			217			273	165	490	4	2
202	BINDERY PREP		183				23		914				83	206	997	5	5
203	MENDING			36			220			113			635	256	748	6	4
204	END PROCESS.		148	163			140		889	478			422	451	1789	10	9
242	PUBLIC PERRE		25						167					25	167	1	1
244	PUBLIC SERRE		5						29					5	29	0	0
257	UNION LISTS		20						138					20	138	0	1
274	STACK MAINT.		49	109			80		243	336			233	238	812	5	4
314	INFO DESK		25				1		128				2	26	130	1	1
		-----	-----	-----	-----	-----	-----	-----	-----	-----	-----	-----	-----	------	------	--	--
		38	2635	817		97	974	438	14636	2418		404	2863	4561	20759		

Example 7. CSUN Labor Report—Cataloging

REPORT 1. HOURS AND COSTS BY ORGANIZATIONAL UNITS FOR 3/31/79NO, ORGANIZATIONAL UNIT NO. 03 CATALOGING

		HOURS BY EMPLOYEE TYPE						COST BY EMPLOYEE TYPE						HOURS	COST	% ORG.	% ORG.
TASK	TASK NAME	LIBRN.	STAFF	STUD.	SUBLIB	SUBSTAFF	W.S.	LIBRN.	STAFF	STUD.	SUBLIB	SUBSTAFF	W.S.	TOTAL	TOTAL	TOT.HRS.	TOT.COST
1	LIB.ADMN.GEN	7	4					63	23					11	86	0	0
2	LIB.ADMN-COM	7	8					59	48					15	107	0	0
3	DEPT. ADMIN.	177	83					1667	477	1				260	2145	5	7
4	CAMPUS ADMIN	11						108						11	108	0	0
8	REGIONAL COO	9						86						9	86	0	0
16	FACLTY P,T,&	47	9					490	54					56	544	1	2
17	PERSNL. GENL	10	10					93	68					20	161	0	1
21	ADMN.SUP.DEP		161	145			56		902	459			164	362	1525	7	5
31	REQ. TRAININ	47	314	106			135	402	1896	334			409	602	3041	12	11
32	OPT. TRAININ	13	16					104	94					29	198	1	1
41	PROF.DEVLPMN	32	16					293	94					48	387	1	1
42	PROF. ASSOC.	10						80						10	80	0	0
51	SPECL.ASSIST	6	23					50	139				1	29	190	1	1
56	AUTHORO. T/O	60	349	32			11	539	2048	103			35	452	2725	9	9
84	NON-REV.MAIN		6	10					36	32				16	68	0	0
103	WITHDRAWING		20	42			1		107	125			4	63	236	1	1
153	PAYROLL		1	14					6	49				15	55	0	0
160	BIB. CHECKIN		13	26			41		78	77			122	80	277	2	1
161	ADAPTIVE CAT	1	152				49	6	969				151	202	1126	4	4
162	ORIGINAL CAT	195	27					1929	150					222	2079	4	7
163	RECATALOGING	8	59					52	365					67	417	1	1
164	ADD HOLD MAN		15						71					15	71	0	0
165	OCLC COPY CA		163	64			34		1007	186			100	261	1293	5	4
166	OCLC ADPT.CA	57	190					545	1096					247	1641	5	6
167	OCLC ORIG.NE	8						62						8	62	0	0
168	OCLC ORIG.RE	190					8	1534					24	198	1558	4	5
169	OCLC RECAT.		27						164					27	164	1	1
170	CARD PREP.		198	112					991	397				310	1388	6	5
171	OCLC INPUTNG		137						758					137	758	3	3
172	ADD HOLD.OCL		1						3					1	3	0	0
250	CATALOG MAIN	1	405	189			213	5	2186	594			619	808	3404	16	12
251	MCHINESHLFLS		203	54			100		1185	187			331	357	1703	7	6
252	AUTHORTY FIL	9	110	82			4	69	716	308			11	205	1104	4	4
		-----	-----	-----	-----	-----	-----	-----	-----	-----	-----	-----	-----	------	------	--	--
		905	2720	876			652	8236	15731	2852			1971	5153	28790		

Example 8. CSUN Labor Report—Circulation

REPORT 1. HOURS AND COSTS BY ORGANIZATIONAL UNITS FOR 3/31/79NO, ORGANIZATIONAL UNIT NO. 04 CIRCULATION

		HOURS BY EMPLOYEE TYPE						COST BY EMPLOYEE TYPE									
TASK	TASK NAME	LIBRN.	STAFF	STUD.	SUBLIB	SUBSTAFF	W.S.	LIBRN.	STAFF	STUD.	SUBLIB	SUBSTAFF	W.S.	HOURS TOTAL	COST TOTAL	% ORG. TOT.HRS.	% ORG. TOT.COST
1	LIB.ADMN.GEN		4						24					4	24	0	0
3	DEPT. ADMIN.	60	116	4				633	682	12				180	1327	4	7
4	CAMPUS ADMIN		2						10					2	10	0	0
17	PERSNL. GENL	11	68					116	444					79	560	2	3
21	ADMN.SUP.DEP		72	74					438	285				146	723	3	4
31	REQ. TRAININ	6	147	97			46	58	737	329			128	296	1252	6	7
32	OPT. TRAININ		6						31					6	31	0	0
56	AUTHORD. T/O	12	102	114			36	127	547	357			113	264	1144	6	6
81	BLDG. MAINT.		26	69			26		126	211			60	121	397	3	2
271	CIRCCTRL&DES	1	306	821			213	5	1592	2928			624	1341	5149	29	28
272	FINES & BILL		167	237			55		796	758			176	459	1730	10	10
273	EXIT CONTROL			205			132			631			389	337	1020	7	6
274	STACK MAINT.		94	577			300		473	1794			876	971	3143	21	17
275	STACK READIN		9	137			113		43	406			325	259	774	6	4
277	SEARCH/HOLDS		42	184			1		240	633			4	227	877	5	5
		-----	-----	-----	-----	-----	-----	-----	-----	-----	-----	-----	-----	------	------	--	--
		90	1161	2519			922	939	6183	8344			2695	4692	18161		

Example 9. CSUN Labor Report—Reference

REPORT 1. HOURS AND COSTS BY ORGANIZATIONAL UNITS FOR 3/31/79MO, ORGANIZATIONAL UNIT NO. 05 REFERENCE

		HOURS BY EMPLOYEE TYPE						COST BY EMPLOYEE TYPE									
TASK	TASK NAME	LIBRN.	STAFF	STUD.	SUBLIB	SUBSTAFF	W.S.	LIBRN.	STAFF	STUD.	SUBLIB	SUBSTAFF	W.S.	HOURS TOTAL	COST TOTAL	% ORG. TOT.HRS.	% ORG. TOT.COST
1	LIB.ADMN.GEN	4						44						4	44	0	0
2	LIB.ADMN-COM	23	2	1			1	201	11	4			3	27	219	1	1
3	DEPT. ADMIN.	110	48			2		1067	306			10		160	1383	4	5
4	CAMPUS ADMIN	37	4					337	26					41	363	1	1
6	EXHIBITS		1						4					1	4	0	0
7	C.O. ADMIN.		40						278					40	278	1	1
16	FACLTY P.T.&	91						742						91	742	2	3
17	PERSNL. GENL	17	11					164	69					28	233	1	1
21	ADMN.SUP.DEP	8	136	22		8	18	60	743	73		42	51	192	969	4	4
22	ADMN.SUP.OTH								1						1	0	0
27	US&CAMPUSMAI		3			27	5		15			136	13	35	164	1	1
31	REQ. TRAININ	30	51	5			49	243	284	15			151	135	693	3	3
32	OPT. TRAININ	2						16						2	16	0	0
41	PROF.DEVLPMN	56						487						56	487	1	2
42	PROF. ASSOC.	20						188						20	188	0	1
43	RESEARCH	111						1142						111	1142	3	4
51	SPECL.ASSIST	29	4				48	262	23				162	81	447	2	2
56	AUTHORD. T/O	238	153	40		91	49	2154	858	117		425	136	571	3690	13	14
84	NON-REV.MAIN		1						5					1	5	0	0
101	DESELECTION	4						38						4	38	0	0
103	WITHDRAWING	6						54						6	54	0	0
111	GENL.SELECT.	31				3		270				15		34	285	1	1
112	APPRVL.SELEC	3						23						3	23	0	0
141	RECVNG.GENL.					9						44		9	44	0	0
147	GOVDOC.PROCS	87	60	161			274	722	418	485			810	582	2435	14	9
202	BINDERY PREP		12						51					12	51	0	0
204	END PROCESS.					16						80		16	80	0	0
220	GENL. INVNTR						1						3	1	3	0	0
250	CATALOG MAIN	18	35			4	3	167	149			18	9	60	343	1	1
274	STACK MAINT.	5	50	128			44	42	214	380			124	227	760	5	3
275	STACK READIN			12			3			34			8	15	42	0	0
310	REF. DESK	472						4154						472	4154	11	16
311	GENERAL REF.	157	3	38				1427	20	111				198	1558	5	6
314	INFO DESK		219	48		58	8		1137	144		292	27	333	1600	8	6
316	THESIS CONSL	15						165						15	165	0	1
318	AOTODATABASE	23						187						23	187	1	1
331	INFORMAL INS	67						631						67	631	2	2
333	BIBLIO. PROD	21	35			5	51	187	196			23	146	112	552	3	2
351	ILL-BORROW	48	122	72			19	454	659	235			53	261	1401	6	5
352	ILL-LEND	4	74	142			42	36	391	443			121	262	991	6	4
		1737	1064	669	-----	223	615	15664	5858	2041	-----	1085	1817	4308	26465	--	--

Example 10. CSUN Labor Report—Curriculum Center

REPORT 1. HOURS AND COSTS BY ORGANIZATIONAL UNITS FOR 3/31/79NO, ORGANIZATIONAL UNIT NO. 10 CURRICULUM CENTER

		HOURS BY EMPLOYEE TYPE						COST BY EMPLOYEE TYPE									
TASK	TASK NAME	LIBRN.	STAFF	STUD.	SUBLIB	SUBSTAFF	W.S.	LIBRN.	STAFF	STUD.	SUBLIB	SUBSTAFF	W.S.	HOURS TOTAL	COST TOTAL	% ORG. TOT.HRS.	% ORG. TOT.COST
3	DEPT. ADMIN.	3						26						3	26	0	0
84	NON-REV.MAIN		21	39		1	56		134	122		4	159	117	419	8	8
103	WITHDRAWING		2						9					2	9	0	0
111	GENL.SELECT.	18						147						18	147	1	3
113	GIFTS SELECT	3						20						3	20	0	0
118	PRE-ORDER CH		1						8					1	8	0	0
131	ORDER.LIB.MA					6						23		6	23	0	0
160	BIB. CHECKIN		2						13					2	13	0	0
162	ORIGINAL CAT	47	60					319	358					107	677	8	12
163	RECATALOGING		21						126					21	126	1	2
170	CARD PREP.					7						29		7	29	0	1
203	MENDING		2	13			23		16	38			64	38	118	3	2
204	END PROCESS.		7	8		20	62		42	25		84	177	97	328	7	6
250	CATALOG MAIN	2	15	35		43	15	13	100	128		181	46	112	468	8	9
252	AUTHORTY FIL	1	2			41		9	11			173		44	193	3	4
271	CIRCCTRL&DES		34	121		1	262		215	361		2	756	418	1334	30	25
272	FINES & BILL		12	23		6	19		75	80		25	55	60	235	4	4
274	STACK MAINT.		11	53			114		74	155			327	178	556	13	10
275	STACK READIN		3	8			32		18	24			92	43	134	3	2
277	SEARCH/HOLDS		4	13			2		27	35			7	19	69	1	1
311	GENERAL REF.		43	46		1	20		269	158		2	56	110	485	8	9
331	INFORMAL INS		3						21					3	21	0	0
		-----	-----	-----	-----	-----	-----	-----	-----	-----	-----	-----	-----	------	------	--	--
		74	244	359		126	606	534	1516	1126		523	1739	1409	5438		

Example 11. CSUN Labor Report—Microform

REPORT 1. HOURS AND COSTS BY ORGANIZATIONAL UNITS FOR 3/31/79NO. ORGANIZATIONAL UNIT NO. 12 MICROFORM

TASK	TASK NAME	HOURS BY EMPLOYEE TYPE LIBRN.	STAFF	STUD.	SUBLIB	SUBSTAFF	W.S.	COST BY EMPLOYEE TYPE LIBRN.	STAFF	STUD.	SUBLIB	SUBSTAFF	W.S.	HOURS TOTAL	COST TOTAL	% ORG. TOT.HRS.	% ORG. TOT.COST
81	BLDG. MAINT.	1						6						1	6	0	0
82	REV.MCH.MAIN	5	1					32	3					6	35	2	3
84	NON-REV.MAIN	3						18	1					3	19	1	1
103	WITHDRAWING	2						14	2					2	16	1	1
147	GOVDOC.PROCS	3	2					21	8					5	29	1	2
204	END PROCESS.	2						14	1					2	15	1	1
220	GENL. INVNTR	1		8			4	7		24			11	13	42	3	3
274	STACK MAINT.	1	17	44			23	7	73	129			67	35	276	22	20
311	GENERAL REF.	6						42						6	42	2	3
312	PHOTCOPY SER	3	2					21	8					5	29	1	2
320	MICROFORMDES	5	16	145			81	35	67	428			240	247	770	63	55
331	INFORMAL INS	2	1					11	2					3	13	1	1
333	BIBLIO. PROD	14						98						14	98	4	7
		-----	-----	-----	-----	-----	-----	-----	-----	-----	-----	-----	-----	------	------	--	--
		48	39	197			108	326	165	581			318	392	1390		

Example 12. CSUN Labor Report—Archives and Special Collections

REPORT 1. HOURS AND COSTS BY ORGANIZATIONAL UNITS FOR 3/31/79NO. ORGANIZATIONAL UNIT NO. 13 ARCHIVES & SPEC.COLL

TASK	TASK NAME	HOURS BY EMPLOYEE TYPE LIBRN.	STAFF	STUD.	SUBLIB	SUBSTAFF	W.S.	COST BY EMPLOYEE TYPE LIBRN.	STAFF	STUD.	SUBLIB	SUBSTAFF	W.S.	HOURS TOTAL	COST TOTAL	% ORG. TOT.HRS.	% ORG. TCT.COST
6	EXHIBITS	21						197						21	197	12	14
8	REGIONAL COO	2						19						2	19	1	1
56	AUTHORD. T/O	15						136						15	136	8	9
113	GIFTS SELECT	8						75						8	75	4	5
142	RECVNG. GIFT	11						103						11	103	6	7
250	CATALOG MAIN	59						549						59	549	33	38
252	AUTHORTY FIL			27						85				27	85	15	6
274	STACK MAINT.			9						27				9	27	5	2
311	GENERAL REF.	28						263						28	263	16	18
		-----	-----	-----	-----	-----	-----	-----	-----	-----	-----	-----	-----	------	------	--	--
		144		36				1342		112				180	1454		

Example 13. CSUN Labor Report—Sci/Tech Reference

REPORT 1. HOURS AND COSTS BY ORGANIZATIONAL UNITS FOR 3/31/79NO, ORGANIZATIONAL UNIT NO. 15 SCI/TECH REFERENCE

		HOURS BY EMPLOYEE TYPE						COST BY EMPLOYEE TYPE									
TASK	TASK NAME	LIBRN.	STAFF	STUD.	SUBLIB	SUBSTAFF	W.S.	LIBRN.	STAFF	STUD.	SUBLIB	SUBSTAFF	W.S.	HOURS TOTAL	COST TOTAL	% ORG. TOT.HRS.	% ORG. TOT.COST
250	CATALOG MAIN	13						97						13	97	2	2
274	STACK MAINT.		81	38			28		407	109			80	147	596	18	11
275	STACK READIN		15	21			18		73	59			53	54	185	7	3
310	REF. DESK	362	174	8			9	3261	872	24			25	553	4182	67	75
311	GENERAL REF.	40						358						40	358	5	6
318	AOTODATABASE	12						94						12	94	1	2
331	INFORMAL INS	3						29						3	29	0	1
		-----	-----	-----	-----	-----	-----	-----	-----	-----	-----	-----	-----	------	------	--	--
		430	270	67			55	3839	1352	192			158	822	5541		

Example 14. CSUN Labor Report—Collection Development

REPORT 1. HOURS AND COSTS BY ORGANIZATIONAL UNITS FOR 3/31/79NO, ORGANIZATIONAL UNIT NO. 19 COLLECTION DEVELPMNT

		HOURS BY EMPLOYEE TYPE						COST BY EMPLOYEE TYPE									
TASK	TASK NAME	LIBRN.	STAFF	STUD.	SUBLIB	SUBSTAFF	W.S.	LIBRN.	STAFF	STUD.	SUBLIB	SUBSTAFF	W.S.	HOURS TOTAL	COST TOTAL	% ORG. TOT.HRS.	% ORG. TOT.COST
1	LIB.ADMN.GEN	9						70		1				9	71	1	1
2	LIB.ADMN-COM	14						141						14	141	1	1
3	DEPT. ADMIN.	84						864						84	864	5	8
16	FACLTY P.T.&	82						809						82	809	5	8
17	PERSNL. GENL		4						20					4	20	0	0
21	ADMN.SUP.DEP		34	2					144	4				36	148	2	1
22	ADMN.SUP.OTH		77	131					381	492				208	873	14	8
27	US&CAMPUSMAI		6	37					28	107				43	135	3	1
31	REQ. TRAININ		17				27		87				79	44	166	3	2
41	PROF.DEVLPMN	32						304						32	304	2	3
42	PROF. ASSOC.	4						46						4	46	0	0
43	RESEARCH	2						23						2	23	0	0
51	SPECL.ASSIST	51						527						51	527	3	5
56	AUTHORD. T/O	82	41	1			1	871	206	4			2	125	1083	8	10
101	DESELECTION	8						70						8	70	1	1
111	GENL.SELECT.	257						2573						257	2573	17	24
112	APPRVL.SELEC	89						850						89	850	6	8
113	GIFTS SELECT	20						192						20	192	1	2
118	PRE-ORDER CH		187	41			121		1034	132			350	349	1516	23	14
119	PREORDCHKOCL		40						216					40	216	3	2
142	RECVNG. GIFT		31						129					31	129	2	1
		-----	-----	-----	-----	-----	-----	-----	-----	-----	-----	-----	-----	------	------	--	--
		734	437	212			149	7340	2245	740			431	1532	10756		

Example 15. CSUN Labor Report—Circulation, South

REPORT 1. HOURS AND COSTS BY ORGANIZATIONAL UNITS FOR 3/31/79NO, ORGANIZATIONAL UNIT NO. 27 CIRCULATION--SOUTH

		HOURS BY EMPLOYEE TYPE						COST BY EMPLOYEE TYPE						HOURS	COST	% ORG.	% ORG.
TASK	TASK NAME	LIBRN.	STAFF	STUD.	SUBLIB	SUBSTAFF	W.S.	LIBRN.	STAFF	STUD.	SUBLIB	SUBSTAFF	W.S.	TOTAL	TOTAL	TOT.HRS.	TOT.COST
81	BLDG. MAINT.		33	48			9		144	148			25	90	317	4	5
271	CIRCCTRL&DES		38	268			119		185	856			340	425	1381	21	21
273	EXIT CONTROL		3	158			137		15	463			397	298	875	15	13
274	STACK MAINT.		22	218			140		102	645			406	380	1153	19	17
275	STACK READIN		7	117			42		31	345			121	166	497	8	7
276	RESERVE BK.R		142	436			87		755	1316			255	665	2326	32	35
277	SEARCH/HOLDS		4	21					21	75				25	96	1	1
		-----	-----	-----	-----	-----	-----	-----	-----	-----	-----	-----	-----	------	------	--	--
			249	1266			534		1253	3848			1544	2049	6645		

Example 16. CSUN Labor Report—Fine Arts Reference

REPORT 1. HOURS AND COSTS BY ORGANIZATIONAL UNITS FOR 3/31/79NO, ORGANIZATIONAL UNIT NO. 28 FINE ARTS REFERENCE

		HOURS BY EMPLOYEE TYPE						COST BY EMPLOYEE TYPE						HOURS	COST	% ORG.	% ORG.
TASK	TASK NAME	LIBRN.	STAFF	STUD.	SUBLIB	SUBSTAFF	W.S.	LIBRN.	STAFF	STUD.	SUBLIB	SUBSTAFF	W.S.	TOTAL	TOTAL	TOT.HRS.	TOT.COST
84	NON-REV.MAIN		4						22					4	22	1	1
204	END PROCESS.		21	56			4		128	182			13	81	323	14	16
252	AUTHORTY FIL		2	38					11	112				40	123	7	6
271	CIRCCTRL&DES	2	59	292			105	20	352	879			303	458	1554	77	75
272	FINES & BILL		1						7					1	7	0	0
274	STACK MAINT.			4						11				4	11	1	1
276	RESERVE BK.R	1		1				5	2	3				2	10	0	0
277	SEARCH/HOLDS								1						1	0	0
311	GENERAL REF.			3						8				3	8	1	0
319	SLIDES DESK						2			1			5	2	6	0	0
		-----	-----	-----	-----	-----	-----	-----	-----	-----	-----	-----	-----	------	------	--	--
		3	87	394			111	25	523	1196			321	595	2065		

SERVICE ANALYSIS

Once the hour and cost data are collected, an excellent tool is available for budget defense and for observing the operational changes occurring within the organization from year to year. The impact of newly introduced automated systems and the results of personnel changes upon services will be more easily assessed. There is, however, another very important program which is necessary to the establishment of a total management system—in addition to knowing the cost of providing a particular service, we also need to know about the quality of that service. Is the quality so poor that we would serve our patrons better by eliminating that service? Is the service of such high quality that we are neglecting other important services in order to maintain it? How does the quality of service in the reference department compare with the quality of service in the catalog department? These are a few of the questions that a service analysis should address.

Every task performed within the library is a service to the patron; if not directly, then indirectly in the form of services to another library unit which provides either materials for patron use or support for library personnel through budgeting, training, and other planning and support activities. An analysis of service quality, therefore, encompasses all tasks performed and determines the extent to which standards are achieved for these services. Service standards is a topic which alone could fill several volumes—there are national standards, state or system-wide standards, local library standards, and individual professional standards. All are important to an administrator's analysis of the quality of service in a library. ALMS emphasizes the development of local library standards through the use of written and agreed upon individual professional standards. These standards may include both national and system-wide standards whenever judged by the individual to be appropriate. Rosemary DuMont, in her article on library effectiveness, expresses an overall philosophy which is consistent with ALMS:

> If the notion is accepted that libraries are unique and pursue divergent goals reflective of their own unique environment, then one must move away from a general conceptual definition of library effectiveness toward a more operational one. Thus it appears to be useful to develop a contingency approach and to define library effectiveness in terms of each library's level of ability in responding to its own unique situational and environmental constraints.[3]

And that, I believe, is precisely the point. Libraries are unique—not even all the libraries under a single funding agency will share all of the same standards or the same day-to-day goals. Academic libraries vary in number and type of individuals served, from small undergraduate colleges to larger universities emphasizing graduate research. Before the quality of service can be analyzed, each library must develop its own local standards.

In addressing the issue of the establishment of local standards, we must begin with the recognition and acceptance of the reality that standards do exist in all libraries. Normally, these standards are unwritten and reside in the minds of the librarians who perform the services, the patrons who utilize the services, and the administrators who are ultimately responsible for the services. However, the three groups may disagree significantly in their definitions. A librarian may focus on quality of information; an administrator may focus on what services the budget will allow; and a patron may focus on omissions in service. In the university setting, library services will be related to the overall mission of the university, whereas in the public library, services will be related to the needs of the community served. Written statements of the kinds and levels of services to be provided should unify librarians, library administrators, and funding agents as to service expectations, and they are vital to the overall smooth operation of a library.

How, then, are such written statements prepared? Begin with the tasks currently performed, those tasks established in accordance with the labor analysis in the first section of this chapter. Select one task, sit down with the person(s) performing the task and his/her supervisor, and construct an analysis of the task following the steps given below. If you are an administrator above the department head level, this responsibility should be delegated to the department head. If a system analyst is on staff, he/she will be able to assist the supervisor with the analysis.

The initial step in an analysis of service adequacy is to determine the actual service provided by a particular task and the beneficiary of the service. In other words, if the service were terminated, who would care? A negative response to this latter question would indicate a possible candidate for service reduction. Let us use the task of receiving library materials in the acquisitions department to illustrate the development of an analysis of service adequacy. Service is provided by the receiving unit to the collection development librarians in the form of physically unpacking shipments and through verification of the materials received; that is, the materials shipped are determined to be exactly as specified by librarians. Further, service is provided to collection development librarians by staff follow-up on incomplete orders, assuring that a maximum number of selected materials will be procured. Reference librarians are served in that materials reach the shelves as quickly as possible, become accessible to patrons and thereby increase the information flow. This task also serves catalog librarians who require a constant flow of materials for manageable, even personnel workloads. Finally, there is service to the accounting section of the library in that invoices are verified for payment in order to update fund balances.

The second step is to determine the criteria to be utilized in discerning the adequacy of the service performed. Is it speed of processing? The number of patrons in a queue? The accuracy of the data provided? The amount of data provided? In the above example, that of receiving library materials for the collection, the criteria will likely be speed of unpacking materials received, consistency and timeliness of follow-up for materials not received, and accuracy and speed of verification of invoices.

The third step in the task analysis process is to determine the level of service provided by current practices. Using the above criteria, the initial statement of service might look like Example 17, in which criteria for adequacy have been italicized.

Example 17. Task Analysis—Receiving Library Materials—Statement of Current Level of Service

Task	*Level of Service*
Receiving Library Materials	Service is provided to the librarians responsible for the selection of materials, the librarians serving at reference desks, the catalog librarians, and to the accounting section. Packages are opened, materials received are checked against the invoice and the order slip, and forwarded to the catalog department *within one week of receipt*. Invoices are sent to accounting *within one week of receipt* of the materials billed. Materials ordered but not received *within six months of the date of order* are queried.

Step four involves an analysis of the adequacy of the level of service provided by current practices. Is one week fast enough for delivering the materials to cataloging? How would service be affected if the time for delivering materials were extended to one month or reduced to one day? What if the invoices were held for two weeks instead of one? If queries were made every three months instead of six, would materials reach the shelves more quickly? Would this result justify the amount of personnel time required to query more often? What is a minimally acceptable level of service? An optimum level? And what do minimum and optimum mean? For the purposes of this exercise, let us assume the following definitions: "Minimally required" is the level below which library patrons regularly express a need for more service,[4] backlogs develop, or quality is inadequate in the judgment of the librarians. "Optimum" is

Example 18. Task Analysis—Receiving Library Materials—Statement of Service Adequacy

Task	*Level of Service*
Receiving Library Materials	Service is provided to the librarians responsible for the selection of materials, the librarians serving at reference desks, the catalog librarians, and to the accounting section. Packages are opened, materials received are checked against the invoice and the order slip, and forwarded to the catalog department *within one week of receipt*. Invoices are sent to accounting *within one week of receipt* of the materials billed. Materials ordered but not received *within six months of the date of order* are queried.

ANALYSIS: The current service is below that which is minimally required. Considering the other processing steps, a week's delay at the receiving point is unacceptable. No processing time in receiving is gained by the delay. No additional staff time is required to process materials on the first day of arrival than to process on the seventh day. Additionally, there is a tendency to group materials and forward them to the catalog departmetn once or twice a week instead of every day, causing an uneven work flow for cataloging staff. The flow of invoices to the accounting section is also too slow. At the end of the month when accounts should be current, there is a flury of last minute posting activity in order to exhibit up-to-the-minute fund balances. Delays in processing also slow payment to the supplier and foster poor public relations.

Based on discussions by librarians and staff, an optimum level of service would be provided by forwarding the materials to the catalog department and the invoices to the accounting section on the day received, and such should be the goal of this unit. Cost studies indicate that an optimum level is attainable by applying 80 hours of student assistant time (@ $3.00 per hour) to catch-up the backlog. After the backlog is eliminated, continuing at the optimum level should be no more costly than the current practice. Three additional booktrucks at $100.00 each will also be required.

The six-month time period allotted to follow-up on orders not received is also too slow. A recent test study illustrates that orders queried within three months yield a 5% greater return than the six-month practice, and requires only a 2% increase in student assistant hours. The total cost increase was $320.00 (40 hours, $3.00 per hour for labor and $200.00 in increased postage and supplies). Following up on orders more frequently than every three months did not substantially increase the amount of materials received, and the cost was significantly greater. Therefore, the latter alternative is too costly to consider. A total cost of $860.00 would raise the service provided by this task to a nearly optimum level.

defined as a level of service which is reasonable and appropriate, in the judgment of the librarians, given the necessary technology and budget support.

"Optimum" should be defined in such a way that attainment is possible; pie-in-the-sky conjecture is of very little utility in this kind of exercise. Example 18 repeats the current level of service shown in Example 17 and adds an analysis of adequacy. Note that the definition of an optimum level of service in the first instance was based upon opinion, while the second was based upon the results of a study. The basis for such assertions should be stated.

Step five represents the inclusion of personnel by type of staff required to provide the current level of service, as well as estimates of the personnel hours necessary to provide both the minimum and optimum levels of service. In some instances, minimum and optimum levels of service may require equal amounts of staff time. Additionally, step five may include the volume of activity in units chosen to best represent the task. The issue of production units is a complicated one, but for purposes of the analysis of a single task, each unit produced should be identified. For the purpose of assessing unit costs, a single representative unit may be selected which represents the overall purpose served by that task. This allows for some measure of costing without creating an overwhelming mass of detail.

Example 19 repeats the current level of service and analysis of adequacy from Examples 17 and 18 and appends the personnel hours and production volume described in Step Five above. Hours are categorized by librarian, library assistant/clerical, and student assistant. Notice in Example 19 that the optimum and minimum levels of service require the same number of hours. Reviewing the analysis of adequacy, we find that querying more frequently than every three months is not cost effective, that is, the increase in completed orders was not significant while the cost was considerable. Also note that the 80 hours of student assistant time required to update the backlog is recorded separately, preventing a distortion of the analysis of ongoing labor requirements for the following year.[5]

With an ongoing cost and service analysis program, changes in the number of hours devoted to the receiving task are recognized and related to possible changes in quality of service (speed in the present example). In other words, it is possible to observe the effects on library service of any addition or deletion of personnel hours. Through such analysis, it is also possible to determine the most useful application of any additional funds that may become available. However, more impor-

Example 19. Task Analysis—Receiving Library Materials—Statement of Personnel Hours and Production Volume

Task	*Level of Service*		*Libn*	*Lib Asst/ Cler*	*Stud Asst*
Receiving Library Materials	Service is provided to the librarians responsible for the selection of materials, the librarians serving at reference desks, the catalog librarians and to the accounting section. Packages are opened, materials received are checked against the invoice and the order slip, and forwarded to the catalog department *within one week of receipt.* Invoices are sent to accounting *within one week of receipt* of the materials billed. Materials ordered but not received *within six months of the date of order* are queried.	current	0	1182	964
		minimum	0	1182	1004
		optimum	0	1182	1004
				(backlog)	80

ANALYSIS: The current service is below that which is minimally required. Considering the other processing steps, a week's delay at the receiving point is unacceptable. No processing time in receiving is gained by the delay. No additional staff time is required to process materials on the first day of arrival than to process on the seventh day. Additionally, there is a tendency to group materials and forward them to the catalog department once or twice a week instead of every day, causing an uneven work flow for cataloging staff. The flow of invoices to the accounting section is also too slow. At the end of the month when accounts should be current, there is a flurry of last minute posting activity in order to exhibit up-to-the-minute fund balances. Delays in processing also slow payment to the supplier and foster poor public relations.

Based on discussions by librarians and staff, an optimum level of service would be provided by forwarding the material to the catalog department and the invoices to the accounting section on the day received, and such should be the goal of this unit. Cost studies indicate that an optimum level is attainable by applying 80 hours of student assistant time ($3.00 per hour) to catch-up the backlog. After the backlog is eliminated, continuing at optimum level should be no more costly than the current practice. Three additional booktrucks @ $100.00 each will also be required.

The six-month time period allotted to follow-up on orders not received is also too slow. A recent test study illustrates that orders queried within three months yield a 5% greater return than the six-month practice, and require only a 2% increase in student assistant hours. The total cost increase was $320.00 (40 hours, $3.00 per hour for labor and $200.00 in increased postage and supplies). Following up on orders more frequently than every three months did not substantially increase the amount of materials received, and the cost was significantly greater. Therefore, the latter alternative is too costly to consider. A total cost of $860.00 would raise the service provided by this task to a nearly optimum level.

PRODUCTION VOLUME = 42,529 items received.

tantly, data from this analysis provide a base from which library administrators may defend the budget. The appropriate budget authorities may be informed of exactly what reduction in service must accompany each proposed budget reduction, or vice versa, what funds are necessary to bring service to an optimum level. For example, a reduction in the library materials budget, that is, the budget for collection development, should be accompanied by staff reductions that do not reduce service. However, cuts in the personnel and/or operating expense (OE) sections of the budget may very well go beyond those related to reductions in the budget for library materials, and library administrators need to respond with a defensible statement of service reduction.

The operating expense budget is also a part of the cost of providing service and is directly linked with the tasks in parts one and two of this chapter—the labor and service analyses. Operating expense funds can be budgeted by each organizational unit or controlled centrally by the library's administration. In either instance, supplies, equipment, service contracts, and operating expenses can be allocated to specific tasks, and the task analyses will form a basis for projecting the operating expense budget. For example, the receiving task detailed earlier in this chapter may result in an operating expense analysis that would read as follows:

> The increase in frequency of orders queried will require an accompanying increase in the operating expense of $200.00 for additional postage, query forms, and envelopes. Other supplies should remain consistent with last year given the projection of a stable materials budget. Supervisors estimate that for each 10% of change (up or down) in the materials budget, postage and supplies will fluctuate by approximately $325.00. Additionally, an increase in the flow of items received from the receiving unit to the catalog department will require the purchase of three additional booktrucks at $100.00 each, a total of $300.00. These trucks are necessary to discontinue the practice of holding trucks until completely filled before moving materials to the catalog department. After adding 10% for cost increases resulting from inflation, other operating expenses are expected to remain constant.

This completes the underlying structure of ALMS: (1) analysis of the purchasing power of the current budget in personnel hours, and (2) an analysis of the quality of service presently provided by these personnel hours. The following chapters will examine the function of ALMS, the use of these analyses for preparation and justification of the personnel and operating expense budgets, personnel utilization, and goal setting.

NOTES AND REFERENCES

1. Ray A. Killian (1978), *Human Resource Development: A Manager's Guide.* New York: American Management Association, Extension Institute.

2. Betty Jo Mitchell, Norman E. Tanis, and Jack Jaffe (1978), *Cost Analysis of Library Functions: A Total System Approach.* Greenwich, Conn: JAI Press.

3. Rosemary Ruhig Du Mont (1980), "A Conceptual Basis for Library Effectiveness," *College and Research Libraries* 41(2):109.

4. Opinion may be solicited through patron survey, comments in a suggestion box, faculty committees, verbal input to staff at information points, and any other means that fit your organization.

5. The Appendix contains an example of a complete service analysis. It represents the first analysis completed at CSUN, requiring nearly a year to develop, discuss and refine. Subsidized staff are not shown separately and reduced the utility of the analysis. Much more analysis and refinement are needed to increase its value as a planning tool.

Chapter 3

Budget Justification and Defense

Budget justification and defense can be more difficult for libraries than for other nonprofit agencies due to the complexities of services rendered and the inability of library administrators to explain library operations in lay terms. Funding agencies usually are comprised of individuals with little or no experience in libraries or library administration. How can these individuals be expected to understand funding needs without a clear idea of library operations?

Libraries operate in terms of services performed, not profit in dollars. Yet, as with any business showing an accounting of its annual profits to the board of directors for possible budget expansion, so a library that can account for its services—demonstrate a profit on its alloted funds—is better prepared to petition a funding agency for an increase in allocation. Or, perhaps more importantly for these budgetary times, the library that can demonstrate the expense of its services may retain its present funding. To assist funding agencies in understanding library operations, library service (and the resources necessary for its provision) must be translated into an accounting exercise that produces debits on one side of the ledger sheet and credits on the other, all focused on an end product of the book-to-patron service. As Thomas Galvin stated the problem:

> We have lacked adequate or effective means of identifying and describing the quality of our institutional product. It is service—by nature largely intangible and difficult to measure. Consequently, we are placed in a difficult posture with respect to accountability. We are neither able to plan on the basis of how much might ultimately be enough, nor have we been able to account in any very satisfactory way to fiscal authorities for precisely what we have accomplished with the resources that have already been made available to us. We have little more to offer than statistics of

> collection size and circulation, and we are discovering that these are data of dubious authenticity and even more dubious significance to funding authorities. The great danger, to borrow a phrase from Robert Munn, is that the library comes to resemble 'a bottomless pit' in the eyes of those who make the ultimate funding decisions.[1]

To simplify such a complex entity is not an easy task, but neither is it impossible. Months, or even years, are required to complete the transition to an accounting system for library services, the time required being dependent upon the budget size. The service analysis will require several months, at the least, to allow staff to consider their activities in terms of actual tasks performed and task definitions.

There can be a natural reluctance on the part of some individuals to spend the time necessary to incorporate ALMS, or "philosophize" as some may view the exercise, when backlogs develop and patron queues form. True, it is the responsibility of each staff member to assure that his/her area of the library is operating with maximum efficiency, while defense of the budget is the responsibility of the administrative staff. But in order to develop a sound management system, the library must operate as a whole unit. Any management system, such as ALMS, requires team effort to provide maximum results, and such effort should include both middle level and upper level management. Without a genuine interest and cooperation on the part of middle management, ALMS will provide adequate budget defense, but will fall short of realizing its capabilities as a dynamic tool for the effective use of personnel and other resources in providing the best possible service for each dollar.

In Chapter 2, the analysis of the receiving task in Example 18 provided a preview of how ALMS data can be used for budget justification:

> An optimum level would be provided by forwarding the materials to the catalog department and the invoices to the accounting section on the day received, and such should be the goal of this unit. . . . A total cost of $860 would raise the service to a nearly optimum level.

By using the above analysis, the funding agency has been informed of two important facts: (1) a reduced budget for this task would produce greater delays in the materials reaching the patrons; and (2) for a moderate budget increase, a significant improvement in service can be realized.

The following question has been posed to me: "If the funding agency is made aware of the precise services purchased with our funds, is it not possible that a service will be declared unworthy of funding and deleted from the budget?" Yes, the budget may be cut, if justification can not be made to the satisfaction of the funding agency. However, during this time of taxpayer protest over high taxes, budgets are being reduced from a simple lack of funds, sometimes due to a conviction that administrators are not utilizing funds in the best possible manner. ALMS, at least, demonstrates that administrators are attempting to exercise sound management practices in the expenditure of funds and to be open and honest with the funding agency and local administrators, adding credibility to arguments for budget support. For academic libraries, often at the mercy of local administrators with a habit of transferring library personnel monies to other areas of the campus, ALMS provides a graphic method for illustrating the impact upon students and faculty of every library position lost to another campus unit. And assuming budget cuts are a reality, ALMS provides sound management data upon which to base decisions concerning the reduction or elimination of services.

Another question sometimes raised is "Isn't it possible that the funding agency will challenge the use of so many staff hours to perform task 'x' or 'y'?" Again, if the use of staff cannot be justified to the funding agency's satisfaction, budget cuts may follow. Such an approach requires that you study the functioning of your organization carefully and be prepared to change what you cannot justify. In some instances the rise and fall of quality of a service may result simply from the speed and accuracy of an exceptional individual and his/her eventual resignation. New employees may require additional hours to complete tasks, at least during the training phase. Accept that reality, but further accept that the loss of an exceptional employee cannot be used as an easy excuse for every deterioration of service. Credibility evolves over a period of time following a series of positive experiences which clearly illustrate a firm grasp of the organization's performance and your honesty in sharing information with your funding agency or local administrators.

The budget process begins with a determination of the total hours expended for all tasks by employee category. Using the tasks listed in Example 2, a recapitulation of the budget indicating the total number of hours at the task level for each employee category is contained in Example 20, the "Task Level Budget Report." The full-time equivalent (FTE) staff for each personnel category may then be determined by dividing the total hours in each employee category by 2080 (40 work hours per week x 52).

Note that under the receiving function, the proposed changes specified in the Task Level Budget Report relate directly to the analysis of service (see Example 18). Similarly, all other changes in the budget report and justification, both increases and decreases, will derive from the analysis of service. Several functions from Example 20 indicating changes in personnel hours are noted below. The analysis of service would contain a full-blown description of the anticipated change such as that specified for the Receiving task in Example 18.

Example 20. Task Level Budget Report—Personnel

Average Rates per hour:			
Librarians	$10.00	Subsidized Librarian:	$8.00
Staff	5.70	Subsidized Staff:	$4.40
Stud. Asst.	3.20	Subsidized Student Assistant	$3.00

Function	*Task*	*Hours* Libn. (10.00)	Staff (5.70)	Stud. Asst. (3.20)	Subdz. Libn. (8.00)	Subdz. Staff (4.40)	Subdz. S/A (3.00)	*Line Totals*	*Projected Changes*
Administration	Library Admin.—General	4,728	192	6	—	—	—		
	Library Admin.—Committees	1,206	132	24	—	—	12		
	Dept. Admin.	5,394	3,198	60	—	42	6		
	Campus Admin.	990	108	—	—	—	—		
	Exhibits	330	18	—	—	—	—		
	Chancellor's Off. Adm.	1,848	264	—	—	—	—		
	Regional Cooperation	210	—	—	—	—	12		
	Total Hours	14,706	3,912	90		42	30	18,780	Add 10% for cost of living increase.
	Total Dollars	147,060	22,298	288		184	90	$169,920	
Personnel	Personnel hiring and evaluation	3,138	1,254	—	—	—	—	4,392	Add 10% for cost of living increase.
	Total Dollars	31,380	7,147					$38,527	
Administrative Support	Typing & Clerical Support: Dept.	120	6,684	2,436	—	132	936		
	Typing and Clerical Support: All other	1,584	5,010	1,926	—	—	2,070		
	Support of Professional Assoc. & Research	84	—	—	—	—	—		
	Mail	48	420	1,416	—	276	654		
	Total Hours	1,836	12,114	5,778	—	408	3,660	23,796	Add 10% for cost of living increase.
	Total Dollars	18,360	69,049	18,489	—	1,795	10,980	$118,673	
Personnel Training	Required Training	750	9,210	5,136	195	498	3,354		Add 300 hrs. @ $10/hr for AACR2 training. Reduce by 195 hrs. @ $8/hr for training of new subsidized librarian, now completed ($780 for library portion). Add 10% of cost of living increase.
	Optional Training	168	498	6	—	—	18		
	Total Hours	918	9,708	5,142	195	498	3,372	19,833	
	Total Dollars	9,180	55,335	16,454	1,560	2,191	10,116	$94,836	

Professional Tasks	Professional Development	1,902	282	—	36	—	—		Add 10% for cost of living increases. Add 25 hours @ $8/hr for library to assume full cost of subsidized librarian.
	Professional Associations	474	—	—	15	—	—		
	Research	936	—	—	—	—	—		
	Total Hours	3,312	282	—	51	—	—	3,645	
	Total Dollars	33,120	1,607	—	408	—	—	$35,135	
Special Assistance	Nonroutine assistance to other departments or units	1,404	456	—	—	—	450	2,310	
	Total Dollars	$14,040	2,599	—	—	—	1,350	$17,989	Add 10% for cost of living increases.
Authorized Time-off	Coffee breaks, jury duty, vacation, sick leave.	8,568	16,320	2,130	220	1,014	1,410	29,662	Add 10% for cost of living increases. Add 110 hours @ $8/hr. for library to assume full cost of subsidized librarian.
	Total Dollars	85,680	93,024	6,816	1,760	4,461	4,230	$195,971	
Systems Analysis	Systems Analysis	1,296	48	—	—	—	—	1,344	
	Total Dollars	12,960	273	—	—	—	—	$13,233	Add 10% for cost of living increases.
Computer Programming	New Programming	120	—	—	—	—	—		Add 10% for cost of living increases. Add 1008 hours @ $10/hr. for addition of one-half time programmer for new programs.
	Reprogramming	36	—	—	—	—	—		
	Program Maintenance	1,044	—	—	—	—	—		
	Total Hours	1,200	—	—	—	—	—	1,200	
	Total Dollars	12,000	—	—	—	—	—	$12,000	
Maintenance	Bldg. Maint. & Security	24	696	1,104	—	—	342		
	Revenue-producing machines: Maintenance	54	486	912	—	—	2,892		
	Non-revenue-producing machines: Maintenance	42	402	456	—	6	696		
	Total Hours	120	1,584	2,472	—	6	3,930	8,112	Add 10% for cost of living increases.
	Total Dollars	1,200	9,028	7,910	—	26	11,790	$29,954	
Deselection	Deselecting	318	—	—	—	—	—		
	Withdrawing	54	264	378	—	—	54		
	Total Hours	372	264	378	—	—	54	1,068	Add 10% for cost of living increases.
	Total Dollars	3,720	1,504	1,209	—	—	162	$6,595	
Selection	General Selection	3,414	—	240	384	18	—		
	Approval selection	888	—	—	—	—	—		
	Gifts selection	264	—	—	—	—	—		
	Pre-order Checking (manual)	12	1,932	480	—	42	1.254		

(Continued)

Example 20. (Continued)

Function	Task	Hours: Libn. (10.00)	Staff (5.70)	Stud. Asst. (3.20)	Subdz. Libn. (8.00)	Subdz. Staff (4.40)	Subdz. S/A (3.00)	Line Totals	Projected Changes
	Pre-order Checking (OCLC)	—	366	—	—	—			Add 192 hours @ $8/hr. to assume full cost of subsidized librarian. Add 10% for cost of living increases.
	Total Hours	4,578	2,298	720	384	60	1,254		
	Total Dollars	45,780	13,098	2,304	3,072	264	3,762	$68,280	
Ordering	Ordering library materials	54	3,924	120	—	72	42	4,212	Add 10% for cost of living increases.
	Total Dollars	540	22,366	384	—	316	126	$23,732	
Receiving	Receiving: General	30	1,452	—	—	72	780		
	Receiving: Gifts	96	330	—	—	—	—		
	Receiving: Approval	—	882	558	—	—	—		
	Periodicals Check-in	—	1,878	756	—	—	636		
	Serials Check-in	—	4,254	90	—	—	1,362		
	Govt. Docs. Processing	930	702	1,182	—	—	2,910		
	Total Hours	1,056	9,498	2,586	—	72	5,688	18,900	Add 120 hrs. @ $3 to catch up backlog and increase querying frequency. Add 10% for cost of living increases.
	Total Dollars	10,560	54,138	8,275	—	316	17,064	$90,353	
Accounting	Library Material Acctg.	—	1,068	—	—	—	—		
	Fiscal Claims	—	1,782	30	—	—	66		
	Payroll	—	666	186	—	—	—		
	Operating Exp. Acctg.	—	108	—	—	—	—		
	Total Hours	—	3,624	216	—	—	66	3,906	Add 10% for cost of living increases.
	Total Dollars	—	20,656	691	—	—	198	$21,545	
Cataloging	Bibliographic Checking	—	192	246	—	—	444		
	Adaptive Cataloging	348	1,662	—	—	—	618		
	Original Cataloging	2,418	1,008	—	—	—	—		

	Recataloging	198	558	66	—	—	—		
	Add Holdings (manual)	—	210	—	—	—	—		
	OCLC Copy Cat/ Checking	48	2,082	582	—	—	360		
	OCLC Adaptive Cataloging	342	1,968	—	—	—	—		
	OCLC Original Cataloging	138	—	—	—	—	—		
	OCLC Recataloging	2,028	252	—	—	—	150		
	Card Preparation	—	2,088	1,104	—	126	—		
	OCLC Inputting	—	1,458	—	—	—	—		
	Total Hours	5,520	11,478	1,998	—	126	1,572	20,694	Add 10% for cost of living increases.
	Total Dollars	55,200	65,424	6,393	—	554	4,716	$132,287	
Physical Processing	In-house Binding	—	—	546	—	—	1,032		
	Bindery Prep. & Returns	—	1,578	—	—	—	312		
	Mending	—	96	636	—	—	2,700		
	Final Processing/Pockets, etc.	30	1,974	2,694	—	342	2,856		
	Total Hours	30	3,648	3,876	—	342	6,900	14,796	Add 10% for cost of living increases.
	Total Dollars	300	20,793	12,403	—	1,504	20,700	$55,700	
Inventory	General Inventory	60	186	108	—	—	42	396	Add 10% for cost of living increases.
	Total Dollars	600	1,060	345	—	—	126	$2,131	
Major and Public File Maintenance	Public Periodical Record Creation & Maintenance	—	240	216	—	—	—		
	Public Serial Record Creation & Maintenance	—	324	—	—	—	—		
	Catalog Maintenance	816	5,262	2,784	—	756	2,622		
	Automated Shelflist Maintenance	—	2,364	612	—	—	984		
	Authority File Maint.	120	1,218	1,500	—	246	54		
	Union List Maint.	—	120	—	—	—	—		
	Total Hours	936	9,528	5,112	—	1,002	3,660	20,238	Add 10% for cost of living increases.
	Total Dollars	9,360	54,309	16,358	—	4,408	10,980	$95,415	
General Circulation	Circ. Control & Desk	48	4,356	15,780	—	66	8,610		
	Fines & Billing	—	2,064	2,478	—	36	570		
	Exit Control	—	24	3,900	—	—	3,138		

(Continued)

Example 20. (Continued)

Function	Task	Hours: Libn. (10.00)	Staff (5.70)	Stud. Asst. (3.20)	Subdz. Libn. (8.00)	Subdz. Staff (4.40)	Subdz. S/A (3.00)	Line Totals	Projected Changes
	Stack Maintenance	42	3,438	11,016	—	—	7,770		
	Stack Reading	—	402	2,634	—	—	2,094		
	Reserve Book Room	30	1,500	5,070	—	—	1,308		
	Search/Holds	—	588	2,412	—	—	186		
	Total Hours	120	12,372	43,290	—	102	23,676	79,560	Add 10% for cost of living increases.
	Total Dollars	1,200	70,520	138,528	—	448	71,028	$281,724	
Reference & Information Services	Reference Desks	9,618	1,896	90	835	—	102		
	General Reference	3,276	552	702	95	6	156		
	Photocopy Service	30	12	—	—	—	—		
	Information Desk	—	2,628	522	—	732	90		($1000 will be provided from the campus general fund for data base searches for faculty.) Add
	Thesis Consultation	294	—	—	—	—	—		
	Automated Data Base searching	474	—	—	—	—	—		

	Microform Desk	30	168	1,716	—	—	894		465 hours @ $8 for full cost of subsidized librarian. Add 100 hours @ $10 for addition of new data bases. Add 10% for cost of living increases.
	Total Hours	13,662	5,256	3,030	930	738	1,242	24,858	
	Total Dollars	136,620	29,959	9,696	7,440	3,247	3,726	$190,688	
Library Instruction	Informal Library Instruction	1,188	78	—	300	—	—		
	Bibliographic & Patron Instructions	366	294	—	—	144	444		Add 150 hrs @ $8 for full cost of subsidized librarian. Add 10% for cost of living increases.
	Total Hours	1,554	372	—	300	144	444	2,814	
	Total Dollars	15,540	2,120	—	2,400	633	1,332	$22,025	
Interlibrary Loan	Borrowing	540	1,290	768	—	—	162		Add 80 hrs @ $5.70 and 100 hrs. @ $3.20 for expected 10% increase in lending activity due to installation of OCLC ILL program. Add 10% for cost of living increases.
	Lending	42	834	1,302	—	—	372		
	Total Hours	582	2,124	2,070	—	—	534	5,310	
	Total Dollars	5,820	12,106	6,624	—	—	1,602	$26,152	
	Total Hours	65,022	110,250	79,116	2,080	4,626	58,026	319,056	
	Total FTE Positions	31.3	53.0	38.0	1.0	2.2	27.9	153.4	
	Total Dollars	650,220	628,413	253,167	16,640[1]	20,347[2]	174,078[3]	$1,742,865	
	Library Share	650,220	628,413	253,167	8,320	0	34,815	$1,574,935	

Notes:
1. One half of this position is paid through the CETA program.
2. All of these positions are paid through the CETA program.
3. 80% of these wages are paid by the Federal Government through the student work-study program.

Personnel Training

With the implementation of the new Anglo-American Catalogir Rules, Version 2, faculty and staff within the catalog department w undergo substantial training. This training time would be reflected the analysis of service by an explanatory statement of why AACR-2 trai ing is required, the estimated number of hours of training required (3(hours for the present example), and a statement of how the number training hours is derived. This increased training time would then l included under the personnel training function of the Task Level Bu get Report.

Professional Tasks

One explanation for a fluctuation in the professional tasks functio would be the amount of time necessary for librarians to attend profe sional association meetings and to research library problems, both keep abreast of current trends in the field and for promotion purpose A statement to this effect would be included in the analysis of servi with the corresponding hours contained in the Task Level Budg Report.

Authorized Time-Off

Hours recorded for the authorized time-off function are general easy to determine since vacation time is normally established librar wide and time allotted to sick leave can be averaged and estimated as percentage of the total hours budgeted for personnel. A statement as t the methodology used to derive these figures should be included in th analysis of service.

Computer Programming

The analysis of service for the computer programming function den onstrates a need for the addition of a half-time programmer positio and this addition is indicated in Example 20 in the task(s) where th programmer is expected to spend his/her time. A justification for th addition of the programmer would be written in the analysis of servic on the basis of either an increased workload or of a new service to b provided. If the 100 hours are to be devoted to the production of a ne computer program for the preparation of the student assistant payro for example, the new programming task service analysis should explain why it is important or necessary to institute such a program. Will future staff savings be received, and/or who will benefit from the added service and how?

Selection/Reference and Information Services/Library Instruction

For another example, assume the elimination of the CETA program by the federal government. If the library does not assume the full burden of the CETA librarian's salary and allows him/her to be terminated, what reduction in service will occur? In this particular example, the tasks of general selection, reference desks, general reference and informal library instruction under the reference function would deteriorate if the CETA librarian were not retained in a nonsubsidized position (see hours recorded on the Task Level Budget Report). Accordingly, an appeal should be included in the analysis of service of the affected areas to retain the CETA librarian based upon the importance of continuing the reference service at the present level, further supported by statements as to the effects upon service to patrons.

Also under the reference and information services function, the addition of 100 hours of librarian time for the augmentation of new data bases must be explained. The analysis of service would discuss the data bases to be added to the present configuration, why these particular data bases are important to library service, and how the 100-hour figure is derived. Example 21, the Operating Expense Budget, which will be discussed further below, includes a projected $500 to cover the cost of the new data bases in excess of user fees collected, that is, the fees collected from patrons to cover the direct costs of operating the data bases in a search. This figure would also be included in the analysis of service as the cost for the improvement of this service. Should a new computer terminal be needed to handle the additional traffic in data base searching, the cost of that terminal will be included in the Operating Expense Budget projection (Example 21 described below), along with the data bases.

Interlibrary Loan

Finally, the interlibrary loan (ILL) tasks have an analysis of service which discusses the installation of a new program for interlibrary loans utilizing the OCLC on-line system. The cost of terminal(s) necessitated by the new program must be included in the Operating Expense Budget

Example 21. Operating Expense Budget

Organizational Unit	*Function*	*Expenditures Last Year*	*Projected Budget*	*Change*[2]
Administration	Support Functions[1]	110,727	121,799	
	Systems Analysis	275	302	
	Computer Programming	800	880	
	Maintenance	2,200	2,420	
	Accounting	500	550	
Acquisitions	Support Functions	7,850	8,635	
	Ordering	4,500	4,950	
	Receiving	500	1,100	Add $500 for changes in level of service
	Accounting	250	275	
	Physical Processing	52,000	57,200	
	Major or public file maint.	500	550	
Cataloging	Support Functions	8,250	9,075	
	Deselection	100	110	
	Cataloging	10,250	11,275	
	Major or public file maint.	57,000	62,700	
Circulation	Support Functions	1,967	2,163	
	Maintenance	2,500	2,750	
	General Circulation	19,452	21,397	
Reference	Support Functions	8,225	9,047	
	Deselection	75	83	
	Receiving	850	935	
	Major or public file maint.	1,250	1,375	
	General Circulation	75	83	
	Ref. & Info. Services	300	880	Add $500 for new data bases—excess over users fees
	Library use instruction	2,675	2,942	
	Interlibrary loan	6,900	14,740	Add one OCLC terminal and use costs: $6500
Collection Development	Support Functions	1,029	1,131	
	Deselection	125	137	
	General Selection	250	275	
	Receiving	50	55	
		$301,425	$339,814	
	Add 10% for inflation.			

Notes:

1. Support functions include administration, personnel, administrative support, personnel training and professional tasks.
2. Explanations of the reasons for change come from the service analysis.

Example 21) and any increase in staffing necessary to handle antici-ated additional activity is included in the Task Level Budget Analysis. dditionally, if ILL is to be maintained as a free service, the projected)CLC charges should be included in the Operating Expense Budget Example 21).

These examples of fluctuations in time required for task performance nd of the demonstrated needs for employment of additional personnel, hile fabricated for our purposes here, will be similar to the situations ncountered in any large academic library. It is hoped that such illustra-ons will provide understanding of how such a budget is developed, but our budget projections may well contain many more anticipated or ecommended changes. For example, our costs in the area of library uilding maintenance are minimal due to the fact that the campus pro-ides the majority of our repair needs through its Department of Plant)perations, leaving optional maintenance costs to the library budget. A brary director responsible for all library maintenance will have a dif-erent breakdown of tasks within the maintenance function and a bud-et allowance to cover the expenses of both personnel and operating xpenses for this area.

Example 21, the Operating Expense Budget, includes supplies, equip-nent leases, maintenance contracts, new equipment purchases, binding, epairs, contractual services, and virtually all other library expenses, xclusive of items within the personnel and library materials budgets. Note that in Example 21 the functions of administration, personnel, dministrative support, personnel training, and professional tasks have een consolidated into a single category, "support functions." The fur-her categorization of the Operating Expense Budget into those five unctions appears to serve no useful purpose. The expenses within the upport function category generally include such items as pencils and aper, typewriters and typewriter maintenance, adding machines, and ll of the supplies and equipment ordinarily supporting office-type op-rations. For purposes of budget justification, the breakdown of expenses y organizational unit within the library is not necessary; however, some evel of breakdown is useful for purposes of internal control. In pre-aring their budget requests, supervisors may opt to analyze the operat-ng expense needs for their departments by tasks, requiring the em-loyee responsible for each task to anticipate such items as equipment eplacement needs, forms depletion, and supply changes due to in-reases or decreases in workload, thus allowing for a higher degree of ccuracy.

Once the Operating Expense Budget has been prepared by major rganizational unit within the library, and by function within the organizational unit, the functional expenses can then be summarized and r corded on the overall Function Level Budget (Example 22 describe below), along with the personnel budget, for a complete budget analysi

To present the budget to the funding agency in a more concise forn the hours recorded for each task in the Task Level Budget Report (E ample 20) may be consolidated by function. Example 22 illustrates th "Function Level Budget," deriving hours from the combining of th individual tasks listed in Example 20 and including a summary of th Operating Expense Budget from Example 21. The total personnel dolla in Example 22 equals the total dollars in Example 20; the total operatin expense dollars in Example 22 equals the total dollars in Example 2 and the analysis of service (such as that contained in Appendix 1) mu justify the hours recorded on the task summary, as well as any chang from the previous year requested on the Function Level Budget. I other words, the Task Level Budget Report provides a summary of th personnel hours indicated in the analysis of service (either at the cu rent, minimum or optimum level, depending upon the level of service t be provided) and the Function Level Budget provides a summary of th Task Level Budget Report as well as the operating expense requiremen by function such that the entire budget, excluding the library materia (books and periodicals) budget, appears on a single report.

It should be noted that if the library depends upon the accountin services of the parent institution, it would be quite useful for the librar and the institutional accounting unit to negotiate an expenditure repo format conforming to the established library categories. However, if reporting format cannot be developed to conform with the library bud get categories established, or if the local accounting reports arrive to late to be useful for management purposes, then the library may opt t develop its own system for expenditure accounting. Because accountin reports are not received from the central accounting office in a timel manner, the CSUN libraries have developed a simple program to main tain a continuous balance on encumbrances and expenditures using a Apple II Plus computer and the VisiCalc accounting package. Throug periodic updates to the Apple files by the budget assistant, the library capable of maintaining up-to-the-minute accounting of the allocation expenditures and transfers for each budget area. This continual moni toring allows the library administration to expend funds more precisel to the budgeted allocations. Without such careful scrutiny, thousands o dollars would remain unexpended at the end of the fiscal year from th CSUN library budget of nearly four million dollars, due to the accumu lation of unanticipated savings on purchases throughout the year. Suc savings can be utilized for additional purchases only if they can be first identified. For example, an item is estimated to cost $1,000 and that amount is encumbered against the budget; however, the actual invoice price is $900, $100 less than the estimated cost. You must have the ability to reincorporate that $100 savings into the budget for utilization in other areas. At CSUN, expenditures are first recorded on the Apple computer at the estimated cost. At a later date, when the actual invoice price is known, the estimated cost is replaced by the actual cost. The Apple computer then recalculates the new balance based upon the corrected figures. The same procedure applies to vacated, budgeted staff positions.

The Function Level Budget in Example 22 is the preliminary exercise for requesting and justifying the budget necessary for at least a minimal level of service. If a funding agency is only willing or able to fund a portion of the amount requested, then you must return to the service analysis to decide which services will be reduced, and a new Task Level Budget Report must be prepared indicating the actual allocations to each task for the coming year. The analysis of service must also reflect the final decision as to the level of service to be provided in the budget. At the end of the year, the labor (hours) report can be compared to the Task Level Budget Report to determine how personnel time was actually expended versus how this time was projected. Those differences between the actual and projected times then become the impetus for the next year's budget request. This year-end comparison can clearly demonstrate the impact of new programs, automation, personnel changes, and workload increases/decreases in library operations. That is one of the most significant advantages of this type of budget based management system. Library organizations are constantly changing at the task level. While functions appear to be more stable, hours devoted to specific tasks fluctuate dramatically during any given year. Example 23 illustrates changes in one library's receiving task during three successive fiscal years.

In order to absorb the full impact of the changes, one needs to know the volume of materials received during those three years. These figures are contained in the analysis of service for each year as illustrated at the end of Example 19.

1976/77 monographs and serials 10,020	other 59,832	total 69,852
1977/78 monographs and serials 11,071	other 49,389	total 60,460
1978/79 monographs and serials 9,858	other 33,221	total 43,079

Example 22. Function Level Budget—Personnel and Operating Expense

Function	*Total Personnel[1] $ Last Year*	*Library[2] Share*	*Personnel $ Projected for Next Year*	*Library Share*	*Change (Library Share)*	*Total Operating[1] Expense Last Year*	*Projected Operating Expense Next Year*	*Library Budget*	*Funds from Other Sources*	*Change (Library[3] Budget)*
Administration	169,920	169,665	186,912	186,631	+16,966	138,048	151,850	151,850		+13,802
Personnel	38,527	38,527	42,379	42,379	+3,852					
Administrative Support	118,673	108,095	130,540	118,904	+10,809					
Personnel Training	94,836	83,773	105,903	94,592	+10,819					
Professional Tasks	35,135	34,931	38,648	38,644	+3,713					
Special Assistance	17,989	16,909	19,788	18,599	+1,690					
Authorized Time-off	195,971	187,247	215,568	206,938	+19,691					
Systems Analysis	13,233	13,233	14,556	14,556	+1,323	275	302	302		+27
Computer Programming	12,000	12,000	24,288	24,288	+12,288	800	880	880		+80
Maintenance	29,954	20,496	32,949	22,545	+2,049	4,700	5,170	5,170		+470
Deselection	6,595	6,465	7,254	7,111	+646	300	330	330		+30
Selection	68,280	63,470	75,108	71,505	+8,035	250	275	275		+25
Ordering	23,732	23,313	26,105	25,645	+2,332	4,500	4,950	4,950		+450
Receiving	90,353	76,385	99,784	84,419	+8,034	1,400	2,090	2,090		+690

Accounting	21,545	21,386	23,698	23,524	+2,138	750	825	825		+75
Cataloging	132,287	127,961	145,515	140,757	+12,796	10,250	11,275	11,275		+1,025
Physical Preparation	55,700	37,636	61,270	41,399	+3,763	52,000	57,200	57,200		+5,200
Inventory	2,131	2,030	2,344	2,233	+203					
Major or Public File Maintenance	95,415	82,223	104,956	90,445	+8,222	58,750	64,625	64,625		+5,875
General Circulation	281,724	224,454	309,896	246,898	+22,444	19,527	21,480	21,480		+1,953
Reference and Information Services	190,688	180,740	210,856	204,006	+23,266	300	880	880	1,000[4]	+580
Library Instruction	22,025	19,126	24,227	22,358	+3,232	2,675	2,942	2,942		+267
Interlibrary Loan	26,152	24,870	29,620	28,210	+3,340	6,900	14,740	14,740		+7,840
Total Dollars	1,742,865	1,574,935	1,932,164	1,756,586	+181,651	301,425	339,814	339,814	1,000	+38,389

Notes:

1. Dollars were transferred from task level budget.
2. This figure comes from the first three columns of the task level budget, plus one-half of the subsidized librarian column, plus 20% of subsidized student assistant column.
3. Explanation of reasons for change comes from the task level budget, which comes from the service analysis.
4. Funds from other sources may include such things as grants, donations and transfers from other campus units or other governmental units. In this instance, $1,000 has been transferred from the campus general fund for the purpose of aiding faculty research efforts.

Example 23. Total Monthly Hours by Type of Staff

						Receiving Library Materials								
	Libn	*Staff*	*S/A*	*Total*		*Libn*	*Staff*	*S/A*	*Total*		*Libn*	*Staff*	*S/A*	*Total*
July 76	1	78	117	196	July 77		125	96	221	July 78	2	53	71	126
Aug		112	131	243	Aug		124	87	211	Aug		86	89	175
Sept		123	100	223	Sept		114	53	167	Sept		81	47	128
Oct		127	169	296	Oct	46	47	54	147	Oct	13	35	51	99
Nov		135	142	277	Nov	18	81	37	136	Nov	8	53	83	144
Dec		131	136	267	Dec		105	20	125	Dec	2	72	72	146
Jan 77		111	128	239	Jan 78		100	101	201	Jan 79	19	13	119	151
Feb		102	119	221	Feb		111	113	224	Feb	5	109	65	179
Mar		115	231	346	Mar		106	113	219	Mar		133	65	198
Apr		140	231	371	Apr	3	90	80	173	Apr		127	46	173
May		140	183	323	May		104	132	236	May		113	37	150
June		108	175	283	June		80	78	158	June		107	103	210
Totals	1	1422	1862	3285		67	1187	964	2218		49	982	848	1879
Average Monthly Hours				273	Average Monthly Hours				184	Average Monthly Hours				156

The correlation between items received and personnel hours devoted o the task over the three-year period from 76/77 to 78/79 is not immedi- ately obvious from the reported statistics:

	Items	*Hours*
76/77	69,852	3,285
77/78	60,460	2,218
78/79	43,079	1,879

From 76/77 to 77/78 items received dropped by 13% while hours de- oted to the task dropped by 32%. The following year a drop of 28% in tems received resulted in only a 15% drop in hours. The overall reduc- ion for the period from 76/77 to 78/79 in items received was 38% while he overall reduction in hours for the same period was 43%. Consider- ble analysis by the immediate supervisor is required for these fluctua- ions to have any meaning for operations planning.

Why did the total hours devoted to this task drop by 43% while the olume in items received dropped by only 38%? Could such a reduction e attributed to a change in procedure which resulted in greater effi- iency? A reduction in accuracy which increased the speed of process- ıg? A staff resignation which led to a new hire who was more productive? partial assignment of receiving staff to another unit, thereby reducing ıe amount of idle staff time? A change in type of material received esulting in less processing time per item? A change in type of staff used, esulting in a higher level of productivity? The drop in personnel hours ould have been caused by any one of those reasons, or a combination. n this example, the final conclusion of the supervisor was that several of ıose reasons applied, but the most significant reason for the dramatic ıcrease in efficiency was the reassignment of staff to another unit for 20 ours per week. This not only reduced the idle time of the staff member, ut it also reduced the number of student assistant hours that could be ıpervised by the staff member, resulting in an overall reduction of the ours devoted to the task. The point is that the number of hours re- uired to perform a particular task varies from month to month and ear to year. Because of these continual changes, spot checks may or may ot provide an accurate representation of the number of hours neces- ıry and the level of staff needed for the receiving task (or any other sk). However, a library opting to use sampling techniques to calculate ıe personnel hours necessary for any one task, could, after a number of ears of gathering data, obtain a rough estimate by sampling during a articular month which is most representative of the previous years' onthly averages. For example, after gathering data for three continu- ıs years, a library may determine that January appears to be the month hich best represents the monthly averages for the previous years for

Example 24. Total Monthly Hours (All Staff)

Selection of Library Materials

July 76	247	July 77	127	July 78	10
Aug	212	Aug	123	Aug	21
Sept	264	Sept	213	Sept	19
Oct	201	Oct	220	Oct	21
Nov	269	Nov	192	Nov	23
Dec	257	Dec	229	Dec	16
Jan 77	287	Jan 78	279	Jan 79	28
Feb	273	Feb	205	Feb	23
Mar	283	Mar	230	Mar	25
Apr	290	Apr	242	Apr	19
May	290	May	247	May	23
June	235	June	217	June	15
Ave. Mo. Hrs.	259	Ave. Mo. Hrs.	212	Ave. Mo. Hrs.	20

Note: September is the only month that represents the three monthly averages closely enough to b considered "typical."

the receiving task (Example 23). However, I emphasize that a samplin month must be determined for each particular task. To illustrate, exam ine the following examples from the same library (Examples 24, 25, 26 and 27). In each, January would not provide the necessary results.

As in the receiving task example above, there are many reasons fo monthly and yearly variances in the number of personnel hours require in each task, and departmental supervisors are in the best position t

Example 25. Total Monthly Hours (All Staff)

Administrative Support—Circulation

July 76	286	July 77	292	July 78	16
Aug	211	Aug	267	Aug	16
Sept	214	Sept	262	Sept	2
Oct	250	Oct	248	Oct	31
Nov	272	Nov	246	Nov	2
Dec	251	Dec	183	Dec	2
Jan 77	278	Jan 78	282	Jan 79	3
Feb	241	Feb	164	Feb	2
Mar	350	Mar	248	Mar	1
Apr	199	Apr	192	Apr	1
May	243	May	224	May	1
June	218	June	205	June	1
Ave. Mo. Hrs.	251	Ave. Mo. Hrs.	234	Ave. Mo. Hrs.	2

Note: No single month represents all three monthly averages well enough to consider it "typical."

Example 26. Total Monthly Hours (All Staff)

Government Documents Processing					
July 76	1199	July 77	754	July 78	654
Aug	1203	Aug	778	Aug	614
Sept	742	Sept	526	Sept	479
Oct	757	Oct	531	Oct	506
Nov	717	Nov	591	Nov	442
Dec	480	Dec	388	Dec	408
Jan 77	775	Jan 78	750	Jan 79	400
Feb	774	Feb	557	Feb	364
Mar	849	Mar	725	Mar	582
Apr	822	Apr	590	Apr	576
May	565	May	535	May	717
June	1807	June	1092	June	1363
Ave. Mo. Hrs.	890	Ave. Mo. Hrs.	651	Ave. Mo. Hrs.	592

Note: No single month represents all three monthly averages well enough to consider it "typical."

assess the reasons for these variances. Cause(s) for variance may range from employee efficiencies/deficiencies to workload increases/decreases, to the introduction of new technology, to new user demands. The point is that in order to budget for workload and technological demands, library administrators must be able to observe the changes in staffing patterns and operating expense demands, along with the corresponding

Example 27. Total Monthly Hours (All Staff)

Original Cataloging					
uly 76	462	July 77	297	July 78	184
Aug	623	Aug	317	Aug	365
ept	507	Sept	382	Sept	151
Oct	536	Oct	442	Oct	106
Nov	593	Nov	427	Nov	74
Dec	426	Dec	257	Dec	61
an 77	622	Jan 78	324	Jan 79	151
eb	484	Feb	341	Feb	176
Mar	580	Mar	437	Mar	222
Apr	477	Apr	291	Apr	229
May	442	May	317	May	134
une	414	June	344	June	200
Ave. Mo. Hrs.	513	Ave. Mo. Hrs.	348	Ave. Mo. Hrs.	171

ote: September is the closest month to a "typical" month but even it varies by some 10% in two cases.

effect of those changes on service to the users. Anything less is to allow the ship to steer its own course.

NOTE AND REFERENCE

1. Thomas J. Galvin (1976), "Beyond Survival, Library Management for the Future," *Library Journal* 101:1835.

Chapter 4

Allocation of Personnel

Human resource management requires a strong and dedicated administrative team, strong in its philosophy of service and dedicated to the development of techniques for detecting knowledge gaps and correcting the deficiencies. Human resource management requires continual analysis of services, continual assessment of the direction and changes in direction of the parent organization, and continual examination of the technological advances in information handling. These ever-changing technologies, such as automated circulation and cataloging systems, have altered the present pattern of library service, requiring equal changes in professional expertise. Today's librarian must have expertise in as many areas of library science as possible to more quickly and effectively address new service needs.

Through utilization of the labor and service analyses, ALMS provides data for human resource management, that is, personnel needs may be determined for each service and employees assigned duties accordingly. And, through examination of these analyses, new service needs may be detected. Should additional personnel be hired to staff these new service needs, or should existing personnel be shifted from services of diminishing utilization or of an ascribed lower priority? In our present financial climate, many managers, if not the majority, do not have the resources necessary to hire new employees and, instead, must decide whether or not new services will be offered and, if so, how to shift personnel to provide these services. An important underlying assumption accompanies this practice of shifting personnel assignments, that is, that the employees involved are willing to accept changes in assignment. Often librarians welcome assignment changes, for such variation broadens their professional experience and increases their salability in the job market.

Or, other librarians, unconcerned with a change in employment, ma find it refreshing just to learn something new, thereby adding a dimer sion to their own assignment. In any case, few libraries today have suff cient budget allocations to simply hire additional librarians as change occur in service needs. Therefore, if the problem of changing servic needs is to be addressed, consideration must be given to shifting prior ties and personnel.

For an example of a perceived service need and possible response review our previous example concerning the discontinuation of CET funds and the displacement of a full-time reference librarian. In Ex ample 20 (the Task Level Budget Report), notice that the budget reques includes an increase in funds to retain the CETA librarian. If the alloca tion increase is denied by the funding agency, either service must b reduced or a staff member(s) must sustain the additional workload. I the latter instance, an hour-for-hour exchange is not always necessary that is, if Librarian *x* works an additional two hours on the referenc desk, Librarian *y* (the librarian assuming part of Librarian *x*'s assign ment) may not necessarily work the two hours of Librarian *x*'s assign ment. If Librarian *x* was providing double staffing of the desk for tha two hours, it may be necessary to revert to single staffing and increas the waiting time for patrons. If *x* supervises an organizational unit, i could mean that a supervisory library assistant under his/her jurisdictio may have to carry a larger share of the supervisorial load for the unit. I *x* is in the collection development area, it could mean that Librarian *y* wil have to reduce personal contact with teaching faculty, and/or that som journal reviews will be completed at the reference desk as time allows. I *x* is in the cataloging department, it could mean that cataloging problem whose solutions require access to the public catalog must be complete while *y* is serving at the reference desk. If *x* in the reference department it could mean that one-on-one patron research assistance will be reduce and/or, in an academic library, that subject bibliographies will be pre pared at the reference desk rather than in a quiet office. If *y* welcome and enjoys the change in assignment, he/she will adjust and redistribut his/her own workload for the least possible reduction in services to th patron. The exchanges of one work assignment for another must b examined to assure that service remains at a maximum level and tha workloads are evenly distributed.

At CSUN, the overall administrative philosophy is to actively encour age voluntary assignment to multiple departments and to make adminis trative assignments to other departments as required by service needs We believe that reference desk experience can greatly aid collection development librarians in their buying decisions, that knowledge of cata loging and of collection development can benefit the reference librarian, that catalog librarians with subject expertise should participate in collection development. We further believe that a knowledge of both cataloging and automated systems is a necessary package for future library development. At Northridge, we have a broad and constantly changing array of combined assignments, and the system works well. The librarians, almost without exception, favor this voluntary approach to altering work assignments, making response to budgetary fluctuations through shifting assignments easier and less traumatic. While assignments are formalized on the basis of tenths of positions (such as .6 Collection Development and .4 Reference; or .4 Systems Group, .4 Cataloging, and .2 Circulation), in most instances the individual librarian decides the portion of time to be spent each day on each assignment, for he/she knows the urgencies of the day and what the priorities should be. Little complaint is heard of one department being slighted in favor of another. And, when such a complaint is made, the workload of the librarian is examined to determine whether or not it is oppressive. In our experience, the librarian usually informs the administration of any inequities in workload, although we have had cases where librarians have pushed themselves to carry burdensome assignments, often because they enjoy all the assignments and are reluctant to give up any one of them.

For each librarian, a department of major assignment is designated; however, all departments to which an individual is assigned submit evaluations for promotion, retention, and tenure. Fractional assignments to library administration have been by administrative appointment rather than by request, although a newly adopted administrative internship program will allow individuals to select the associate and assistant directors, as well as department heads they will understudy. These internships will normally cover a three-month period for each position studied and will require an average of four hours per week. Interns will attend administrative meetings and observe day-to-day activities of the mentor. This program is not designed to serve the same function as the fractional appointment program, which is expected to utilize individual talents and interests to fill specific library needs. The internship program is intended primarily to provide nonadministrative librarians with an opportunity to observe the kinds of problems that administrators deal with, the types of decisions that must be made, and hopefully to study a variety of administrative styles. The success of this program is yet to be assessed.

The shifting assignment concept in personnel utilization, while not at all contrary to the subject specialist concept, does tend to de-emphasize the use of subject specialities in some respects. While subject specialization is very much in evidence at CSUN, particularly in the collection development processes, the CSUN libraries rely heavily on the services of subject area generalists. Broad subject areas generalists (humanities, sciences, social sciences) are the chief strategists for the overall development of the collection, with subject specialists serving as available on limited assignment from other departments. The utilization of broad subject area generalists provides a balanced and constant approach to collection development. The subject specialities change as librarians resign and are replaced with new employees with different subject backgrounds, while the overall collection strategy remains stable. In many cases, emphasis upon subject area generalists avoids the necessity of limiting recruitment to a librarian with a specific subject background. The obvious problems with emphasizing subject specialties is that it is unlikely that libraries will ever be funded well enough to provide specialists in all subjects. Given that limitation, the real benefits of specialization can never be realized.

Betsy McIlvaine, in her remarks concerning librarians and advanced degrees, identifies some specific advantages of subject specialties:

> Reference departments in large university libraries already specialize to some extent. But think of the quality of service that could be offered if the staff had a range of advanced degrees spanning many of the areas of the university. Librarians with subject expertise could aid faculty and graduate students in planning and conducting the literature searches so necessary to the beginning of serious research. New students would be aided by the enhanced ability of the librarian to translate their actual query into proper terms to facilitate the search. Librarians could team-teach courses in addition to providing more cursory bibliographic instruction.[1]

However, the reality of the library budget suggests that faculty and graduate students will continue to conduct their own literature searches, and bibliographic instruction will continue to be provided by those who are most convinced of its importance, regardless of their level of subject expertise. The ability to reassign librarians to multiple service areas as changing needs and budget reductions dictate may be more valuable to the library's clientele than subject specialities. That is not to say that advanced degrees are not beneficial to library service; any form of continuing education is useful even though the subject itself may not be the focal point of an individual assignment.

Automated systems is one area of specialization, however, that has gained considerable importance over the past years. The need for an on-line public access catalog that will replace the card catalog has become more and more urgent, requiring specialists with new expertise in both cataloging and the techniques of programming and automated systems. Reference librarians also need expertise in information retrieval through automated systems to access bibliographic data and to provide user training in automated systems.

This type of personnel utilization—shifting assignments—is of benefit to the individual librarian and to the profession. For the individual, librarianship becomes the challenging, dynamic career suggested by its world-encompassing scope. With shifts in job duties, librarians no longer have time to perform the myriad of subprofessional tasks that are so necessary to the functioning of a library, but so damaging to the professional image. Rather, technical library assistants must be trained to perform these subprofessional tasks efficiently, thereby adding new dimensions to their positions as well in the process. The body of knowledge that is common to all libraries and all library positions is the essence of our profession, that is, in addition to technical knowledge, (1) a common philosophy of library service, (2) the background knowledge which enables us to identify our knowledge gaps, and (3) the techniques for investigating and filling those knowledge gaps. The essence of library service should be captured and taught in library schools to enable the graduate to enter any position in any type of library and function effectively. Through such instruction, we would become true library generalists, and at the same time, true professionals. In the context of personnel utilization, we would be better able to respond to new service requirements throughout the library. That does not mean that we should not have or cannot utilize a specialty, but merely that we should not lose sight of the importance of an overall knowledge package of which the specialty is only an integrated part. A "generalist" is defined, for purposes of this discussion, as a librarian who has a firm enough grasp of the body of knowledge described above to be able to serve in any library position in any library. This requirement would address the need of librarianship for a "discrete body of knowledge" and would eliminate the promotion of staff, highly trained in a narrow technical area, to full professional status.

Thus far, discussion has focused upon the reassignment of professional librarians to meet changing service needs. Yet, shifting service needs also affect other library staff members. The reassignment of clerical and technical staff on the basis of organizational need is more complicated than librarian reassignment. In many instance, certainly in libraries such as CSUN, such staff members are subject to employment codes that specify duties to be performed within that classification. In order to assign different duties, a totally new job description often must be written for the individual followed by an audit by an outside agency within the system to determine whether or not the new assignment is properly within the limitations of that classification. The auditing process alone is time-consuming, and training in the new duties adds further to the reduction of productivity. At times, the high turnover of clerical and technical staff renders the training too expensive for the shifting of assignments to be profitable. Additionally, our experience has shown that noncareer staff are often uncomfortable and insecure with too much shifting between departments. This may be due to loyalties which develop at the department level, or to simply fear of something new and unknown. In the university setting, the use of student assistants can provide the needed organizational flexibility, allowing permanent staff to remain relatively static. In other libraries, temporary hourly rate employees may be the answer to organizational flexibility. There are some obvious disadvantages to the use of temporary, part-time employees, the major ones being the increased training required by high turnover, a lesser degree of commitment to the job than career employees have, and special skills needed by the supervisor for motivation.[2] At the same time, it is easier to reassign them to meet shifting priorities and, equally important, for routine jobs fewer hours often mean higher productivity. In other words, there is less time to become bored.

In the CSUN library, we have instituted a program allowing library assistants and clerical staff to understudy positions at the next higher level of classification. Such cross-training is only permitted when the level of productivity of the requestor exceeds by 10% the minimum level required in his/her present job description. The employees then may opt to devote four hours per week to learning another position.

In order for such a program to work, the job description must be defined in such a way that performance expectations are clear to both supervisor and employee. These job standards are difficult to establish but once they have been set, eligibility for the intern program is easy to judge and, in addition, the evaluation of an individual's performance becomes easier and more fair. The supervisor is responsible for developing the standards with the assistance of the incumbent employee. Subsequent employees in that position will either verify the standards or they will reveal a need for revision up or down. The 10% requirement is not a hard and fast rule, but it is intended to protect the supervisor from a loss of productivity that will create backlogs in the unit. Example 28 is a job description which includes some performance standards. Cross-training within departments works extremely well, but movement across departmental lines is less well received by supervisors and staff. Our program should serve as a career development program, as well as a training program, but considerable time and attention must be given to individual counselling before the cross-training program can function successfully at CSUN. Utilization of such a program for career development would require the expertise of specialists in both counselling and affirmative action in order to assure fairness and equity for all employees. For that reason, the CSUN program has remained as simply a job enrichment opportunity with no attempt made to direct an individual toward a job for which he/she might be acceptable on a permanent basis. When a position is vacated, it is opened to all who wish to apply and those who have interned compete on an equal basis with those who have not. It is naturally a disappointment to those employee/interns who are rejected in favor of one who has not interned. The benefits in terms of job enrichment, however, outweigh the disappointments.

The management of personnel resources requires the flexibility to shift assignments as necessary, otherwise, greater numbers of employees must be continually added to the staff to manage new requirements, while present employees, whose services are less in demand, become idle. As budgets become tighter, the easy option of hiring additional employees is no longer viable. Library managers need to examine methods for achieving personnel flexibility through the shifting of assignments.

Within the ALMS system, decisions regarding the reassignment of personnel are developed after careful examination of the services analyses. The following analysis of automated data base searching activities (Example 29) serves to illustrate this decision-making process.

The service analysis in Example 29 provides information that an additional 100 hours of librarian time is required to provide minimally adequate data base service. Obviously, it would be difficult to hire an additional librarian to work only 100 hours per year. Therefore, unless other library needs constitute at least a half-time librarian position, existing library resources must be examined closely for the additional 100 hours needed to provide access to the *New York Times Index.* In reviewing present resources, first examine other library tasks for possible personnel savings at the librarian level. If sufficient hours can be saved from other tasks to support the data base service, examine the talents and interests of the librarians involved for a reasonable prospect for reassignment. Unfortunately, the reality is that often those librarians most capable and most eager to accept new assignments are also the most overloaded with work. Multiple reassignments, as opposed to the reassignment of a single librarian, are an alternative to realize the most positively received and productive arrangement of responsibilities. If careful scrutiny of other library tasks does not reveal personnel savings from other tasks, a decision must be made as to service priorities. Is the addition of the *New York Times* data base a higher priority than the maintenance of other services at optimum or current levels? Assuming the addition of the data base is of a significantly high priority, a service with a lower priority can be

Example 28. Job Description with Performance Standards

CATALOG DEPARTMENT

POSITION: Catalog Maintenance Assistant

CLASSIFICATION: Library Assistant I

DUTIES:
Under the supervision of the Catalog Maintenance Supervisor to input cataloging data on a CRT terminal to the OCLC On-line Share Cataloging System, process books recataloged or reclassed and update records for library materials withdrawn from the collection, file in the various card catalogs, type catalog cards, review the work of others and assume other duties as assigned.

After an initial training period of one year, the Catalog Maintenance Clerk will be expected to perform the duties and meet the requirements listed below. Periodic performance evaluations will be based upon how well the employee meets the requirements specified.

I. *Process Materials Recataloged or Withdrawn* (45%)

Search for an charge out books and catalog cards from public and technical service areas, verify and update library records for books missing or destroyed, process books recataloged or reclassed, submit notices to update the library's machine Shelflist Record, and maintain the Search/Hold file for missing items to be recataloged. This task requires knowledge of Library of Congress classification and filing systems as well as knowledge of local cataloging procedures.

Minimum Requirements: Recatalog an average of 75 books, remove an average of 100 card sets from the card catalogs, and update an average of 100 records per month. an error rate of 1% or less is acceptable in recataloging and updating records.

II. *Input Cataloging Records* (25%)

Search OCLC data base for Library of Congress cataloging, input cataloging data from revised computer printouts and original workforms for monographs, music scores, and sound recordings. Modify bibliographic records on-line, revise records input by other staff members, and alert the system to print catalog cards and create an archive tape record. This taks requires experience in operating a CRT terminal for accurate input of data, it requires a thorough knowledge of OCLC searching procedures to avoid inputting duplicate records, and it requires a good enough understanding of the OCLC tagging system for monographs, music scores, and sound recordings to allow identification and correction of tagging errors that would affect the system's card printing program or the subsequent retrieval of records.

Minimum Requirements: Search and input an average of 100 cards per month. Music scores and sound recordings input should not backlog for more than a week. The searching task for duplicate records should be error-free. An error rate of 1% is acceptable for records input and produced on OCLC.

(Example 28.—Continued)

III. *Card Catalog Maintenance* (25%)

File catalog cards into the various catalogs in the library following Library of Congress filing rules, correct or return filing errors found in the process of filing and return subject cards that require authority checking, revise the work of other filers, process OCLC card shiments, and assist with related file maintenance activities.

Minimum Requirements: File an average of 2500 cards per month and revise an equal amount. An error rate of 1% or less is acceptable.

IV. *Miscellaneous* (5%)

These duties are irregular and performed as they are required. They may include typing and revising catalog cards and training new staff and student personnel in the section.

---

reduced or eliminated and the personnel reassigned. The idea of asking for volunteers to undertake a particular assignment is one that needs careful thought. If you do so and you get no volunteer, you are then in the uncomfortable position of having to issue an order to someone who may ask "why me?" If instead, you select someone whose talents most fit the assignment and make clear that this is the reason you are asking, you are more likely to get a positive response. If you still get a negative response, you must weigh carefully the advantages and disadvantages of forcing the person to accept the assignment. If you have no one else available, then the decision is indeed a difficult one.

The optimum use of personnel resources requires an enormous and continual balancing and juggling act. It is one of the most important of management's responsibilities, and certainly one that requires a great skill and patience. Human resource management can also be one of the most rewarding of management skills, for not only are library patrons receiving the best service possible, but, as experience at CSUN has shown, the lives of librarians and staff are enriched through continued professional growth.

The importance of ALMS in the area of personnel utilization lies in the data from the labor analysis which illustrate clearly how existing personnel are being utilized, and the assessment of need found in the service analysis which should indicate where personnel shifts are desirable. When dealing with human beings, the transactions are never as simple as assessing need and assigning someone to fill it. Individual personalities and personal needs must be carefully considered and dealt with. Only

Example 29. Task Analysis—Automated Data Base Searching—Use in Assignment of Personnel

Task	Level of Service		Staff Hours Libn	Lib. Asst. Clerical	Stu. Asst.
Automated Data Base Searching	Activities reported here include the interview of users to establish the parameters of the search strategy, terminal operation, consultation with the user after the search, calculating and collecting fees, and planning and coordinating the service. The service is available during the hours of 12-2 P.M. daily and 6-8 P.M. Monday through Thursday and includes only the DIALOG and MEDLINE data bases.	(Current)	300	0	0
		(Minimum)	400	0	0
		(Optimum)	3,000	0	0

Analysis: Because no queueing and no user pressure for additional hours of service have been reported, it is assumed that the hours of availability are adequate at the present time. However, there is considerable agitation by faculty and graduate students for the addition of the *New York Times Index*. A poll of faculty indicates strong support for its addition, and a six-month tally of student requests resulted in average of 15 requests per month.

The addition of the *New York Times Index* is estimated to require approximately 100 additional hours of librarian time and $500 for continuatin of the policy to provide partial library support of the use charges. Any further addition of data bases may also bring about the need for some clerical staff time for assistance in correspondence with users. This should be carefully watched during the coming months. Reference librarians consider the addition of this data base to be essential to upgrade our service to a minimum level of adequacy. The addition of approximately 20 data bases would be required to upgrade our service to an optimum level, at a cost that would be prohivitively expensive at the present time. However, the addition of data bases should not be dismissed as unimportant simply because funds are unavailable to support this much needed service. Eventually, if additional funds are not made available, shifts within traditional services may be required to expand data base capabilities.

Production volume: 225 searches

when individual desires clearly conflict with the needs of the institution should they be denied, and only then after every effort has been made to satisfy both. Too often managers either totally ignore the needs of the individual, or always cater to the individual at the expense of the institution. Neither extreme is acceptable. It is possible, with considerable effort and thought, to maintain a balance that serves most of the requirements of both. ALMS can assist with the achievement of that objective.

NOTES AND REFERENCES

1. Betsy McIlvaine (1981), "Librarians and Advanced Degrees," *College and Research Libraries News* 12: 47.
2. Michael D. Kathman and Jane M. Kathman (1978), "Management Problems of Student Workers in Academic Libraries," *College and Research Libraries* 39:118-122.

Chapter 5

Goal Setting

The exercise of goal setting is probably one of the most frustrating, and unfortunately often fruitless, of all the necessary management system components. Goals are often so vague that it is difficult, if not impossible, to determine what activities, resources, and expertise are needed for their achievement and to determine when the goal actually has been achieved. Yet, in spite of the possible failure of written goals to move us toward a higher state of accomplishment, they are a necessary part of a good management system. As stated in Hamberg, et. al:

> A logical starting point in the development of a managerial system is specification of what the organization is attempting to achieve. In order for managers and administrators to evaluate alternative courses of action in planning and decision making, the following are needed:
>
> 1. Statements of objectives should be explicit, unambiguous, and operationally meaningful.
> 2. Suitable measures must be developed for evaluating the degree to which objectives are obtained.
>
> In most organizations, including libraries, these statements tend to be quite vague, providing little or no guidance to the planner or decision maker. Hence, it is generally impossible to determine degree of success in pursuit of the objectives. Also, the objectives usually are in conflict. Objectives calling for different aspects of better service are in conflict among themselves for scarce funds and against objectives calling for lower costs. Organizational units following conflicting objectives tend to act in competition with each other rather than in cooperation toward a common purpose.[1]

In addition to providing a base for planning and decision making, goal setting also serves to establish library administrators as managers who are in control of the library direction and who are altogether capable of expending the library's resources in the best interest of its patrons.

> 'The concept of planning is going to have to become part of everyday library management,' states Palmour. 'The economic situation is about to reach the stage where libraries are going to have to justify their expenditures. Having goals and objectives puts libraries in the position to do this for their funding bodies.'[2]

But why are library goals so difficult to define? This difficulty may be a result of the lack of a clear definition of service expectations. Library goals should be service-oriented; however, it may be argued that the majority of goals that lie gathering cobwebs in administrators' desk drawers *are* service-oriented. The question then becomes: Why do library administrators appear unable to write goals that are active tools in the decision-making process? This inability to write meaningful goals may be attributed to at least four causes:

1. Lack of specificity. Goals tend to specify an improvement in service but fail to include statements defining specific activities which must occur before the goal is reached; that is, changes in present tasks, staffing changes, new individual responsibilities, cost, additional equipment needs, and a timetable for converting to the improved service.
2. Failure to relate goals to all services provided by the library. Unless we are addressing an obvious public service function, we neglect to define how the goal relates to service. As stated in Chapter 2, every task performed within the library provides a service, whether directly in serving patrons or indirectly through support to another library unit. The nature of a service must be narrowly defined such that its relationship to a specific goal is apparent.
3. Lack of mechanisms for periodic update. Library service requirements change continually to meet patron needs, and consequently, elements within a goal statement may become obsolete in a relatively short period of time. Therefore, in order to provide meaning and utility, a mechanism must be developed for a periodic update of the goal statement.
4. Failure to utilize goal statements in decision making. Library administrators frequently are not goal-oriented and, therefore, lack the necessary commitment to continued revision and utilization of goals as a decision-making tool. Response to an immediate crisis based upon the best data available is easier than planning for prevention of the occurrence in advance. That is not to say that goal-setting prevents crises; it should, however, reduce their frequency and, more importantly

perhaps, direct any related decision making. It is naive to think that no decision will or should be made without reference to a specific goal. Sometimes the goals of the library must give way to the needs of the parent institution or to unavoidable political pressures.

The reality of political pressures must be understood, accepted, and taken into account throughout the planning process. Jeffrey Raffel's article on the political aspects of library decision making is a must for nonadministrative librarians who aspire to an understanding of the decision-making process.

> The basic political problem with economic analysis transcends operational and day-to-day difficulties and political intrigue. The basic political problem centers on political conflict inherent in all our institutions, including libraries. It is this conflict that is inappropriately dealt with or ignored in economic analysis.[3]

While political considerations must always be acknowledged, they should be the exception rather than the rule as a basis for decision making. There are undoubtedly other reasons why library goal-setting exercises are often futile. The four suggested above, however, emphasize the need for a new approach.

ALMS expands the traditional goal statement to include the individual tasks performed within the library and specific service goals to be realized for each of those tasks. The ALMS goal-setting process is dependent upon the labor and service analyses described in Chapter 2. Each task is to be linked directly to a goal or goals and relates very closely to the budget preparation process, as will be illustrated below. Specifically, goal setting for ALMS requires:

1. The preparation of an overall mission and goals statement;
2. the development of task action statements from the analysis of service;
3. an annual accounting of personnel utilization by task;
4. an annual analysis of service adequacy;
5. an annual review of priorities and goal achievement and a rewrite of goals and action statements as appropriate; and
6. the daily use of the goals and action statements as decision-making tools.

The requisites above will produce a mission/goal/action document that is easily utilized as a handbook for decision making. If not used for that purpose, the goal-setting exercise quickly becomes a waste of time and effort, transforming into a game of "let's write some goals and then see how nearly we reach them without really trying." If this is the case, then a general statement of library purpose, or philosophy of service, is all that is required. Each administrator then reaches daily decisions on the basis of that overall mission statement and operates in concert with his/her own personal, unwritten goals for the unit (s) under his/her responsibility. Many library administrators appear to operate on the basis of unwritten goals, whether or not a formal, written goal statement exists. Decision making is far easier, and far more enjoyable, on this informal basis. Decisions can be changed frequently and without explanation as political pressures shift. And, perhaps more importantly, the tedious and time-consuming process of analysis necessary to true goal-oriented decision making is eliminated. For those administrators in the nonprofit sector, who will know or ask the reasoning for certain decisions? There are no stockholders to scrutinize a profit and loss statement. Decisions must be completely disastrous before reaching the attention of the user community, and even then, there are many scapegoats—the recent budget cut, a turnover in personnel, the Library of Congress, the computer. It is virtually impossible to prove error.

There are many administrators however, who actively seek methods for developing tools for goal-directed decision making. How, then, is a goal statement developed to such precision and completeness as to be used for the decision-making process?

The first step is the definition of the library's mission or statement of purpose, and the library objectives and goals that relate to that mission. We should establish the role of the library in the context of the community served. The university library, for example, should be examined as a "task" of the university, much as "receiving library materials" is a task of the library. What service is the library expected to provide within the university setting?[4] To whom should services be provided and what criteria should be used to judge service adequacy? How can we measure service adequacy against those criteria? At another level, the university itself should be examined as a "task" of the community and, on a larger scale, the society served. What are the needs of society that the university can and should serve? What criteria should be used to judge its adequacy, and how can adequacy be measured? Once again, as is the case with library tasks, answers relative to service must be formulated through a combination of user opinion, the experience and judgment of the professionals responsible for its operation, and the ability and willingness of the funding agency to provide adequate budget allocations. Unfortunately, university administrators, like city and county governing boards, can be as phlegmatic about planning as library administrators.

And, there is a great temptation to use that fact as an excuse not to attempt such planning for the library. After all, if the university does not have a clear statement of purpose, how can the university library make a clear statement of its role in the larger university community? The task level goal/action exercise described below can serve a useful purpose even without integration with established university goals, although admittedly, well-defined university goals do increase the utility of library goals. The point is that the lack of higher level planning must not be offered as an excuse for the lack of goals developed within the library.

The mission statement is the most broad, general definition of why the library exists and the clientele that it serves. The objectives begin to focus on less general statements of long-range intent, the goals are still more specific statements of direction, and the action statements reveal the specifics of goal achievement. The objectives and goals sections serve to reduce the scope of the mission to bite-size ideas and may be developed in two layers or in several, depending upon the complexity of the issue.

At this point, the statement of objectives and goals resembles so many others of which I have spoken. It is vague. It is merely a collection of statements relating to desired outcomes—adequate service, trained personnel, appropriate collection development. But, it is at this point where ALMS deviates from the traditional goal-setting exercise, appending library tasks and specific actions related to each. The goals provide direction; they bridge the gap between current operations and desired results through specific actions. The action statement, that is, the blueprints for execution of the goals and objectives, must be developed within the various organizational units of the library, for only at that level is there enough knowledge to produce statements of specificity sufficient for decision making. That is where the real work begins. Once those action statements have been completed, library administration, with representation from all units, should examine them for possible conflicts among the units and should integrate the projected budgetary increases/decreases into the formal budget process. Priorities should be set and staffing reassignments should be considered.

Once again, the service analysis serves as a foundation. Let us follow one specific task through the entire process.

Consider the following objective:

Personnel. To recruit and maintain a staff of highly qualified individuals to carry out the functions of the library; to accomplish this through effective screening and interviewing techniques and programs for staff development and training which promote job satisfaction and provide promotional opportunities.

And, consider one of the goals of the personnel objective:

> To train new employees to fulfill the requirements of their job descriptions with the least possible expenditure of trainer and trainee time.

In the previous chapters, we learned to identify and define specifi library tasks, and later, to analyze the service adequacy of each. Review ing those tasks, it is apparent that the task of "required training" relate to the library goal above. This task is then appended to this goal, bu further, the task analysis provides a basis for the development of specific action statement, the effect of the action on service, how it will b attained, the individual(s) responsible, a timetable, cost, and the effect upon other services. In Example 30, I have illustrated how the servic analysis can be expanded for use in the development of action statements

In addition to a statement of how the actions are expected to affec service, Example 30 describes *how* the actions are to be undertaken, *wh* is responsible for each activity, *when* each activity is to be completed, *ho much* each activity is expected to cost, and *what effect* these will have o other existing tasks. Only after all of these questions are answered an the responses carefully considered, can a determination be made as t whether or not the stated actions should be pursued or discontinued.

Having completed the action statement for training, it is easy to un derstand why goal setting may become mere administrative exercise with little practice value. A first impulse would be to define the relevan goal for the training task as follows:

> Relevant Goal: To reduce the percentage of total personnel hours devoted to required training from 6% to 2%.

Such a service goal is too simplistic. It ignores the cause(s) of the turn over or the state of the current training program. It is unknown whethe or not a reduction in training time can be effected realistically or is, i fact, desirable. A study of training aids may reveal the exercise of pre paring new materials with periodic revisions is not cost effective, that is the cost of providing new training aids exceeds the cost of present per sonnel training time. Or, an investigation may reveal that the substantia amount of personnel time devoted to training is not linked with turn over or with deficient training aids, as suspected. Rather, we may dis cover that increased training time is due to a larger percentage of hourl wage employees versus permanent salaried employees. And, if hourl wage employees prove to be more productive than permanent salarie employees, additional training time may be justified by the increase service. Indeed, under such circumstances, it may be desirable to in crease training time from 6% to 8% instead of instituting a 4% reduction. In other words, the goal of reducing the personnel hours for required training from 6% to 2% is meaningless. Such a statement provides no insight into causal factors of a problem, and in fact, offers little to establish that a problem exists. In the present case, we do not even know whether or not a reduction in training time would improve or impair service.

Unfortunately, many such vague statements may be found in the goals and objectives of libraries, indicative of the degree of our commitment to planning. We plan and devise our goals, but in fact we are reluctant to devote the time necessary to render such planning meaningful, to develop a dynamic set of objectives/goals/actions capable of lending direction to the decision-making process. Consider the following observation: If planning is not meaningful, it is not worth the expenditure of a single hour. That assertion is debatable, of course, for one could contend that such planning serves an external purpose, if not an internal one, by signaling funding agencies and outside observers that we are progressive administrators, well in control and steering a well-calculated course. Such argument is not totally without merit. However, for a statement of goals to be a truly useful tool, it must include a clear statement of how, who, when, how much, and what effect, as outlined above.

Let us again examine the receiving task from Chapter 2 and explore goal development for a task that produces tangible units. In this case, the analysis of service actually contains the majority of elements necessary for goal development.

Example 31 illustrates the symbiotic nature of the budget justification, personnel allocation and goal-setting processes. The three are interwoven, interdependent and simultaneous in construction, and each is equally dependent upon the labor and service analyses for development. As the budget is prepared for the following year, each task should be examined from the vantage point of the previous goals and action statements. Yet, an evaluation of goal achievement requires an update of the labor analysis and the analysis of service. Fluctuations in the expenditure of personnel hours should be reviewed carefully, changes in service should be analyzed and projected, and the effect of these shifts upon goals should be documented in a revised statement. Some changes in the expenditure of personnel hours or service will not be sufficient to warrant a change in the goal statement; however, other changes will be monumental.

The change from the traditional card catalog to an on-line catalog, for example, will be a monumental shift in the type of service offered to patrons, as well as an impetus for changes in the expenditure of personnel hours. All cataloging tasks will be affected by the transition to an on-line catalog, as will reference services, systems analysis and program-

Example 30. Task Analysis—Required Training— Use in Goal Development and Action Statements

Task	*Level of Service*		*Staff Hours* *Libn.*	*Lib. Asst. Clerical*	*Stu. Asst*
Required Training	Time is recorded against this task by both trainer and trainee and includes the reading and writing of training documents, attendance at workshops and orientation programs, and se training exercises. Training is administered to all new personnel and existing personnel with changes in assignment.	(Current)	750	9708	849
		(Minimum)	855	9700	840
		(Optimum)	670	2300	840

Analysis: No standards for judging training adequacy exist at present, and therefore t appropriateness of the personnel hours expended here must be judged for the time bei on the basis of the percentage of *total* personnel hours devoted to training. A five-mon study of twelve libraries indicated that, in most libraries, training does not exceed 2% the total personnel hours. Training hours represent nearly 6% of the total hours record in this library, slightly more than 1% for librarians, 8% for library assistants and cleri staff, and 6% for student assistants. The high percentages were a result of an unusua high turnover of library assistants and clerical staff, and a higher than normal availabil of work/study students. The utilization of work/study students requires additional traini due to the high attrition rate and to the tendency of supervisors to hire more individu than necessary in anticipation of the resignations. Due to the low cost of work/study pe sonnel to the library (20 cents per dollar), an overall training figure for student assistar of 6% is not unacceptable. According to statewide studies, the percentage of library ass tants and clerical staff should not exceed 2%. Librarians will normally average about 1 However, next year a net increase of approximately 100 hours is expected due to ad tional training for AACR2 (an increase of 300 hours for AACR2 and a decrease of 195 f completion of training of a new librarian). Therefore, if the library wishes to conform the statewide average, a reduction in the total percentage of training for all staff by 3-4 should be realized over the next few years. However, at the present time there is n sufficient data to determine whether conforming to the statewide average is a desirab goal. The same number of hours will continue to be budgeted to this task until the rate turnover is reduced, training techniques are improved, and/or additional study negates t desirability of a reduction in training time. It is expected that backlogs will continue grow in the catalog department where the majority of the turnover is occurring, until son degree of stability is realized.

Relevant Goal: To train new employees to fulfill the requirements of their job descriptio with the least possible expenditure of trainer and trainee time.

Action Statement: The actions relevant to the training task are (1) an investigation of t reasons for turnover among library assistants and clerical staff and (2) an investigation the level of efficiency of the current procedures for training both staff and student assistan

Effect on Service: The effect on service of these actions is expected to be an eventu reallocation of hours saved on training to other tasks, both for additional service a reduction of backlogs. A projection of the personnel time to be saved, if any, cannot assessed until studies have been completed.

(Example 30—Continued)

---

rocedures: (1) Exit interviews will be conducted with staff terminating employment with he library in order to determine whether or not the reasons for termination are attribut-ble to poor management practices within the library or other correctable conditions. A eport of the interview results will state the reasons for termination and possible preventa-ive action(s) by the library to avert future terminations for the same cause. (2) A library-vide study of training practices and training aids will be conducted. Supervisors will be equested to write a brief statement for each task under their supervision describing how raining is conducted and attaching any training aids (lengthy procedures manuals will be eferenced only, but should be made easily accessible). Training aids will be analyzed for ompleteness and clarity of instruction. Trainer techniques will be examined for efficiency nd effectiveness. The final report detailing the results of the study will outline recom-nended changes in training aids and/or trainer methods for each task, accompanied by an stimate of the number of training hours to be saved by the implementation of each ecommendation.

esponsible Person(s): (1) Exit interviews—associate director; (2) Study of training prac-ices and aids—systems analyst.

stimated Date of Completion: (1) Exit interviews—January 1, 1982 (one year); (2) Study of raining practices and aids—January 1, 1982 (one year).

ost: (1) and (2)—No additional personnel funds required. No additional operating ex-ense funds required. No capital outlay for facilities or equipment required.

ther Tasks Affected: (1) The associate director is solely responsible for the implementation f exit interviews and will absorb the time expended for this task under the "administra-ion function." The time devoted to exit interviews will not be sufficient to displace other lanning activities. (2) The systems analyst will require approximately 8 hours per week to tudy the supervisorial training practices and aids, delaying an investigation of a possible OM backup for an on-line catalog by approximately 3 months. However, because imple-nentation of an on-line catalog is not planned for another 3-5 years, this delay does not ppear to be unduly disadvantageous. The potential savings from this training study war-ant the delay in the COM investigation.

---

ning. The overall effects of the change upon each task will be difficult to redict. Therefore, at the end of each year, the labor analysis should be tudied carefully so that changes deriving from the shift to an on-line atalog are separated and recorded. Action statements associated with omplex tasks, such as development of the on-line catalog, should be ursued in stages similar to the action statements for training in the bove example. To begin with a goal such as "to install an on-line catalog y 1985" is, again, meaningless without relevant action statements. Such goal makes no provision for implementation. As with previous exam-les, action statements should answer the questions of "how, who, when, ow much, and what effect." The installation of an on-line catalog may e viewed as an hypothesis, with the individual action statements as the esting of that hypothesis. Consider the training example. To lower the

Example 31. Task Analysis—Receiving Library Materials—Use in Goal Development and Action Statements

Task	*Level of Service*		*Libn.*	*Lib. Asst/. Cler*	*Stu Asst*
Receiving Library Materials	Service is provided to the librarians responsible for the selection of materials, the librarians serving at reference desks, the	current	0	1182	96
		minimum	0	1182	100
		optimum	0	1182	100
				(backlog)	8

catalog librarians and to the accounting section. Packages are opene materials received are checked against the invoice and the order slip, a forwarded to the catalog department *within one week of receipt*. Invoices a sent to accounting *within one week of receipt* of the materials billed. Materi ordered but not received *within six months of the date of order* are querie

Analysis: The current service is below what is minimally required. Considering the oth processing steps, a week's delay at the receiving point is unacceptable. No processing ti in receiving is gained by the delay. No additional staff time is required to process materi on the first day of arrival than to process on the seventh day. Additionally, there is tendency to group materials and forward them to the catalog department once or twic week instead of every day, causing an uneven work flow for cataloging staff. The flow invoices to the accounting section is also too slow. At the end of the month when accour should be current, there is a flurry of last minute posting activity in order to exhi up-to-the-minute fund balances. Delays in processing also slow payment to the suppli and foster poor public relations.

Based on discussions by librarians and staff, an optimum level of service would be pr vided by forwarding the material to the catalog department and the invoices to the counting section on the day received, and such should be the goal of this unit. Cost studi indicate that an optimum level is attainable by applying 80 hours of student assistant tir ($3.00 per hour) to catch-up the backlog. After the backlog is eliminated, continuing optimum level should be no more costly than the current practice. Three additional booktruc @ $100.00 each will also be required.

The six-month time period allotted to follow-up on orders not received is also too slow. recent test study illustrates that orders queried within three months yield a 5% great return than the six-month practice, and require only a 2% increase in student assista hours. The total cost increase was $320.00 (40 hours, $3.00 per hour for labor and $200. in increased postage and supplies). Following up on orders more frequently than eve three months did not substantially increase the amount of materials received, and the cc was significantly greater. Therefore, the latter alternative is too costly to consider. A to cost of $860.00 would raise the service provided by this task to a nearly optimum level

PRODUCTION VOLUME = 42,529 items received.

Objective: To provide for the speedy processing of new materials.

Goal #1: To speed the flow of materials and invoices through the Receiving Unit.

Action Statement: The action relevant to this goal is to forward materials from the receivi unit to the catalog department and invoices to the accounting unit on the day of receip

Effect on Service: The effect on service will be to equalize the work flow of the tasks of t cataloging, adaptive cataloging, final processing, library materials accounting and fisc claims sections. Additionally, attainment of the above goal is expected to deliver materi to the shelves for patron use one week earlier.

(Example 31—Continued)

---

rocedures: (1) Eighty hours of student assistant time will be added to the budget to iminish the existing backlog. (2) The receiving area will be examined each morning upon rival. If any trucks of materials or any invoices remain in the unit overnight, with the xception of incorrect shipments, the reasons for delay should be determined and correcve actions taken. (3) Three additional booktrucks will be purchased.

esponsible Person(s): (1) Reduction of backlog—The library director will seek a budget ugmentation of $240 for the additional 80 hours of student assistant time. If such augentation is not forthcoming, savings from vacated staff positions (savings beyond the rojected savings) will be allocated for the addition of 80 student assistant hours. The ceiving supervisor will then hire 80 additional hours of trained student assistant time. (2) xamine receiving area—receiving supervisor. (3) Purchase booktrucks—library director ill seek a budget augmentation of $300. If no augmentation is received, savings from acated positions will be used (savings beyond the projected amount). The library assistant r purchasing will order the booktrucks.

stimated Date of Completion: (1) November 1, 1981. (10 months). (2) Ongoing (3) April 1, 982 (15 months).

ost: (1) $240 (80 hours, $3 per hour). (2) No additional personnel cost. Receiving supersor will absorb. (3) $300 (3 booktrucks, $100 per truck).

ther Tasks Affected: The task of cataloging, adaptive cataloging, final processing, library aterials accounting and fiscal claims are directly affected by the expeditious movement of aterials and invoices from the receiving unit. However, discussions with the affected pervisors suggest that no increase or decrease in staff will result from this change. The verall effect will be to balance the work flow of all five tasks and to shelve materials one eek earlier for patron use.

oal #2: To reduce the number of orders cancelled by vendors due to depleted stocks.

ction Statement: The action relevant to this goal is for the receiving unit to query undelived orders after 3 months instead of 6 months, as is now customary.

ffect on Service: The estimated effect on service will be to increase the materials available r patron use by an estimated 1,500 titles per year.

rocedures: (1) The student assistant budget will be increased permanently by 40 hours.) The operating expense budget will be augmented by $200 per year. (3) The responsibily for additional queries will be assigned to a student assistant.

esponsible Person(s): (1) and (2) library director will seek additional funding. If this fundg is not obtained, this action will not be pursued further until corresponding savings are alized from the reduction of training costs or from other targeted cost reductions. (3) ceiving supervisor.

stimated Date of Completion: (1), (2), and (3) September 1, 1981 (8 months).

ost: (1) $120 per year, (2) $200 per year, (3) Cost included in (1).

ther Tasks Affected: The tasks of ordering library materials and library materials counting should be affected in a positive way, with fewer cancellations being required. e suspect that vendors may be slow to complete single copy orders, while larger, more crative orders are supplied. In this manner, stock quickly dwindles, and items sell out, aving the single copy order unfilled. The amount of savings to be realized is unknown at is time, but after a year's experience with the new query procedure, an examination will e made of cancellations, both before and after implementation, providing information on e percentage of decrease, if any, in cancellation volume. The major overall benefit, of ourse, is the increase in materials available for patron use.

---

percentage of hours spent in training from 6% to 2% appeared to b
an appropriate goal; however, until studies are completed, the need f
a reduction in required training time is debatable. Although it is u
likely, in the case of the on-line catalog, studies could reveal that oth
options, such as the hiring of additional personnel to file catalog car
and attend to patron needs, would be more cost effective than goir
on-line.

The on-line catalog example illustrates another point previously state
that is goal statements, if properly written, may provide a valuable to
for decision making. Also, the advanced planning necessitated by suc
goal statements may stave off future crises. Unfortunately, library ad
ministrators sometimes tend to depend too heavily upon intuition, whic
is at least one of the reasons why goal setting in libraries can be a futi
exercise. In any organization with the depth, breadth, and complexity
a library, intuition must defer to reason, and goals and objectives mu
build a pathway of individual actions required to provide a particul
service or overcome a specific problem. This more detailed approach
goal setting has not been adopted in the past because long-range pla
ning is generally considered to be the responsibility and domain of to
administration while operational detail is the legacy of middle and low
level management. The development of successful, decision-oriented goa
and objectives, with their accompanying action statements, requires n
only a totally committed management team, but a committed *library* tea
as well. The recording of hours in each task for the labor analysis, th
review and assessment of services for the service analysis, the extrapol
tion of goals from the service analysis, the development of specific a
tions to fulfill the goals, and the subsequent studies of goal achievemen
all require the dedication and attention of librarians and staff at th
working level. The management team must encourage and guide, ap
plaud and assist, suggest and advise, but the knowledge bank for accom
plishment lies at the unit level.

The maturity and professionalism exhibited by the organization as
whole will play a major role in the success or failure of the plannin
process. The willingness and ability to respect individual points of vie
to admire strengths and to forgive weaknesses—these are the qualities
a true professional, and these are the qualities that will determine th
success or failure of planning and goal setting within the library env
ronment. Unlike many businesses whose products are tangible and whos
production process is a matter of routine, planning for libraries cann
be viewed as the sole domain of upper level management; everyon
must contribute to assure quality service. To follow past methods and t
assign goal setting to administrators alone will yield yet another colle

n of lofty statements of intuitive intent, with little direction as to the tails of implementation. But, how is such a library-wide planning team ganized? This question is a topic for an entire book. However, the ccess of a planning team will depend upon the character and commit- ent of the individuals involved, upon the degree of professionalism of ch team member, and upon the amount of credibility the library-wide nning team attributes to upper level management. John Baird, man- ement consultant for Positive Personnel Practices, Inc., says of credi- ity:

> While managers commonly assume that credibility is a single unified judgment which subordinates make about them, research indicates otherwise. When assessing a manager or a supervisor, subordinates seem to make specific judgments based on six characteristics; competency; character; intent; dynamism; personality; and admirability.[5]

Few of us past the age of six are able to substantially change either our rsonality or our character. We can, however, continue to improve our mpetency, demonstrate our intent to act in the best interest of our ployees whenever possible, and seek to earn the respect of both supe- rs and subordinates. A successful management system requires not ly techniques to create and interpret the system itself, but also ac- owledgment by the entire staff of the system's importance to the over- functioning of the library. Its success or failure depends upon both, ereby making communication and team building essential components the continuing educational process.

Warren Bennis, while president of the University of Cincinnati said of blic administration, particularly universities:

> Unquestionably, universities are among the worst-managed institutions in the country. Hospitals and some state and city administrations may be as bad; no business or industry except Penn Central can possibly be. One reason, incredibly enough, is that universities—which have studied everything from government to Persian mirrors and the number '7'—have never deeply studied their own administration.[6]

Perhaps, the same is true of library administration. We have devel- ed goals and objectives which provide purpose, our *raison d'être*. But, ese goals provide only a mirror image of what should be. Library ministrators must delve further, must identify our present state and sist in the development of strategies to attain our goals. Let us not wait r others to lead us. Rather, let us begin to study the administration of r libraries at the lowest level if we must, and progress to the higher levels, for that study will provide the basis for the development of achi able service goals.

NOTES AND REFERENCES

1. Morris Hamburg, Richard C. Clelland, Michael R. W. Bommer, Leonard E. Ram Ronald M. Whitfield (1974), *Library Planning and Decision-Making Systems.* Philadelp University of Pennsylvania Press, p. 9.

2. Susan Spaeth Cherry (1980), "Who is King Research and Why are They Saying Those Things About Us?" *American Libraries* 11: 477.

3. Jeffrey A. Raffel (1974), "From Economic to Political Analysis of Library Decis Making," *College and Research Libraries* 35: 414.

4. A statement of mission, objectives and goals for the CSUN library can be found Appendix 2. It is derived from campus and statewide planning documents and fr national standards of service. Service adequacy criteria are addressed in the self-anal found in Appendix 1.

5. John E. Baird, Jr. (1980), "Enhancing Managerial Credibility," *Personnel Jour* 59(12): 1001.

6. Warren Bennis (1976), *The Unconscious Conspiracy: Why Leaders Can't Lead.* New Yo AMACOM, American Management Association, pp. 25, 26.

Chapter 6

Conclusion

The preceding chapters have been an attempt to share with all who are interested in active management in the nonprofit sector, a library management system (ALMS) that integrates the budgeting and planning processes. This integration is vital to a management system. It relates each service to all other services, each change in personnel to service, each goal to both service and personnel. This integration of the budgeting and planning processes creates a coordinated whole, without which it is difficult to make administrative decisions and to communicate the meaning of library service to staff and funding agencies.

ALMS is based upon the concept of effectiveness as a fundamental and continuous element of the planning and budgeting process and upon the conviction that effectiveness relates directly to the needs of a particular user community and the ability of a specific staff to interpret and fulfill those needs. Rosemary DuMont states this premise clearly:

> Library responsiveness to expectations is an increasing task. In view of the changing nature of inputs, administrators have a continuing responsibility to recognize changes in the environment, to restructure available resources, to modify technologies, to develop employees, and so forth, in order to best employ the resources of the library to fulfill expectations that are themselves constantly changing.[1]

ALMS situates administrators and supervisors in the position of active management, where constant analysis and adjustment to a changing environment are routine, as opposed to the position of passive management where administrators and supervisors await a crisis and then react. Active management is difficult work, but the rewards are substantive, the central reward being the knowledge that the best service possible has been provided within limited resources. You, the management team, are in control of the ship, and the course is calculated and not a result random winds.

Such control must begin with a thorough understanding of how p sonnel are being utilized and what is being produced as described Chapter 2. It is difficult, if not impossible, to plan for what "ought to l if you do not know what "is." In order to defend and justify furtl budgets, you must begin with a defense of the existing budget as a b: for proposing either change in or maintenance of current levels of fur ing. Definitions of existing service levels are necessary for both bud defense and for the most effective assignment of personnel to m service needs. Planning and goal setting form the bridge between wl "is" and what "ought to be." The bridge outlined in this book rests up the labor analysis for a description of what "is" and service analysis statements of both what "ought to be" and what "is."

Our discussions have offered little concerning how to measure eff tiveness for purposes of analyzing service adequacy, but discussions how to evaluate library services are available in other works, such those by F. W. Lancaster and Ching-Chih Chen.[2] Responsibility lies w each librarian to explore and consider various means of measuring fectiveness in his/her area of responsibility. One librarian may empl time and motion studies of processing times, while another may opt f patron surveys and usage studies. The method for determining eff tiveness is not important, but the ability to analyze the service itself important. If the specific service can be identified, then criteria may established for judging the adequacy of that service. And once the ac quacy criteria have been established, the appropriate methodology f measuring and testing adequacy will become more easily recognizab Such measurement and testing for service adequacy will be time-consumi and often costly. Conducting an opinion survey, for example, can quire considerable personnel expertise and time to develop the surv instrument, to define the sample, to administer the survey, and to reco the result. And, because costs may be substantial, the estimated impc tance of the results must be weighed carefully before assigning the su vey funds. For example, if it is expected that a survey will cost $3,0 and the maximum savings to be realized from survey results is limited $300 a year, then, ten years will be required just to pay for the surve Such a venture is probably not worth the time and expense. However, the survey is expected to result in improved service but little or savings in personnel time or operating expenses, a decision must made, based upon the availability of funds and the relative merit of th improvement versus other possible service improvements.

In the first attempts to judge the effectiveness of service at the ta level, the intuitive judgment of librarians and staff performing the tasks may be the only available criterion. In this instance, intuition may provide a beginning. If a librarian says "I think we should be able to move materials through this unit within one month of receipt instead of three," then begin by accepting that statement as a criterion for judging adequacy. Experience will either provide supporting evidence for that assertion, prove the statement is incorrect, or reveal that further studies are needed. The important point is that intuition alone should be used as a starting point only. The next step is to refine, expand, and improve intuition into logical, reasoned assertions. The "I think" or "I feel" approach is not acceptable to any professional, but such statements do provide a hypothesis with which to begin an investigation.

This book would not be complete without some discussion of the status of ALMS at CSUN. Does ALMS really work? Or, is it just another interesting theory which in practice falls under its own weight? At CSUN, we completed both the labor analysis and the service analysis before a number of librarians refused to fill out data collection forms and thereby halted the labor analysis upon which ALMS is totally dependent. Only the catalog department continued with a modified version of the labor analysis. Continued refinement of the CSUN service analysis is still possible, but measurement of change is not. To alter the data collection process to sampling is not workable, for as illustrated in Examples 23 through 27, sampling is not valid for the measurement of change. Data from last year or two years ago will not serve today's planning needs. Granted, not all tasks change as dramatically as those in the above examples, but a sufficient number of tasks do change that the current collection of data is essential to this type of dynamic management system.

Because little objection was raised to the program by CSUN librarians during the first four years of the labor analysis (Function Cost Analysis) development, the eventual rebellion was a surprise to administrators. When it first became evident that a serious problem existed, the question of continuing the program was directed to the Librarian's Advisory Committee for Planning, composed of nonadministrative librarians. A long series of hearings of the committee followed, resulting in five recommendations:

1. A suitably modified FCA program should be retained for a trial period of one year.
2. Duplicate statistics should be investigated at the department level.
3. A mechanism to provide necessary input for continuing refinement of FCA should be established.

4. Limitations of task measurement should be addressed at the department leve after extensive departmental consultation.
5. Each department should re-conceptualize the activities performed by librar- ians within that department.[3]

Despite these recommendations from their peers, some ten months la 14 of 32 librarians signed a letter to the director stating that they wo no longer participate in the data collection (Function Cost Analysis) p gram because:

1. We believe that a compulsory and perpetual FCA project violates academic freedom.
2. FCA was never mandated by a policy making committee.[4]
3. FCA has caused morale problems which interfere with the performance of our jobs.
4. We view the FCA project to be professionally demeaning.

Meanwhile, the CSUC systemwide program was underway, and library director requested, and received, cooperation from the majo of librarians for the duration of the system-wide program. At the end that five months, however, data collection was discontinued for the lal analysis. One of the local faculty unions was called into the discussions a librarian who charged that FCA was a violation of academic freedo Union representatives also charged that the program was nothing m than a simple time and motion study, a technique that had been c carded by modern management long ago. After one informal conf ence with the director, however, the union pursued the matter further.

Library administrators may question the advisability of allowing libr ians to simply terminate a project as they so choose. At CSUN, t answer lies in the existing reward system. Promotion, retention, a tenure actions rest upon three recommendations: the department ch the library personnel committee, and the library director. Disagreem among the three may be appealed by the individual to the campus P sonnel Planning and Review Committee, composed of nonadminist tive faculty. At the writing of this book, the Personnel Planning a Review Committee has yet to uphold any personnel decision made the library director when such a decision was at variance with the r ommendation of the library personnel committee. Therefore, unli other managers, the library director may not use the promotion a tenure system for reward purposes. Rather, the library director has lit power outside the power of persuasion.

In retrospect, it may be said that too little of the power of persuasi by the library director was used to convince the librarians that the labor analysis was a tool of the Service Domain, as well as of the Management Domain. Perhaps more time should have been devoted to a complete explanation of how the labor analysis was to be used as a part of the overall management system, and more specifically, of the dependency of the system on the professional expertise and judgment of those in the Service Domain. A program of more frequent discussions with faculty and staff might have reduced the degree of opposition to the program in its final stages of development. ALMS is not, in fact, a threat to the professional. To the contrary, ALMS emphasizes the importance of the professional to the planning process and the dependency of management on the professional opinion of those who comprise the Service Domain. ALMS transfers responsibility for the planning process to both the Management and Service Domains and provides a truly collegial atmosphere for library management.

Currently, the circulation and cataloging departments have reinstated the full labor analysis program in order to study the effects of OCLC and CLSI on staffing. But the future of ALMS at CSUN remains uncertain. Full restoration of the program relies upon the ability of management to demonstrate the usefulness of ALMS to the Service Domain; perhaps this volume will serve to clarify its value.

One last philosophic indulgence, if you will. Managers and supervisors in nonprofit organizations have a tendency to operate as if an individual is either born with the knowledge of how to manage effectively or automatically acquires such knowledge upon appointment to an administrative position. In actuality, the techniques for effective management are developed slowly over time through continual reading in the field (particularly current management and personnel journals), observation and analysis of cause-and-effect relationships, attendance at management workshops and seminars, in-depth discussions with other managers, and a determination to learn about all aspects of organizations and the people that make them function. Advanced degrees are always beneficial to the individual by providing the latest concepts in management theory, but advanced degrees do not assure managerial effectiveness. Rather, effective managers are produced through a combination of experience, continual study, and individual effort to grow professionally.

While using the term "managers" to describe those responsible for library operations, it should be clearly understood that managers must also be leaders, a concept that is equally as difficult to practice as it is to define. Bennis made several observations regarding leadership that are useful for purposes of reflection:

> But what is it that prevents me from being as good a leader as I want to be? The biggest obstacle, of course, for you as well as for me, is the turbulent, unstable world. It is the explosively changing environment in which we have to function.[5]
>
> Leadership is as much an art as a science, and the key tool is the person himself, his ability to learn what his strengths and skills are and to develop them to the hilt.[6]
>
> So why are 'leaders' not 'leading'? One reason, I fear, is that many of us don't have the faintest concept of what leadership is all about. Leading does not mean managing; the difference between the two is crucial. There are many institutions I know that are very well managed and very poorly led. They may excel in the ability to handle all the routine inputs each day, yet they may never ask whether the routine should be preserved at all.[7]

However difficult the task of leadership, we must continue the attemp to grasp its meaning and fulfill its obligations.

In 1970, a study of university library management conducted by Booz Allen, and Hamilton, Incorporated, pointed out the need for improvements in planning and control:

> Impediments to effective management of university libraries exist in a number of areas:
>
> Planning—The need for more comprehensive library planning and budgeting systems, which, for the near and longer term, specify (1) the role and requirements of the library in relation to the academic program of the university; (2) the library's objectives and plans in support of academic programs; and (3) the library resources (financial, personnel, and physical materials, facilities, and equipment) needed to implement agreed upon plans.
>
> Objectives and Requirements—The need for improved library statistics for use as tools to determine the cost and effectiveness of library programs and services in relation to the academic program requirements.
>
> Operations—The need for standards to measure and control the flow of work in the library; the need to explore feasible applications of automatic data processing which are transferable from one library to another; and the need for greater codification of operating policies, systems, and procedures for use in training library personnel, controlling operations, and delegating responsibility.
>
> Organization—The need to strengthen the service delivery capacity of university libraries through formal organizational recognition of several management functions, such as planning and research, budgeting, and personnel development, which are vital to effective and efficient resource utilization, delivery of services, and communication flow within the library.[8]

While other impediments to management were identified by the Boo Allen, and Hamilton study, ALMS directly addresses the impedimen listed above. The labor and service analyses provide the base for pla ning and budgeting, as well as serve to determine cost and effectiveness of library programs and services and to establish standards for measurement and control of work-flow.

Booz, et al. also underscore the need for organizational recognition of the importance of personnel development and training for managerial techniques and skills. How important is the development of managerial skills? Bennis, again, puts the problem into perspective:

> A scientist at the University of Michigan has recently discussed what he considers to be the ten basic dangers to our society. First on his list of ten, and most significant, is the possibility of some kind of nuclear war or accident which would destroy the entire human race. The second basic challenge facing us, is the prospect of a world-wide epidemic, disease, famine, or depression. The scientist's No. 3 in terms of the key problems which can bring about the destruction of society is the quality of the management and leadership of our institutions.[9]

The challenge of providing quality management is nearly overwhelming. It is to know intimately the purpose, structure, strengths and weaknesses of our organizations and, beginning with ourselves, to strengthen our weaknesses and to examine our strengths for appropriateness of purpose; to ever seek new ways of acquiring and analyzing data to help us to understand ourselves, but to ensure that the collection of data does not become an end in itself. The ultimate goal is the marriage of organizational and individual needs: the development of organizations which serve the needs of their communities and of individuals who serve the needs of their organizations.

NOTES AND REFERENCES

1. Rosemary Ruhig DuMont, "A Conceptual Basis for Library Effectiveness," *College and Research Libraries*, Vol. 41, March 1980, p. 110.
2. F. W. Lancaster, *The Measurement and Evaluation of Library Services*, Information Resources Press, Wash. D.C. 1977. Ching-Chih Chin, *Quantitative Measurement and Dynamic Library Service*, Oryx Press, Phoenix, Ariz., 1978.
3. California State University Northridge Libraries, Librarians' Advisory Committee for Planning, "Report on Library Function Cost Analysis Program," April 19, 1978. See Appendix 5 for the full report.
4. The 1973-78 statement of CSUN Library Goals and Objectives states the "the Associate Director will develop a system of work measurement statistics." That document was approved by all library departments.
5. Bennis, p. 127.
6. Bennis, p. 134.
7. Bennis, p. 154.
8. Booz, Allen & Hamilton, Inc., *Problems in University Library Management*, Association of Research Libraries, 1970, Washington D.C., pp. 5-6.
9. Bennis, p. 145.

Appendix 1

California State University—Northridge, University Libraries: Service Analysis and Self-Study Report for Reaccreditation October, 1979

The following service analysis represents the first attempt by librarians and staff of the California State University, Northridge, Libraries to define the service provided by each established task and to identify the standards against which quality could be measured. Much work remains to be done and the refining process will be ongoing. Professional judgment about existing service quality is an acceptable way to begin.

The study of service adequacy in the CSUN Libraries was begun early in 1978 under the direction of the Associate Director of University Libraries in cooperation with the chairs of the five library departments and members of the library's administrative offices. The Function Cost Analysis Report of June, 1978, was used for the purpose of determining the total staffing for one year and the required level of staffing for each of the major tasks performed in the library.

Once the criteria for determining the adequacy of our current service were established for each task, or related group of tasks, a collective judgment was made as to the relationship between our current level and that which we consider to be a minimally required level.[1] An estimate was then made of staffing requirements, by type of staff, to provide that level of service. Further, a collective judgment was made as to the definition of what constitutes an optimum level of service and the staffing requirements for providing that level.[2] In some cases we discovered that we are currently below the minimum and in others we are above the minimum. We also learned that in some instances the minimum and optimum levels are the same. In other words, we provide all that is needed but any less would mean inadequate support for the educational programs offered by the campus. The following analysis represents the first, and admittedly less than perfect, attempt at self-examination.

NOTES

1. "Minimally required" is defined as the level below which library patrons regularly express a need for more service, backlogs develop, or quality is inadequate in the judgment of the library faculty.
2. "Optimum" is defined as a level of service which is reasonable and appropriate, in the judgment of the library faculty, given the necessary technology and budget support.

INDEX

ACQUISITIONS/SERIALS

ADMINISTRATION

ADMINISTRATIVE FUNCTIONS

BIBLIOGRAPHY

CATALOGING

CIRCULATION

REFERENCE

ACQUISITIONS/SERIALS

Task	*Level of Service*		*Staffing* LIBN	*LA*	*CLER*	*SA*
Ordering an Approval Rev.	Orders for library materials are typed and sent to vendors within four to six weeks of receipt of the request. Materials arriving weekly on approval are put up for review by bibliographers within two weeks.	(current)	52	1685	3655	139
		(minimum)	52	1685	3655	139
		(optimum)	52	1685	4655	219

ANALYSIS: The current level is the minimum. An optimum leve would see orders out to vendors within one week. Approval shipmen would go up for review every week as shipments arrive.

PRODUCTION VOLUME 77/78 = 38,878 titles ordered.

Task	*Level of Service*		*Staffing* LIBN	LA	CLER	SA
Automated Accounting	All transactions for encumbrance, receipt, payment of orders are keypunched, including cancellations and returns. Runs are submitted four to eight times per month for the current year and once a month for the two prior fiscal years. End-of-the-month financial reports are balanced and distributed within one week of the end of the month.	(current)	0	1155	0	521
		(minimum)	0	1155	0	521
		(optimum)	0	1155	0	521

ANALYSIS: Current level is both minimal and optimal. Timely reports are essential for budget control. The library could be, and probably would be, seriously overspent if campus accounting reports (often several months in arrears) were the sole source of budget data. Also, constant interaction with Receiving and Order Sections is required, thus making the possibility of accounting at a remote location extremely time consuming and difficult.

PRODUCTION VOLUME 77/78 = 38,104 transactions.

Task	*Level of Service*		*Staffing* LIBN	LA	CLER	SA
Receiving	Packages are opened, material verified and put on trucks for review by bibliographers within one day of receipt. Invoices are processed for payment and sent to the Accounting Section within one week of receipt. Queries regarding materials ordered but not received are sent after the order is 6 months old; queried again at 12 and 18 months for domestic publishers. Foreign publishers are claimed at 12 months.	(current)	67	1182	0	964
		(minimum)	67	1182	0	964
		(optimum)	67	1182	0	1500

ANALYSIS: The current level is minimum. Regular orders should be queried every month after the order is 60 days old. This would lessen the likelihood that titles would be lost due to the publisher running out of stock.

PRODUCTION VOLUME 77/78 = 11,899 volumes received (nonbook, serials and approval not counted).

Task	*Level of Service*		*Staffing* LIBN	LA	CLER	SA
Fiscal Claims	Invoices are processed for payment by Sacramento, and balance sheets are produced monthly so	(current)	0	1612	41	832
		(minimum)	0	1612	41	832
		(optimum)	0	1612	41	832

that accounting records can be balanced with campus accounting. Invoices are held for processing for ten days on the average.

ANALYSIS: Current level is the minimum as well as the optimum. Holding up invoices for payment causes vendors to request prepayment before shipment and this creates more work.

PRODUCTION VOLUME 77/78 = 9,054 claims

Task	*Level of Service*		*Staffing* LIBN	LA	CLER	SA
Periodical Processing	Periodicals are checked in and forwarded within 20 working hours of receipt. Claims are mailed every three months. Since no record of issues received is available to the Reference Department, that information is	(current)	0	621	2137	1642
		(minimum)	0	621	2137	1642
		(optimum)	0	621	2137	4600

made available by telephone during normal working hours. Supervision includes problem solving and serving as liaison between the State Bindery and the library staff.

ANALYSIS: The current level is the minimum except for the lack of availability of the periodical record to Reference during evening hours and on weekends. No way has been found to provide this without addition of so many hours that it cannot be considered with the other below minimum activities. Optimum service would therefore include staffing the periodical record 81 hours per week and reducing the time for forwarding periodicals to eight hours of receipt.

PRODUCTION VOLUME 77/78 = 47,089 issues checked in; 1,616 claims; 1,773 Linedex entries typed

Task	*Level of Service*		*Staffing* LIBN	LA	CLER	SA
Bindery Preparation and returns	This volume varies with the size of the budget for binding. Three weeks are required for preparation and record maintenance of an average size shipment. Six weeks are required for binding and shipment.	(current)	0	506	1502	528
		(minimum)	0	500	1500	500
		(optimum)	0	100	2000	700

ANALYSIS: Here are suggested two possible options for reducing staffing costs. Both would require considerable discussion and study. One option would be to send nothing to the State Bindery for which microform is available and use those bindery funds for the purchase of microform copies. This would involve a systematic approach with the analysis of each title for its usage and mutilation problems, its practicality in microform, with the loss of color, graphs and charts. Additional costs impact on the book budget is unknown. Another option is to bind everything the bindery budget allows during semester break and summer school, supplementing with public service staff necessary hours needed. This would devastate resources for summer school and special arrangement would be required with the State Bindery to handle such large shipments. The current level is considered optimum with the bindery budget allocation available. We would increase the processing hours as we are permitted to spend more money on binding. If we could break away from legal restrictions of the State Bindery, local vendor binding would be less expensive and allow for faster processing of materials.

PRODUCTION VOLUME 77/78 = 10,562 units bound

Task	*Level of Service*		*Staffing* LIBN	LA	CLER	SA
Periodical Record Set-up	Records are established for new, reclassed, cancelled, withdrawn, and ceased periodicals. Illness of staff has created a backlog here, but normal processes should be established within the 78/79 fiscal year. Normal time for set-up is two days.	(current)	0	888	67	0
		(minimum)	0	888	67	0
		(optimum)	0	888	67	0

ANALYSIS: Current (without staff illness) is the minimum level. It is also optimum. Any delay keeps materials from being used by patrons when they are current.

PRODUCTION VOLUME 77/78 = 1,141 records set up.

Task	*Level of Service*		*Staffing* LIBN	LA	CLER	SA
Serial Processing and Record Set-up	All serial items arriving on standing order are identified as to proper cataloging entry. Those which cannot be identified or which carry special problems of entry become part of the "problem serials" backlog of 30-40 titles (average). Material is checked in within four to six weeks and claiming is done every four months. Records are kept of serials sent to the Bindery	(current)	0	1106	3451	1907
		(minimum)	400	1106	4400	1907
		(optimum)	400	1106	4400	1907

and of Reference pamming. The sets file is maintained also. At present there is a records backog which is being worked on by the department secretary and should be eliminated by mid-spring.

ANALYSIS: We are currently below minimum here; we should be processing all materials within two weeks and claiming every three months. We need .2 of a serials cataloger to deal with problems. A .5 CAIIA has been added recently to help bring us up to a minimum level, but the backlog is likely to remain for some time. It would be of great benefit to other sections, as well as this one, to establish a "floater" at the LAI level who could follow a backlog all the way through the technical services departments so that the minimally required level could be maintained at all times. Working off a backlog in one section usually creates one in another section. This person would have to be familiar with all sections so that assistance could be applied as needed. The 1106 hours recorded under LA time on the optimum line above does not include the floater's hours.

PRODUCTION VOLUME 77/78 = 625 bound volumes; 1,246 loose issues

Task	*Level of Service*		*Staffing* LIBN	LA	CLER	SA
Periodical Reading Room Stack Maintenance	We have staff available to shelve and reshelve periodicals 52 hours per week.	(current)	0	46	577	1586
		(minimum)	0	46	577	1586
		(optimum)	0	0	0	4200

ANALYSIS: Current level is the minimum. We would prefer to have shelving and reading of stacks all hours the library is open (81 hours).

PRODUCTION VOLUME 77/78 = 99,739 new and reshelved items; 15,163 discards; 1,610 pulled for bindery

Task	*Level of Service*		*Staffing* LIBN	LA	CLER	SA
Periodical Reading Room Desk	Desk staff assist patrons with problems six hours per day. Staff leaves and illness have made this impossible recently but full staff will bring hours back to normal. Usually there are no queues.	(current)	0	1028	123	29
		(minimum)	0	3400	600	0
		(optimum)	0	3400	600	0

ANALYSIS: We could limit

service even further by cutting back to five hours per day, 10:00 A.M -3:00 P.M., Monday thru Friday. However, since this is a heavily used area we would prefer to be able to provide the same service here as at other service desks, that is, 81 hours per week. This is the minimum recommended for the library with the importance of periodical literature. 81 hours would require two full-time staff members and more considering miscellaneous time costs. The level should be LAI to provide continuity and expertise, with back-up clerical.

PRODUCTION VOLUME 77/78 = 10,004 questions.

Task	*Level of Service*		*Staffing* LIBN	LA	CLER	SA
Mends	All damaged or worn books from the collection or incoming new titles are repaired according to instructions or as appropriate; indexes, errata, and missing pages are tipped in, pictures are glued down, pockets are made for loose	(current)	0	27	0	1984
		(minimum)	0	50	0	4300
		(optimum)	0	50	0	4600

materials, and special actions are performed as necessary for hard bound books and paperback and coverless works not to be pammed or togiced. Reference and Reserve Book Room materials are given priority processing. Circulating materials are organized in call number order for availability in case of a specific request for any given title, coded by month received, and processed in order as received. The number of incoming "mends" from the collection depends on the availability of staff in other departments to locate, pull, and process damaged and worn books. Consequently, End Processing has no control over the number of books waiting to be processed at a given time. The workload is extremely heavy after the end of each semester, with the return of books by students and the release of reference materials for repair. Since it is cheaper to mend than to replace with a new purchase, the trend in mends will probably be toward such processing as the collection gets older. However, both Reference and Circulation should investigate the possibility of sending materials for mend regularly throughout the year, avoiding the seasonal overload.

ANALYSIS: Since mends are normally high usage, our present 60-90 day turn-around time is below minimum. Even though such titles will be processed on a demand basis from the Circulation Department, few patrons would have the knowledge to request such materials. Since this is very much a seasonal operation, in order to reduce turn-around time to 30-45 days we would have to increase the student hours to 4,300. Optimum service would be more in the vicinity of one or two weeks turn-around time.

PRODUCTION VOLUME 77/78 = 3,773 units.

Task	*Level of Service*		*Staffing* LIBN	LA	CLER	SA
End Processing	All new titles, copies, volumes, serial issues, mended books, pammed and togiced materials, "re-labels," records, cassettes, and microfilm reels are labeled, property stamped, pocketed, due slipped, tattle-taped, etc., as required; book cards are keypunched for circulating materials. The processed materials are proofed to make certain that all requirements have been met and data are correct. The materials are then separated according to type of material, classification, or special instructions from bibliographers and catalogers. Such categories as rushes, reference, "re-labels," mends, periodicals (not in the low-use category), serials (both reference and circulating), state bindery shipments, records, microfilm, and cassettes are given priority processing when possible. Other materials are processed as soon as possible in order as received. The average time for new books to be processed is five days. The difference in the number of units processed during any particular year depends upon the library's purchasing power and the catalog department's ability to keep up with the cataloging of purchased materials.	(current)	0	192	53	3390
		(minimum)	0	1200	0	4000
		(optimum)	0	1200	0	5000

ANALYSIS: We are currently operating at bare minimum for turnaround time. We have no formal quality control at this time so that aspect of service is unanalyzed. In 76/77, we received many public service complaints on the delay of materials to the stacks. The time-lag study also indicated an exhorbitant amount of time between the date of cataloging and the date processed in the circulation department. By adding more students, we have reduced the complaints but added to our cost per unit produced. Certain types of materials should have still higher priority in processing. We feel that the key element in production, where the volume of material fluctuates so dramatically with workflow from other departments, may be supervision. In the past, this area was part of a larger unit, and supervision was spread very thinly over the entire unit. It is expected that having a supervisor dedicated to this area alone will improve our service. A conversion of student assistant hours to staff hours should also be considered. Our experiences in 78/79 will begin to demonstrate whether this is correct. An optimum turn-around time would be two to three days, but this would require a sizeable increase of student assistant hours, and the added service would not warrant the expense.

PRODUCTION VOLUME 77/78 = 36,626 units.

Task	*Level of Service*		*Staffing* LIBN	LA	CLER	SA
Pam and Togic Binding	Covers are affixed to all incoming paperback and coverless works and periodicals with instructions	(current)	0	39	0	3367
		(minimum)	0	39	0	3367
		(optimum)	0	39	0	3367

to "pam," "togic," or "process as appropriate." Material is pocketed, pages are cut, material is typed in, and pictures are glued down, as required. The fluctuations in total units processed and time per unit are directly related to the different categories of materials processed during a given period of time, the number of units in a specific category, the type of processing necessary, the availability of students to do the work, and the experience and expertise of the students. A leveling off of periodicals to be togiced can be expected as the three or four year backlog of units is processed.

ANALYSIS: Periodicals that are togiced are low-usage titles. Therefore, turn-around time could be longer than we have now. It is now approximately one week for the togic periodicals and five days for End Processing. The togicing could be postponed during work-flow surges. The time then could possibly be extended because of usage patterns, but there would be no time savings; the same amount of time would be required to accomplish the task later. Monograph pamphlets currently take approximately three weeks. This is an acceptable minimum since public catalog records are not yet available. Cards now are filed in approximately four weeks and automated title and author listings are now produced once a month for the reference department. Therefore, minimum could be optimum unless time sequences for record updates are reduced, then pamphlet making would have to increase appropriately. Again, there is no staff saving; processing will require as much time if done later.

It might be possible to reduce the amount of pamming through a more careful review of all items defined as pamphlets before requesting cataloging, and by providing better subject access to the pam file. Savings in personnel time would be proportionate to the number of pams eliminated. Assuming a 20% reduction in pams, 600 hours of student assistant time would be saved with very little time added to End Processing. The apparent trend toward the purchase of "cheaper" materials (paperbacks) by collection developers saves in the book budget but adds significantly to personnel costs. Therefore, titles available in hard copy should normally be purchased in hard copy rather than paperback. A total of one week is probably optimum in terms of turn-around time, and an emphasis on supervision of student assistants is aimed at both reducing errors and speeding processing time.

PRODUCTION VOLUME 77/78 = 15,130 (9231 pams, 5899 togiced)

Task	*Level of Service*		*Staffing* *LIBN*	*LA*	*CLER*	*SA*
Missing Issues	Lost or mutilated pages or issues are replaced as they are discovered. Backfiles on microform and cumulative indexes are ordered.	(current)	0	1591	145	601
		(minimum)	0	0	1000	500
		(optimum)	0	0	1500	500

ANALYSIS: Reduction of search and investigation for supplementary material as well as simplification of record keeping could reduce the current time requirements.* Ideally we would add some $20,000 more budget for backfiles and purchase back-up copies on microform for all heavily used titles. This would add some 500 hours to the order section, 500 to receiving and 200 to the bindery shelflist. There should be offsetting savings in the Bindery task.

PRODUCTION VOLUME 77/78 = 1,120 missing issues and volumes

Note: *As of Spring, 1979, this has been done

ADMINISTRATION

Task	*Level of Service*		*Staffing* LIBN	LA	CLER	SA
Systems Analysis Programming, Reprogramming, Program Maintenance	Consultation and advice is provided to the library administration regarding general library operations and planning, acquisition of proprietary automation systems and hardware. This service is provided on demand as are	(current)	3438	0	150	0
		(minimum)	4000	0	0	0
		(optimum)	7500	0	0	0

the following: analysis and evaluation of Chancellor's Office automation systems and related documents, consultation services to the Chancellor's Office on development of management tools, programming new systems, reprogramming and program maintenance. Systems analysis for new automation systems and manual operations is possible only on a very limited basis. We are only able to complete required new automation programs (such as OCLC) and only the most seriously needed inhouse automation development (such as the combined serials/periodicals list). There is no time at all for the systematic analysis of manual operations.

ANALYSIS: Minimum service requires the maintenance of existing programs and the necessary systems analysis, technical and programming expertise to permit the library to implement and maintain systems mandated by the Chancellor's Office or proprietary library automation systems. It is also necessary to spend some time analyzing those manual operations where our intuition and/or experience suggest that our service might be substantially improved through changed procedures or that staff savings might be realized through such changes. Optimum service would provide the necessary systems analysis, planning, development, technical/programming, and training expertise to enable the library to (1) develop or adopt, implement and maintain an integrated general purpose, interactive bibliographic control system, (2) Systematically analyze all library operations for improvement in efficiency and service. This would require an additional programmer and one full time librarian/analyst.

PRODUCTION VOLUME 77/78 = not available.

Task	*Level of Service*		*Staffing* LIBN	LA	CLER	SA
Building & Copy Machine Maintenance	This task includes the various routine functions of building care, security, and inspection. However, the majority of time is spent in copy machine maintenance. This service includes high quality, five-cents-per-page coin	(current)*	0	256	159	1380
		(minimum)*	0	256	159	1380
		(optimum)*	0	356	159	1580

copiers on each floor of the library and fifteen-cents-per-page microform copiers. As a separate category (086) in July to December 1978, this took 1236 subsidized hours which were paid for by revenues generated by the coin copying service. In addition, some subsidized hours of coin copy workers go into answering office phones in exchange for library assistant work spent on managing coin copy operations (approximately 200 hours). Based on this information, it can be assumed that 2,978 student assistant hours in org. unit 008 during 1977/78 went into basic coin copy maintenance and were self-funded by photo copy revenue. Opening and closing the building requires about 1,450 hours per year. Three-fourths of that time is spent clearing patrons from the library, the remainder on a daily routine of turning lights and machinery off and on, opening doors, inspecting for problems and security checks. The remaining 365 hours in this category is spent in routine equipment checking and resupply and periodic building inspections.

ANALYSIS: Current copy service staffing does not allow for a copy maintenance person in both buildings. In some cases, response to repair requests is slower than ideal, creating a few patron complaints. By more direct library management over the past three years, problems and complaints have diminished due to better machines and more responsible help. Copy volume has grown steadily and the price has been maintained. Therefore, the copy service is basically meeting minimum needs. Optimum requirements would include more and less expensive microform hard copy services, and perhaps color copying. Continued success of the coin copiers may generate enough funds to add these services. Opening and closing consume minimum time as needed, less time spent would cause security or safety problems. An extra 300 hours per year for security checking and recording of problems would be optimum. Given continued IMS technician support, equipment maintenance time is minimum and optimum.

Note: *Assuming revenue producing subsidized help will be supported elsewhere in future years, it is not included in these figures.

Task	*Level of Service*		*Staffing* LIBN	LA	CLER	SA
Equipment Maintenance and Repair	This task includes obtaining maintenance contracts on equipment; utilizing such contracts, warranties or other means to maintain equipment in good repair; and monitoring equipment condition. The total time spent is minimal.	(current)	0	58	0	26
		(minimum)	20	150	0	25
		(optimum)	20	200	0	25

ANALYSIS: The large increase of optimum and minimum projections over 77/78 is due to the fact Reference and I.M.L. were not reporting into this category in 77/78. The July through December 1978 figures show Reference and I.M.L. minimum figures about as estimated for a full year as minimum. Optimum would include an extra 50 hours LA time to analyze closely how much better maintenance would improve quality of equipment performance.

Task	*Level of Service*		*Staffing* LIBN	LA	CLER	SA
Building Maintenance	This represents work needed to determine or relieve reports of needed building repairs, request or requisition such repair, then repair or verify work completion.	(current)	1	171	0	0
		(minimum)	0	170	0	0
		(optimum)	0	170	0	0

ANALYSIS: The work is done as necessary and currently is at optimum and minimum.

Task	*Level of Service*		*Staffing* LIBN	LA	CLER	SA
Accounting/ Payroll—OE	Preparation of student assistant payroll includes preparation, distribution and calling in of time sheets; preparing raise list from approved evaluations; recording of raise approval or denial on file card; updating the rate of pay;	(current)	0	160	412	97
		(minimum)	0	160	412	97
		(optimum	0	160	412	97

totaling the hours worked and the total earned; obtaining delinquent signatures; checking time sheet for recording errors; preparation and distribution of payroll sheet for recording errors; preparation and distribution of payroll summary and budget memos; posting and calculating monies left in work study; typing lists of persons eligible for raises; processing reclasses; sending termination evaluations and processing new students. The number of student employees averages approximately 280.

OE and equipment accounting includes recording encumbrances, charges, allocation transfers, etc. Also, the monthly reconciliation with the campus accounting ledger and the correction of errors.

The current level is considered to be both optimum and minimum.

PRODUCTION VOLUME 77/78 = not available.

Task	*Level of Service*		*Staffing* LIBN	LA	CLER	SA
Exhibits	New exhibits are set up in the Oviatt Library approximately every two months. There are two travelling CSUN exhibits, on the average, circulating at any given time.	(current)	307	0	0	26
		(minimum)	150	0	0	15
		(optimum)	500	0	0	50

ANALYSIS: Minimum is con-considered to be half as many as are currently displayed (or three per year with one travelling). Optimum would be to add the same number of exhibits in the South Library as exist now in the Oviatt.

PRODUCTION VOLUME 77/78 = not available.

Task	*Level of Service*		*Staffing* LIBN	LA	CLER	SA
Special Collections: Selection, Processing, Filing, Service	Consultative service is provided Monday-Friday between the hours of 10 A.M. and 3 P.M. Processing and filing are done during those hours with supervision and selection during 8 A.M.-10 A.M. and 3 P.M.-4 P.M. hours as well.	(current)	1187	0	0	557
		(minimum)	800	0	0	500
		(optimum)	1180	0	2000	0

ANALYSIS: Minimum service would be to limit all activities to 10 A.M.-3 P.M., Monday-Thursday. Optimum service would provide for staffing the room for public use of the collection from 8 A.M.-5 P.M. This would require a full time CAIIA in place of student assistant hours.

PRODUCTION VOLUME 77/78 = not available.

ADMINISTRATIVE FUNCTIONS

Task	*Level of Service*		*Staffing* *LIBN*	*LA*	*CLER*	*SA*
Administration (All Departments	In 77/78, this task included attendance at department meetings and work-related in-house library committees such as Library Council, the Executive Board and specialized task forces (either departmental or those estab-	(current)	15,813	3468	685	1176
		(minimum)	Experience will determine			
		(optimum)	15,000	3800	500	100

lished by the Library Administration). It also includes other administrative duties such as (1) planning and developing new projects; (2) the scrutiny of operations, work flows or files; and (3) adjusting differences between individuals by counseling. Later FCA programs separate this task into five tasks: (1) Library Administration, General—planning and reviewing library operations, directing activities of subordinates by the Director, Associate Director, and Assistant Directors. Planning for buildings, space, physical facilities in general. Budget planning and review for library materials, personnel, OE, and equipment. Interaction related to the above between department chairpersons and the three levels of library managers. Developing management tools. Directing administration and office staff. (2) Library Administration, Advisory Committees—activities related to Library administration—generally carried on by permanent or ad hoc committees (Executive Board, Library Council, Library Faculty (nonpersonnel matters), Student Rep Board, Standing and other committees). (3) Department Administration—generally the same as Library Administration General but confined to the department. Any departmentally constituted committees, groups, or meetings concerning the department as a whole, particularly its policies, budgets, and staffing. (4) Campus, Chancellor's Office and other Administration—Faculty Senate Committees, PP & R, EPC, ERC, etc. Campus advisory committees and task forces. CCAB, fair employment practices, Dean's Council, Chancellor's Office Committees: LDAC, regional cooperation groups, responding to Chancellor's Office technical and administrative proposals and positions. (5) Assigned library representation—library director's representation to both campus and off-campus groups (or those assigned by him t represent the library).

Using the December 1977 cumulative FCA reports, the total hours shov that, on the average, 45% of the administrative hours for the year hav been expended by the end of December. Applying that to the Decembe 1978 cumulative FCA reports, we can project the following hours for th 78/79 year:

Library Administration, General	2183	÷	45%	=	485
Library Administration, Advisory Committees	787	÷	45%	=	174
Departmental Administration	5803	÷	45%	=	10,67

Campus, Chancellor's Office and other administration	804 ÷ 45% = 1786
Assigned Library Representation	187 ÷ 45% = 415
Total hours	19,473

ANALYSIS: If the percentage holds through the last half of 78/79, this represents a reduction in total hours devoted to administration from 77/78. The reduction of 1669 hours represents a little under 8% of the total 77/78 administrative hours. One possible explanation for the reduction is that in July, 1978, when we began to record administration hours by type of activity, the tendency to use Administration as a dump for time not otherwise accounted for was lessened. Also, fewer directives from the Chancellor's Office have been received since the publication and discussions associated with the A. D. Little Report. Considering that the above 19,473 hours do not include personnel actions, training time or supervision time, the total, amounting to slightly under 10 full positions, seems to be an optimum level or even excessive. Some consideration should be given to reducing the number of people reporting in the administrative categories through reorganization, reassignment or a more accurate recording of time on the part of individuals. To cut back to a minimum level in Administration, we should consider the following methods:

A. Attempt to reduce General Library Administration and Campus, Chancellor's Office and other administration by: (1) limiting the number of people attending statewide or regional meetings to one from each appropriate department, (2) asking the vice president for academic affairs for a direction to comply with any requests from the Chancellor's Office for information requiring a significant amount of time to compile (more than one hour). This would not apply to currently established statistical reports.

Time saved by Central Administration should be used to assist the departments by relieving them of as much administrative responsibility as possible (i.e., shift to central decision making whenever possible). After appropriate consultation and data gathering, the library director or his designee would write up a proposed action and send to all library faculty and Library Council, asking for a response by a given date from those who wish to comment. Meetings would only be called on items where considerable disagreement is evident.

B. Attempt to reduce Library Advisory Committee time by (1) preparing agendas in advance of meetings, (2) writing information items and announcements to be distributed in advance, (3) limiting Executive Board and library-wide planning meetings to the first and third Wednesdays of each month from 2 P.M.-5 P.M. Library-wide planning from 2:00 P.M.-3:30 P.M. and Executive Board would be held from 3:30 P.M.-5:00 P.M., (4) limit all other advisory committees to three hours per month and limit the number of people attending to one per department and one from central administration.

C. Attempt to reduce departmental administration by reducing number of people reporting in the administrative categories throug reduction in the number of people performing administrative ta

In 78/79 most of the time was reported by librarians and library as tants. Considering that the definition of this category includes prima activities and committees dealing with departmental policies, bud and staffing, it would seem appropriate to limit the participants, beyc one monthly staff meeting, to the chief departmental administra plus one LAII or LAIII representing each major section or group related activities. A total of 1,000 hours per year per department librarian time (5,000 hours total) and 400 hours per year per dep ment of LA time (3,000 hours total) should be our long range goal, t saving at least 3,000 hours or 1½ full positions. The savings should used to reduce backlogs and service deficiencies in the department they are realized.

Task	*Level of Service*		*Staffing* LIBN	LA	CLER	S.
Personnel	This task includes all appointment, promotion, retention, tenure activities (time spent interviewing candidates, evaluating personnel, writing new job descriptions, handling exit interview, setting up personnel files	(current)	2509	2509	246	1
		(minimum)	2500	2000	200	1(
		(optimum)	2740	2500	200	1(

and attendance records, etc.). The 78/79 FCA Program requires a bre down of time recording into two tasks: (1) Faculty PRT and (2) Facu and staff personnel, general. Using the December 1977 FCA cumulat reports, we find that 48% of the personnel time recorded in 77/78 recorded through the end of December. Using December, 1978 F cumulative reports and applying the 48% factor, we arrive at the follc ing projection for 78/79:

Faculty PRT	302	÷	48%	=	629 ho
Faculty & Staff Personnel General	1489	÷	48%	=	3102
Total hours					3731

ANALYSIS: If the percentage holds, the total number of hours in p sonnel activities in 78/79 will be 1,641 less than the total in 77/78. Thi due for the most part to a change in time reporting by the person assistant who now records in the category of administrative support stead of personnel. Taking that into account, the reduction is about 5 hours. This seems like a reasonable amount and is dictated by turnover a large extent. I would propose leaving this alone, considering 78/ projections to be minimum. Optimum should include considerably mc work on reviewing and updating job descriptions for staff, perhaps much as 40 hours per department of librarian and LA time.

Task	*Level of Service*		*Staffing* LIBN	LA	CLER	SA
Training	Time spent as both trainer and trainee is recorded here. It includes time spent reading and writing training documents, in attendance at workshops and orientation programs, and in self-training exercises. In 78/79,	(current)	1422	5065	3775	5641
		(minimum)	1400	3400	3400	5500
		(optimum)	1900	5000	4400	5500

the FCA Program was changed to distinguish required training and optional training, the latter being job-related training initiated by the employee (not professional development). Using the December 1977 FCA cumulative reports, we see that 54% of the training for 77/78 was recorded through the end of December. Using December 1978 FCA cumulative reports, we project the following totals for 78/79.

Required training	6859 hours	÷	54%	=	12,701
Optional Training	512 hours	÷	54%	=	948
Total hours					13,649

ANALYSIS: If the percentage holds, a reduction of 2,274 hours will be realized in 78/79. Since the total is made up, for the most part, of required training, due either to turnover or new technology procedure, the 78/79 figures must be considered minimum. An optimal level would include more time for cross-training of personnel at all levels. This would allow for maximum flexibility in the reassignment of staff to avoid layoffs resulting from projected declining enrollments or other budget cuts. At least 8 hours per week per department.

Task	*Level of Service*		*Staffing* LIBN	LA	CLER	SA
Professional Activities	Time used to enhance professional expertise is recorded here. It includes attendance at professional workshops and association meetings, projects growing from involvement with professional associations, visits to other libraries,	(current)	4883	380	32	13
		(minimum)	5000	100	0	0
		(optimum)	6400	400	0	0

researching and reading professional literature, and attendance at faculty governance activities. The new FCA program in July 1978 created a breakdown of this task into three:

1. Professional development—Reading and studying professional and technical literature to keep up with one's professional field, attending (as a listener) meetings of professional societies and lectures they sponsor, participating in workshops sponsored by professional organizations.

2. Professional Associations—Work as an officer or committee member.

3. Research—Preparation of papers, speeches, demonstrations for presentations at professional meetings or for publication in professional literature. Design and conduct of actual research projects including background reading, writing a professional book and related activities performed by the author. All research must be job-related.

Using the December 1977 FCA cumulative reports, we see that 44% of the time recorded in 1978 was recorded through December. Using December, 1978 FCA cumulative reports and applying the 44% factor, we project the following for 78/79:

Professional development	940 ÷ 44% =	2136 hours
Professional Associations	413 ÷ 44% =	938
Research	296 ÷ 44% =	672
Total		3746

ANALYSIS: If the percentage holds, the total number of hours in these tasks will decrease by 1562. Since we do not have the same breakdown for 77/78, we cannot know which of the three is showing the greatest reduction. The hours recorded here should be almost entirely librarian hours, and since we have 32 librarians at present, we feel that the hours recorded in 77/78 are less than bare minimum. Optimally we would expect something like 10% of a librarian's time to be spent in these activities (four hours per week). However, the vacant librarian positions which we are forced to keep in salary savings have made it impossible to spend the hours needed for proper research and development.

Task	*Level of Service*		*Staffing* LIBN	*LA*	*CLER*	*SA*
Problem Solving	This task is defined as any activity not regularly scheduled and not part of one's job description, of relatively short duration, and that benefits people other than those in one's own immediate work group. It was included in order to	(current)	1674	640	180	1156
		(minimum)	2200	1000	100	700
		(optimum)	2200	1000	100	700

encourage staff to be helpful to others by not forcing staff to charge th time to their own tasks and thereby inflating their unit costs.

ANALYSIS: This is not an activity that can be predicted as it is based o people's needs as they arise. Using the December 1978 FCA cumulativ reports and projecting the remainder of FY 78/79 from the rate of ex penditure through December 1977 (46%), we should expect an increas in hours from 3650 (77/78) to 4380 (78/79). A yearly average of 4,00 hours seems both minimum and maximum.

Task	*Level of Service*		*Staffing* LIBN LA CLER SA
Miscellaneous	This task records nonproduction activities for which the State pays: vacation, sick leave, compensating time-off, holidays, coffee breaks, nonproduction meetings (Staff Association), departmental parties, and jury duty. These fig-	(current)	12,784 11,866 10,764 5037
		(minimum)	Should remain relatively consistent
		(optimum)	Should remain relatively consistent

ures can never be checked for accuracy because we do not keep separate records of vacation and sick leave used. However, using averages for those items as well as coffee breaks we conclude that hours recorded here should not exceed 36,000 plus 1,000 hours for jury duty, etc.

ANALYSIS: Using the monthly averages of (1) 10 hours for coffee breaks, 8 hours for vacation, 8 hours for sick leave (60 staff); (2) 10 hours for coffee breaks, 16 hours for vacation, 8 hours for sick leave (30 librarians); (3) 415 hours for breaks (all student assistants), we produce a yearly figure of some 36,000 hours. Using the same percentage as expended through December 1977 (53%), we project 42,320 total hours for 78/79, as follows (this compares with 40,451 hours for FY 77/78):

Librarians	15,569
Library Assistants	11,005
Clerical	11,994
Student Assistants	3,752

If the 53% factor holds, this will require investigating; it should not be rising while staff is going down (167,172 total hours recorded July-December 1977, 155,287 hours recorded July-December 1978). One might speculate that time which properly belongs to another task is being incorrectly recorded here.

Task	*Level of Service*		*Staffing* LIBN LA CLER SA
Administrative Support	In 77/78, this category included typing done as an administrative assignment (correspondence, memos, reports, etc.), maintaining departmental correspondence files, compiling monthly workload statistics, departmental	(current)	1734 3325 9414 9831
		(minimum)	unable to determine
		(optimum	unable to determine

scheduling, handling student assistant budget, supplying forms production, sorting and distributing mail and ordering and receiving supplies and equipment. The 1978/79 programs record six tasks under administrative support: (1) Administration—departmental: All clerical and typing activities in support of the "Administration—departmental" task. (2) Administration—library and all others: All clerical and typing activities in support of all the other "Administration" tasks. (3) Support of professional associations and research: All clerical and typing activities in support of those two tasks. (4) Coin copier: Obtaining maintenance service and all associated typing, clerical, and record-keeping activities. (5) Coin typewriters: Obtaining maintenance service and all associated typing, clerical and record-keeping activities. (6) Building and other equipment maintenance: Obtaining maintenance service and all associated typing, clerical, and record keeping activities.

The hours recorded through the six months ending December 1978 in the six tasks detailed above were:

Administration—departmental	6502	÷	46%	=	14,134
Administration—Library and all others	4893	÷	46%	=	10,636
Support of professional associations and research	200	÷	46%	=	434
Coin copiers	451	÷	46%	=	980
Coin typewriters	34	÷	46%	=	73
Bldg. & other equipment maintenance	59	÷	46%	=	128
Total	12,139	÷	46%	=	26,385

ANALYSIS: Outside of Central Administration, which accounts for nearly one-third of all hours in administrative support, the library-wide average at the end of December 1977 was 5% of the total hours spent in all tasks. At the end of December 1978, the percentage was slightly above 4%. This reflects the loss of CETA and work-study personnel and will likely not increase in 79/80 unless our vacant CETA positions can be filled and the availability of work-study students improves. Funds from nonstate sources will be providing an estimated 1,200 hours per year for the administrative support categories in Central Administration, representing a 400 hour per year increase over 78/79. We do not know at this point in time what effect the nearly 1% reduction in this function will have on service. A careful monitoring of problem areas as they develop will eventually allow us to establish a minimum level. Since all areas in the library report in this function, it will be difficult to determine the optimum except to say that enough support should be provided to prevent librarians and library assistants from using their time for the performance of routine clerical duties. This is not true in all cases currently, but a length survey would be required to determine the exact deficiencies. We will be carefully reviewing the six months system-wide FCA reports for other libraries of comparable size in order to compare our level of support in this function.

BIBLIOGRAPHY

Task	*Level of Service*		*Staffing* LIBN	*LA*	*CLER*	*SA*
'election and Approval Selection	Materials are selected both to support the curriculum and for independent study needs. Based on our surveys of students and faculty, we estimate that 85% of expressed student needs and 80% of expressed faculty needs	(current)	3400	0	0	0
		(minimum)	3400	0	0	0
		(optimum)	4500	0	0	0

are filled. Considerable time is spent by bibliographers in consultation with faculty regarding selection policies. Students make input through suggestion boxes in both libraries.

ANALYSIS: The current level of complaints of inadequacy of the collection is within reason, and so the current level is considered to be at the minimum level required. However, complaints from the faculty regarding the consultation process related to selection policies were regarded as significant enough to rate us below minimum. These complaints are being dealt with by the library administration through publication of a series of information bulletins and by the bibliographers through emphasis on meetings with teaching departments, thus allowing for more extensive contact without an increase in hours of librarians.

An optimum level would require filling at least 90% of expressed student needs and 82% of faculty needs. 500 hours a year added to area coordinators' support would allow more in-depth attention by librarians in their areas of specialization and give area coordinators more time for remaining subjects. This assumes the current budget level for library materials; reduced budgets will require more selection time. An additional 700 hours spent in consultation with teaching faculty would largely eliminate faculty complaints of lack of communication.

An optimum level would require additional means of evaluating the effectiveness of our library's collections. Such methods include checking lists, catalogs, and bibliographies; direct examination of the collection; compilation of statistics; citation analysis studies; and the application of standards and document delivery tests. These methods, when used in combination with one another, can demonstrate with reasonable accuracy how well our collection meets its goals. At this time, we are not able to make an estimate of the additional hours required to implement the above evaluation procedures.

PRODUCTION VOLUME 77/78 = not yet established.

Task	*Level of Service*		*Staffing* LIBN	LA	CLER
Gifts, Receiving, Selection and Processing	We accept and process some 10,000 gifts per year. About 10% of the titles received are added to the collection. Dollar value of titles added to the collection is estimated at $10,000 per year.	(current)	200	0	500
		(minimum)	100	0	400
		(optimum)	200	0	500

ANALYSIS: The current level is considered to be minimum since we do not actively advertise for d tions. (78/79 will require some fewer hours than 77/78). There is curre a backlog of some 20,000 titles to be reviewed, representing about $20 to the collection. However, these are likely to be low-demand items sc backlog does not seriously reduce service. Optimum service would incl advertising for gifts and pick-up service, particularly collections of tiquarian books which would fit in with special needs of our teac program. An example of such a collection already received is the Mc mott Collection. We do not now have the time to actively search out solicit gifts of this type. This would probably triple our receipts and about $30,000 in titles to the collection.

PRODUCTION VOLUME 77/78 = 791 volumes added

Task	*Level of Service*		*Staffing* LIBN	LA	CLER
Deselection	Deselection decisions are necessary in order to keep the library's collection relevant to library users' concerns, to eliminate outdated materials in rapidly changing fields, and to keep open-stack areas free from overcrowding.	(current)	127	0	0
		(minimum)	200	100	100
		(optimum)	400	100	100

These goals will be increasingly difficult to meet as library mate growth and reductions in capital expenditures for buildings combin create insufficient space and a need for stabilizing the number of volu housed in the library. Coping with this situation requires collecting compiling data for making informed deselection decisions. These d sions should be based on such information as how (and how often) libr materials are used, by whom, the usage pattern over time, cost, cost creases to be expected, and general information on publication patte The library has no formal system established for collecting this d There are no staff allotments for this task, and the information collecte gathered by librarians in the time diverted from their other resp sibilities. Present deselection decisions must be based on less than satis tory data and are, themselves, less than satisfactory in guiding the libra development.

In attempts to improve this situation, title-by-title circulation statis have been collected since 1975, preparatory to deselecting. In additio library task force is studying the space needs of a growing collecti taking into account use of central storage facilities and library networki on-campus compact storage, acceptable delay time in materials retrieval, factors which determine location of specific titles, as well as the teaching faculty's strong reservations about weeding.

ANALYSIS: To bring the library's deselection function up to a minimally satisfactory level, the following activities are required:

1. The periodical use study data must be analyzed;
2. The reference serial use study must be analyzed;
3. Information on circulating serials must be incorporated into our present data base;
4. Periodical locations must be coded and keypunched;
5. Analyzed serials must be tagged so that the reviewing librarian is aware that further data will have to be hand-compiled;
6. Programs must be written (500 librarian hours) to analyze title-by-title circulation statistics in order that optimum book storage decisions can be made.

In addition, we need to develop and write programs which will allow for consistent storage and processing of data and for the identification of categories of materials suitable for weeding.

Optimally, satisfactory service for deselection would require an established policy, functioning procedures, and cumulated and accessible data. It would also require local storage for low-use titles and a functioning mechanism for returning used materials to the circulating collection. Teaching faculty and librarians would interact in removing titles from local storage to CSUC storage (should this alternative develop) or to another location.

Task	*Level of Service*		*Staffing*			
			LIBN	*LA*	*CLER*	*SA*
Out-of-print Ordering	Out-of-print ordering includes wantlists of materials which are sent to vendors specializing in supplying such materials and answering the correspondence generated concerning specific titles on the wantlists. These tasks have	(current)	0	0	0	0
		(minimum)	0	0	100	0
		(optimum)	0	0	100	0

been performed by student assistants in the past. Approximately one-third of the out-of-print titles are generated by requests from subject-specialist librarians; the other two-thirds of these titles are generated by the circulation department's inventory process. The correspondence concerning individual wantlist titles must usually be responded to within three weeks, since vendors have only a limited time available for holding titles for CSUN.

ANALYSIS: Currently no out-of-print orders have been made since August 1978. There are 825 titles backlogged to be ordered. In addition, no correspondence has been answered since that time, meaning the loss o previously ordered titles and the effort that went into obtaining informa- tion on those titles. We are receiving complaints from library patrons an teaching faculty on the lack of out-of-print buying. It is the opinion of th librarians involved in collection development that an out-of-print pro- gram must operate in order to provide our clientele with materials of thi type. We are currently functioning at below a minimum level. To functio optimally, the out-of-print should be assigned to a staff person who woul have the time to handle the sporadic correspondence and compile th wantlist once a month. The permanence of the staff position would in- crease the effectiveness of the program by providing for continuity o experience with individual vendors, who do not perform consistently.

PRODUCTION VOLUME: = of 1,300 titles reviewed, 908 were sent ou and less than 200 titles were receive

Task	*Level of Service*		*Staffing* LIBN	LA	CLER	SA
Pre-order Checking	Order requests are checked through our card catalog and in-process file for duplicates. Of every 1,500 checked, 600 go to the order section within a period of one week to one month as follows: priority 1s within two	(current)	0	1000	500	300
		(minimum)	0	1000	500	300
		(optimum)	0	1000	1000	480

weeks, priority 2s within three-four weeks, priority 3s within four week About 360 titles per year go out of print before we can get the orders ou representing about $5,400. The rate of unintended duplication is approx mately 440 per year; about one half of those can be returned for credi leaving a net effect on the budget of about $1,650. We feel that increase checking for dups would cost more in labor than the $1,650 to be save

ANALYSIS: The current level is considered minimal. Increasing tin for requests to get to the order section would increase duplicate orde cause the loss of prepublication discounts, increase the likelihood that titl will be out of print, and increase the probability that catalog orders will sold elsewhere.

Optimum service would allow (1) all requests to go to the order section three weeks, (2) checking of scholarly bibliographies to improve the qua ity of the collection, (3) check missing lists on all gifts and "library ha titles to insure that we add titles missing from the collection but still in o files, (4) survey reading lists for classes against our collection, and (5) c duplications in half. An on-line catalog and an on-line file of materials order would allow us to accomplish the five criteria listed above. We a not, however, able to make staffing projections for the on-line alternati at this time.

PRODUCTION VOLUME 77/78 = total requests checked not availab

CATALOGING

Task	*Level of Service*		*Staffing* LIBN	LA	CLER	SA
Original Cataloging	Librarians catalog all materials purchased and gifts as time allows for which LC or other acceptable copy is not available. Normal books in process, excluding gifts, average 1,000 currently purchased titles at any given	(current)	4792	0	0	0
		(minimum)	6000	0	0	0
		(optimum)	9000	0	0	0

time. The current backlog of gifts is 12,500 books, 3,200 phonorecords, and 22,316 of unanalyzed microform series. Due to staff resignations and cuts, the backlog of purchased titles is expected to climb to 4,000 by the end of June 1979. During 1979/80, new hires should be trained and the backlog is expected to be reduced to 500. 1974/75 studies show that after four months only 73½% of our titles received have been cataloged; 96% after one year (this includes all titles, not just original cataloging).

ANALYSIS: We are currently below minimum and backlogs are growing. The addition of two new catalogers should bring us back to past levels and, hopefully, below. (In past years, the normal backlog was near 3,000. During the past two years we have reduced that backlog to an average of about 1,000). Continued complaints from reference librarians make us aware that past levels are not adequate. We feel that in order for patrons to make the best use of our resources, no more than one month (500 titles) time lag is acceptable. In order to eliminate the backlog of current materials only, we would need approximately 3,500 hours of librarian time (3,500 titles). The remaining backlog of gifts should be steadily decreased by at least 100 titles per month. It should be noted that the adoption of AACR2 will require training and slow down cataloging. An optimum level of service would provide full cataloging for every item added to the collection. This would include full cataloging for IML materials and the analyzing of all series and collections. Time lag should be no more than one month (500 titles backlog). This assumes that OCLC has the MARC data by that time. At the present time the data is not available that quickly so the optimum is not possible.

PRODUCTION VOLUME 77/78 = 4,352 titles

Task	*Level of Service*		*Staffing* LIBN	LA	CLER	SA
laptive ıtaloging	Library assisants catalog all materials with LC and other acceptable copy. The normal backlog of current purchases is about 3,000	(current)	307	5589	14	1353
		(minimum)	0	6380	0	1000
		(optimum)	0	7380	0	1000

titles (two months). This backlog is projected to 6,900 by June, 1979, due to the extensive training required for use of the OCLC terminals. An unacceptably high erro rate has caused the necessity for a special study to identify the problems resulting in a further slowing of titles cataloged. We expect these prob lems to be identified and corrected by the end of the fiscal year and b that time the normal backlog of 3,000 can be maintained. However, w estimate that more than half of that old 6,900 backlog would remai (some 3,900) as well as those gifts that fall under the jurisdiction of th adaptive catalogers.

ANALYSIS: We are currently below minimum but familiarity wit OCLC procedures should begin to reduce the backlogs by June, 197 However, several years may be needed to reduce it to an acceptable lev of 1,500 (one month). The new librarians may be able to contribute som time to the reduction of the backlog once they are trained and befo being assigned part-time to other parts of the library. To eliminate th current materials backlog only would require about 1,950 extra hour The adoption of AACR2 will create an additional staff drain for trainin but we are not able to predict the extent at this time.

Optimally we should also be able to eliminate the backlog of gifts. Sin the number of gifts that fall into this category is unknown, we have arb rarily added 1,000 hours for the optimum level.

PRODUCTION VOLUME 77/78 = 16,396 titles.

Task	*Level of Service*		*Staffing* LIBN	*LA*	*CLER*	*SA*
Recataloging	We must recatalog those materials for which the classification has been changed by LC, for which holdings have changed, or, as in the case of serials and periodicals, those titles which have ceased or changed and require the revision of descriptive cataloging. We currently do not ha sufficient staff to reclassify when the number of volumes to be relabele very large or to revise descriptive cataloging unless the change is signi cant.	(current)	137	459	184	85
		(minimum)	137	459	184	85
		(optimum)	137	459	184	85

ANALYSIS: The current level is considered to be minimum. Howev in order to stop the increasing backlog, we will have to be more selectiv establishing that which is "significant" enough to recatalog.

The optimum service would be to recatalog everything that needs it wi out being selective.

PRODUCTION VOLUME 77/78 = 793 titles.

Task	*Level of Service*		*Staffing* *LIBN*	*LA*	*CLER*	*SA*
Withdrawing	Titles noted for withdrawal by the circulation department are processed in the catalog department by withdrawing all cards for those titles from the various card catalogs, annotating the machine shelflist records with a "W," and	(current)	0	18	269	241
		(minimum)	0	18	1160	1000 (temp)
		(optimum)	0	18	269	241

annotating and filing a card for each title in our Withdrawn file. Volumes or copies of multivolume or multicopy titles noted for withdrawal are processed by annotating the shelflist cards with the missing volumes or copies and annotating the machine shelflist records with a "W." Books which have to be destroyed are pulled and destroyed along with the appropriate catalog cards, and the machine shelflist records are deleted.

Currently, we have a backlog of about 4,000 titles. These titles are the remainder of the 1970 Star Inventory which, because of lack of staff, were not withdrawn at the time. The department is keeping up with current circulation requests for withdrawals and the backlog is not increasing.
ANALYSIS: To eliminate the Star Inventory backlog, the department would need an additional 1,650 clerical and student hours. Having once eliminated the backlog, keeping up with the present level of withdrawals can be done with present staffing. The hours shown under minimum level of service reflect the added hours needed to eliminate the backlog.

If the library were to engage in a major deselection program, 412 additional hours would be needed for each 1,000 volumes to be withdrawn.

Task	*Level of Service*		*Staffing* *LIBN*	*LA*	*CLER*	*SA*
ard Preparation	Cards are typed for the public and technical services catalogs. Only about 20% must be fully typed since the rest are provided through OCLC. Those which are provided by OCLC must be input through the terminals and this is	(current)	0	325	4578	2397
		(minimum)	0	325	4578	2397
		(optimum)	0	325	4578	2397

equivalent to the time required for typing masters (the Xerox reproduction and the typing of headings and cross references are estimated). Some 1,500 hours per year have already been saved by this process (since 75/76) and by 1980 we expect that as much as 1,200 additional hours of student assistant time may be saved due to improved utilization of OCLC and new OCLC programs. Also, OCLC savings will help offset the loss of our CETA clerk without a significant increase in the backlog which now stands at some 3,700 cards (two months). It should also be pointed out that revised procedures have reduced the backlog from 15,000 in 76/77 8,000 in 77/78. Normally, cards are typed within two months of recei data.

ANALYSIS: Backlogs are currently developing while the staff is le ing OCLC input technique. We had hoped that by June, 1979, the bac would be worked down to a minimally acceptable time lag of one m (1,800 cards). This would also be considered optimum. However, lo the CETA clerk will extend that time into the 79/80 fiscal year.

PRODUCTION VOLUME 77/78 = 306,054 cards typed.

Task	*Level of Service*		*Staffing* *LIBN*	*LA*	*CLER*	
Catalog Maintenance	This task includes filing catalog cards into public and technical service catalogs, expansion and division of catalogs, making corrections requested by reference department. The backlog has been averaging 32,650 cards,	(current)	11	554	2734	5
		(minimum)	50	1500	2300	5
		(optimum)	50	1500	2300	5

which is down from 53,467 in 76/77 and 41,463 in 77/78.

ANALYSIS: A minimally acceptable backlog is 22,500 cards (month). The LAI's on the Sci/Tech Reference Desk have helped presorting during slow periods and OCLC's prefiling of cards has hel to reduce past backlogs considerably. However, some improvement is needed to assure that the cards are filed by the time the book is on shelf. The optimum acceptable backlog is 11,000 cards (2 weeks).

PRODUCTION VOLUME 77/78 = 334,403 cards filed.

Task	*Level of Service*		*Staffing* *LIBN*	*LA*	*CLER*	
Machine Shelflist Maintenance	Maintenance of the machine shelflist tapes requires deleting records from tape, coding records on tape, and adding corrected, changed, current and missing records to tape. Maintenance involves conversion of rec-	(current)	0	617	2298	
		(minimum)	0	756	1666	2
		(optimum)	0	756	5150 or 1666	2 4

ords of holdings to machine readable form, proofing the converted d submitting batches of the converted records with programs designe perform specific transactions to the computer for processing the data to tape. The programs that perform specific transactions, e.g., deleting/coding records and adding/merging records, supply printed lists of the input records with program generated messages on certain types of transactions and on transactions that could not be completed during the processing of the record data. The transaction lists must be edited and all program-generated messages checked out, messages of transaction failure analyzed, and the problems solved so the record data can be processed. The basic shelflist tapes are updated with tapes containing records for current/changed records cummulated on tape during a given period of six months. The Sci/Tech class shelflist tapes are updated regularly every six months to produce new catalogs of holdings. The A-P, Music and Juvy class shelflist tapes are updated whenever the transaction lists from the previous runs have been edited and corrections made on the record data.

ANALYSIS: In July 1977, all class tapes had been updated to include current/changed records through January 1977. In June 1978, Sci/Tech, A-G class tapes had been updated to include current/changed records through January 1978, with H-P, Music and Juvy class tapes backlogged for updating. The backlog has grown steadily since June 1978, and now the Sci/Tech class tapes are the only ones updated with our latest current tapes containing records through January 1979; A-D class tapes are updated with current records through August 1978; E-P, Music and Juvy are updated with current records through January 1978, a year behind.

Ideally, all class tapes should be updated with the latest current tape when the new six months current tape is closed.*

Note: *May be revised in light of forthcoming automation plans.

CIRCULATION

Task	*Level of Service*		*Staffing* *LIBN*	*LA*	*CLER*	*SA*
Search Hold	When a patron cannot locate a needed title, he reports it missing to the circulation desk and requests that when it is returned (if checked out) or found (if missing) he/she be notified and the title held for him/her. These requests	(current)	0	679	295	2104
		(minimum)	0	679	295	2284
		(optimum)	0	679	300	2013

are processed each weekday morning with response time varying from ten hours to sixty hours (Friday P.M. until Monday A.M.). Patrons are notified by mail the same day the item is located and put on hold. Unlocated items are searched twice more at weekly intervals. If item is still not located, the patron is informed, and the item is put into the Missing Inventory; the patron is referred to interlibrary loan. Items in Missing Inventory a searched after seven months, thirteen months, and three years, and th noted for withdrawal. Re-order requests are sent to bibliographers review for re-order, generally at seven to thirteen months. Books to held for patrons are listed on a hold list which is up-dated once ea weekday evening. Time delay is 24 to 60 hours from time of search/ho request. All books circulated are checked against the list before reshe ing.

ANALYSIS: We feel that this is a minimally required level of service. delay searches would not reduce workload and would add greatly to t inconvenience of the patron. Not offering the service at all would leave systematic method for replacing titles missing from the collection. Op mally, we would process requests twice each weekday and once ea weekend day and follow up searches once a day for three days. We wou trap holds at charge and discharge time through an on-line bibliograph control system which would reduce searches by immediately placing hol at the time of request. This accounts for the slight reduction of stude assistant hours under optimum staffing above.

PRODUCTION VOLUMEfor 77/78 = 12,383 items searched.

			Staffing			
Task	*Level of Service*		*LIBN*	*LA*	*CLER*	*SA*
Circulation Control and Desk	Books are charged out at both the Oviatt and South Library Circulation desks. Normal waiting time in Oviatt is 0-2 minutes, in South it is minimal. Books are paged on request for handicapped students. There is normally a 2-3	(current)	188	1029	1815	17,2
		(minimum)	188	1234	2020	19,5
		(optimum)	188	1029	1875	21,4

minute wait for the issuance of library cards. Address files are maintain and updated 5-6 times per semester. Books are returned to the sta areas within 24 hours of return, and normally shelved within 1½ to 2 days of return (2½ to 3½ days during busy times). The South Library slightly faster.

Transactions are batched to the Computer Center each weekday afte noon and run overnight or over the weekend. The average time lag f charge and discharge transactions to appear is 24 hours with a maximu of 72 hours (weekend). The Oviatt charge desk provides full service 78 hours per week during the regular semester and partial service for additional 4 hours per week. The South charge desk offers full service f 83¼ hours per week.

ANALYSIS: Constant patron requests for longer hours of opening i dicate that our service is presently below the minimally required lev Our surveys indicate that the additional hours most needed are Fridays

P.M.-8 P.M. (add) and Sundays 10 A.M.-10 P.M. (instead of 1 P.M. - 10 P.M. South). Some time might be saved at the charge desk by reducing the stations staffed at busy periods from 3 to 2 in Oviatt and allowing queues to form. South only has one station, so no reduction could be made there. Charge desk workers shelve or file during slow periods. The number of library cards issued cannot be reduced unless a campus-wide ID card were to be issued at registration which could be used as a library card. Reducing the speed of discharging and shelving would not save any staff because it takes no more time to discharge and shelve in a timely fashion than after an elapsed period of time.

An optimum level of service would require an additional charge-out station at Oviatt and one additional student assistant at South Library during busy periods (14 hours per week more in Oviatt and 40 in South). More significantly, optimum service requires an on-line system featuring a photo ID isued by the campus and validated at registration each semester, on-line access and updating of all patron records, additional book drop pickups, as well as an on-line system with inventory file, in-circ file, patron files, financial obligation information, hold-trapping, and exception status for bad IDs. An optimal level of service would also require an extension of hours to meet most patron requests, (i.e., Monday-Friday 7 A.M.-12 midnight and Saturday/Sunday 8 A.M.-10 P.M.).

PRODUCTION VOLUME 77/78 = 280,351 titles circulated.

Task	*Level of Service*		*Staffing* *LIBN*	*LA*	*CLER*	*SA*
Fines and Billing	Overdue notices are sent 14 days after the due date and Billed-as-Lost 5 weeks after due date. (A complete search is done first.) If no response, 4 weeks later an encumbrance notice is sent. If no response, 10 days later an encumbrance request is sent to Cashiering.	(current)	0	228	2500	2159
		(minimum)	0	228	2500	2245
		(optimum)		unable to predict		

Lost book reports and contested item searches are initiated once each weekday. Accounting for money is done once each weekday. Excessive use fees are cumulated by patron until a $3.00 minimum is reached, then a payment request is sent, followed in four weeks by a fee bill (if unpaid), and if there is no response, the student's records are encumbered.

ANALYSIS: We could save approximately 120 student assistant hours per year (715 bills at 10 minutes each) by delaying BALs by one week. We could save 50 student hours per year if the encumbrance process were delayed two weeks (instead of 10 days). However, minimal service in 1978/79 will require an additional 250 hours for additional faculty Billed-as-Lost searches and notices. This year will also have a one-time cost of 250 hours to convert old type encumbrances to the B.O.S. System in spring 1979.

Optimum service would require an on-line patron file which includes all patron information and all outstanding obligations, itemized. The file would be updated by terminal in real time. The capability would exist to immediately update the machine record of amounts due and paid. There would be automatic generation of encumbrance notices for students with past due obligations, complete and current student address information, immediate on-line updating of the in-circ file, and generation of a cumulative itemized record of paid obligations for auditing purposes by date, indexed by name. We are unable at this time to estimate, with any satisfaction, the staffing requirements for such a system. However, we expect to pursue it with our long-range planning for automation.

PRODUCTION VOLUME 77/78 = Fine notices and fee bills 14,455
Books Billed as Lost 5,767

Task	*Level of Service*		*Staffing* LIBN	LA	CLER	SA
Exit Control	There is one exit in Oviatt and two in South Library (North door and main entry). One student assistant monitors each exit each hour that it is open. Handicapped use the bypasses as needed. The north door, South Library, is	(current)	0	5	52	7417
		(minimum)	0	5	52	7417
		(optimum)	0	5	52	9267

open 8 A.M. to 5 P.M. during the academic year, and 10 A.M. to 3 P.M. during holidays and summer. When open, the north door is used more heavily than the main entry (about 200 exits per hour vs. 100 exits per hour).

ANALYSIS: There are some complaints when the north door, South Library, is closed, and about the differences in exit control between the two libraries. Some 1,850 hours of student assistant time would be required to open the north door during all library open hours. However, complaints are not numerous enough to consider the present level to be below minimum. Optimum service, however, would include this. Patrons much prefer the Oviatt system because, due to the theft detection system there, only persons with briefcases or packages need stop for examination. Money has been granted for installation of the same theft-detection system in the South Library and installation is now in progress. This system will also improve wheel chair access. One exit would probably suffice in South, but the exit that is least used is the main, or south, exit and in order to close that one considerable remodeling of the building would be required. Closing the north door completely would likely cause a large volume of complaints of inconvenience due to the heavy traffic there, but it would save 1,700 hours per year. Completion of Phase II would save some 4,000 hours of student assistant time if only one exit were maintained.

PRODUCTION VOLUME 77/78 = 1,470,486 exit count.

Task	*Level of Service*		*Staffing* LIBN	LA	CLER	SA
General Stack Maintenance	Library materials are shelved once daily throughout the libraries. This task is showing a steady increase in volume. Bound periodicals were up 4.2% and books used in-house are up 7.3%. Volumes received from technical	(current)	0	56	200	10,792
		(minimum)	0	56	200	10,792
		(optimum)	0	56	200	14,792

processing are processed at the rate of about 36,000 per year. Processing time has been speeded up from one week to two days by a new procedure of leaving them on librarians review shelves for only one or two days. Once a year the stacks are shifted to allow for growth of the collection. This will have to be done more extensively as the collection expands. Minor shifts are made throughout the year. Major shifts require about 350 student assistant hours annually.

ANALYSIS: The current level is considered to be minimum. If books are not shelved in a timely manner, no major time saving results and the number of search/holds increases dramatically and adds staff requirements in that area. No staff savings can be realized by diminishing service here. Optimum service would require shelving books and periodicals every four hours we are open.

PRODUCTION VOLUME 77/78 = 490,878 books reshelved.

Task	*Level of Service*		*Staffing* LIBN	LA	CLER	SA
General Stack Reading	Reading of the stacks (some 600,000 volumes) for misplaced books and keeping unbound science periodicals in order allows an average error rate of 2.35 to 3.96 per section in Oviatt and 1.57 to 3.93 in South. This repre-	(current)	0	50	265	4300
		(minimum)	0	50	265	4300
		(optimum)	0	50	265	7800

sents an increase over 76/77 averages due to an increase in hours spent on in-house shelving resulting in a decrease in sections read.

ANALYSIS: Minimum service means a maximum average of 4 errors per section. Actual maximums were very near this. For errors to exceed this level would represent a real disadvantage to the library user, since those books which are out of order are likely to be the ones which are most heavily used. An optimum would be one to two errors per section.

PRODUCTION VOLUME 77/78 = 33,525 sections read.

Task	*Level of Service*		*Staffing* LIBN	*LA*	*CLER*	*SA*
Reserve Book Room	Hours of opening are the same as library open hours. 10,000 volumes, 3,000 articles and professor's personal copies are housed here. In 77/78, there was an increase of 15.5% in desk circulation. Materials are discharged	(current)	0	1528	33	5709
		(minimum)	0	1528	33	5709
		(optimum)	0	1528	50	9426

and reshelved within the hour, and the queues are usually no longer than three persons per station at any given time. Reserve request lists are processed within one week of receipt.

ANALYSIS: An added workload is expected here due to the new copyright law (ordering reprints, requesting permission to copy, maintaining logs of materials copied). The current level is considered to be the minimally required level. An optimum level would provide a 24-hour reading room for reserve materials; automated circulation; a browser terminal for on-line catalog display of library owned books; and a computerized listing of personal copies in professor, course number, and title order. It would also be of much greater service to the campus if the RBR were located in Oviatt, since 75% of the materials housed in the RBR fall into classes housed in Oviatt.

PRODUCTION VOLUME 77/78 = 18,221 volumes used in RBR
52,506 circulated

REFERENCE

Task	*Level of Service*		*Staffing* LIBN	*LA*	*CLER*	*SA*
Fine Arts Circulation	Check out materials for in library use; phonorecords, headphones, audiocassettes, art slides, art illustrations, videocassettes and reserve music scores. Single staffed except 9 A.M. - 5 P.M. Monday thru Friday during which time there is	(current)	44	930	0	5024
		(minimum)	44	930	0	5024
		(optimum)	44	930	0	5806

double staffing. An equipment inventory is taken first thing in the morn ing and the last thing in the afternoon. Basic equipment maintenanc includes cleaning cassette heads twice a week and headphone cushion daily. Record stacks and cassette drawers are read two to three times pe year.

ANALYSIS: for the most part our current service level is minimal. Thi material is used in-house so service must be prompt. If double staffin were cut back, reshelving would pile up, thus adding time for locatin materials, and increasing the possibility of misfiled materials, lost student IDs, and unhappy patrons.

Optimum service would call for double staffing the desk additionally on Saturday and Sunday, with triple staffing 11 A.M. - 1 P.M. Monday thru Friday. This would allow not only for faster service, but also for checking materials returned for proper ID (that is, phonorecords are in correct jacket). Also, each set of headphones and each record could be cleaned before giving to the patron. Reading of the record stacks should be done weekly.

PRODUCTION VOLUME 77/78 = 11,223 questions; 53,828 items used; 1,773 items circulated.

Task	*Level of Service*		*Staffing*			
			LIBN	*LA*	*CLER*	*SA*
Government Documents Processing (U.S.)	Currently, U.S. Documents processing is below the minimal level. Various tasks are either backlogged, done intermittently rather than regularly, or not done at all. Tasks and current status are outlined below.	(current)	386	618	0	5628
		(minimum)	728*	1664	0	5628
		(optimum)	1999	1664	1546	6413

Task	Not Done At All	Intermittently	Backlog	Acceptable
I. Selection				
A. Surveys (received & processed)			X	
B. Maintain Item Cards		X		
C. Review of Montly Catalog, Selected Lists, etc.		X		
C. Systematic review of selection profile	X			
II. Ordering				
A. Missing Issues from:				
1. Periodicals			X	
2. Acquisitions/Serials			X	
3. Government Documents			X	
4. Cataloging			X	
B. Added Copies			X	
C. Claims of items never received				X
D. Special offers				X
E. Replacements		X		
F. Nondepository items			X	
G. Depository items not received by CSUN		X		

(Continued)

	Task	Not Done At All	Inter-mittently	Backlog	Accept-able
III.	Documents Processing				
	A. Receipt, Review & Check-in of depository items			X	
	B. Label, Property stamp and tattletape			X	
IV.	Bibliographic Searching				
	A. Documents Expediting		X		
	B. Separate Mailings			X	
	C. Claims and Orders from:				
	1. Acquisitions/Serials			X	
	2. Bibliography			X	
	3. Periodicals			X	
	4. Cataloging			X	
	D. Errors from the Government Printing Office		X		
	E. Faculty Requests				X
V.	Shelflist				
	A. Documents Holdings			X	
	B. Items returned from cataloging			X	
	C. Separate Mailings		X		
	D. Documents Expediting		X		
	E. Recataloging				X
	F. Items sent to other areas (a librarian, newsletter, pams, IML, Placements Office, Geog. Map Library, etc.)			X	
VI.	Corrections				
	A. In the Monthly Catalog	X			
	B. On the Shipping Lists	X			
	C. On the Documents			X	
	D. Shelflist			X	
	E. Errata		X		
VII.	Collection Maintenance				
	A. Shelving			X	
	B. Inventory	X			
	C. Deselection and Withdrawal		X		
	D. Reading	X			

Note:
*Listed in job description.

Some of the contributing factors for U.S. Documents Processing bein[g] currently below the minimum level are:

1. Increase in workload
   75/76 37,122 documents processed
   76/77 61,755 documents processed
   77/78 66,005 documents processed
2. Increase in time spent training student assistants

   A. High turnover (over 70%) due to graduation, higher paying jo[b] elsewhere, and terminations (inadequate skills and performance[)]

B. Work study students, on whom we rely, have smaller allotments (six to eight hours per week). More students have to be trained and supervised for the same number of work hours.

This results in the library assistant spending more time on training (and less on other duties). A student assistant cannot work effectively/efficiently until trained, but when the student assistant quits, the training must begin again with someone new. A solution might be to hire a clerk who, hopefully, would stay longer and contribute more in terms of continuity and quality for the training time invested.

In the division of duties, student assistants do most of th processing; the library assistant supervises, trains and solves problems; the librarian makes professional decisions (selections, etc.) and solves problems. Since the decisions and problems are not easy to reduce (though we've tried), any cuts would have to be made in student assistants.

If a cut in staffing were to be made, a reduction in the number of U.S. documents to be processed would have to be achieved by determining not to receive certain titles which we receive at present. A reduction in the number of items to be processed would reduce student assistant hours. However, considerable professional time would be involved in determining which titles would be cut and in continuing cuts to maintain the reduction as important new titles are selected and added. Staff time would be involved in the resulting correspondence with the Superintendent of Documents and updating our records.

At a minimal level, U.S. documents should be selected, acquired, processed, maintained, and user assistance provided in accordance with the guidelines and standards adopted by the Depository Library Council (see attached). To implement these, the U.S. documents unit should do, regularly and in a timely manner, the documents processing tasks outlined under the CURRENT levels of service.

At an optimal level for U.S. documents processing, all minimum level tasks would be accomplished in a more timely manner, and the following additional activities would be accomplished:

1. Comprehensive, cumulative, and current subject/author/series access to U.S. documents would be provided. Potentially, this could be accomplished by various means (on-line searching of *Montly Catalog* tapes, CoDoc, using OCLC to catalog all U.S. documents, etc.), all of which would require considerable additional staffing and equipment.
2. The U.S. documents shelflist would be an on-line file. All depository documents would be processed and on the shelflist within seven days of receipt.
3. Documents staff would have on-line access to the *Monthly Catalog, NTIS*, and other documents data bases. These data bases would be used to do bibliographic searching to identify documents received as separate mailings or through the Documents Expediting Project and to resolve documents serials/series problems more rapidly and adequately than is possible at present.
4. Professionals and staff would have time to provide timely responses

to administrative requests for statistics and other information and to plan, conduct, and analyze cost and procedural studies. Professional documents journals such as *Government Publications Review* would be available at California State University—Northridge and studied for improvements in our treatment of documents. The documents processing manual would be complete and up to date.

Since this optimal level clearly would require considerable additional funding which does not appear to be available, no serious analysis of the staff necessary to achieve optimal level has been done. However, it would appear that most of the increase in staff would be at the professional and clerical levels with a possible decrease in the student assistant hours.

PRODUCTION VOLUME 77/78 = 73,960

Note: *Listed in job description.

Task	*Level of Service*		*Staffing* LIBN	*LA*	*CLER*	*SA*
Government Documents Processing (California)	California documents processing involves the ordering of non-depository items, searching of documents in California State Publications, typing and filing of cards, shelving and claiming of nonreceived and lost items. It also consists of stamping and numerically shelving of bills.	(current)	750	0	0	780
		(minimum)	700	0	0	1040
		(optimum)	600	0	0	1560

The ordering of documents and handling of serial claims are done by the librarian, the other tasks by student assistants. One student assistant works five hours/week processing documents and another ten hours/week exclusively handling bills. The volume of documents and bills processed is approximately 100-125 documents and 750-1,000 bills per month.

With the growing demand for documents, and especially bills on current legislative action, the current level of service is below minimum. Bills are shelved approximately one week after arrival, documents from two to three weeks.

Although there have been no steady complaints from patrons, there is always a pile of unprocessed documents (30-40) and bills (100-150). Occasionally patrons check in the librarian's office to examine an unprocessed document. This happens when the California State Publications list has already been shelved in the Reference Room, but the actual document has not been shelved yet. Various minor tasks, although less important but still necessary for a well-functioning documents collection, have already been given low priority; e.g., the discarding of the superceded daily and weekly histories, which are on the shelves with the most current ones, the weeding of superceded documents, etc. Also, the storage area (backup area for duplicates) is often a pile of unsorted documents. The newly processed duplicates are arranged by sudoc numbers only when there is time. A minimally required level of service would require at least an additional five hours/week student assistant time.*

Ideally, documents should be on the shelves a week after arrival, bills in three to four days. Optimum service would require more student assistant hours: ten additional hours/week for documents and five hours/week for bills. At the current level, the librarian is too much involved with tasks which can be handled by a student assistant. With more student assistant hours available, the handling of claims and the searching can be done by student assistants. With less time spent on routine tasks, the librarian cold spend more time minimizing the steadily growing items not listed in the California State Publications for which call numbers have to be made up. More student assistant hours would enable regular weeding of the document collection and periodic shelving of documents in the backup area so that a missing document in the reference area can be immediately replaced.

Since California documents has its own card catalog in the Reference Room by author, title and subject, the KWIC index now being prepared at CSU, Long Beach ($65 per copy) is at this stage a luxury item.

PRODUCTION VOLUME 77/78 = 14,374 documents and bills processed, 267 withdrawn.

Note: *As of September 1, 1979 there has been some improvement in the processing of California documents. The student assistant number of hours for handling documents has been increased from five to eight hours/week (work study). It is expected that the production volume will increase five to 10%. Also, the shelving backlog has somewhat improved. Documents are now shelved three to four days after being processed.

Task	*Level of Service*		*Staffing* *LIBN*	*LA*	*CLER*	*SA*
Reference Selection	Review new titles suggested for addition to the Reference Collection. Consult with appropriate specialists on potential candidate	(current)	277	0	60	15
		(minimum)	555	0	119	29
		(optimum)	555	0	119	29

titles for addition/selection/deselection/location/relocation. Select and order general and multidisciplinary reference titles. Transmit clientele suggestions to bibliography department. Address clientele complaints, demands, and suggestions about the Reference Collection. Participate in formal and informal discussions and consultations involving budget, space, and other planning for the existing Reference Collection. Solve problems resulting from processing, record, decision and publishing discrepancies. Coordinate maintenance activities with acquisition/serials and cataloging departments' personnel to assure availability of collection for clientele demand. Initiate inquiries in response to client demand for anticipated materials.

TRENDS: Developments in general selection policy and acquisitions and cataloging procedures impact on this function, which produces service. Reference File Maintenance and Reference Stack Maintenance increase workload of this function if they are not performed above minimum levels.

			Staffing			
Task	*Level of Service*		*LIBN*	*LA*	*CLER*	*SA*
Reference Processing	Supplying all physical identifiers (location labels, dots, dummies) to items new to the collection and to items returned to the collection; removal of physical identifiers from volumes for routine relocation. Filing of looseleaf and loose issues serials. Supplying, when permanent records have not yet been received for a title, a temporary record for the reference shelflist. Tallying of items received. Verification of all numbers from accompanying process flyer. Return or re-routing of "error" items.	(current)	342	0	1434	2045
		(minimum)	0	0	1450	2045
		(optimum)	Unable to determine			

Impacts on: Reference File Maintenance
Catalog Maintenance
Impact from: Reference Inventory and Deselection
Reference Selection
Bibliography: Selection, Approval Selection, Deselection
Cataloging: Recataloging

TRENDS: For the 1978/79 year, training task costs should be added to this task, to Reference Inventory and Deselection, and Reference File Maintenance for a valid cost picture for the year. The "impact from" list has probably generated less work than in years previous to 1977/78. This can be expected to reverse as work is generated by the coalescence of deselection and weeding policy and procedures.

The 1978/79 figures will show hours for librarian because of work accomplished preparatory to training a clerk. Since the workload varies, the minimum is currently defined in terms of backlog. Backlog exists when items to be processed have not been processed the third day after being received.

Task	*Level of Service*		*Staffing* LIBN	LA	CLER	SA
Archives Processing	At present, there is limited bibliographic access to archives. There is a card catalog for archival material classified by issuing agency and a card catalog for theses classified by author and department. Maintenance of both	(current)	350	0	0	60
		(minimum)	175	0	0	180
		(optimum)	350	0	0	360

collections is on a catch-as-catch-can basis. Archival materials published on campus are acquired as they become known to the archivist. Access to the collection is by appointment during the normal work day. Theses are delivered to departments, students and cataloging within two months of return from the bindery.

ANALYSIS: The current level is considered minimum except that maintenance of the collection should be orderly and not catch-as-catch-can.

An optimum level would provide complete bibliographic access to archives, including the card catalog plus a computer listing of archival material classified by issuing department or agency and by subject where feasible. In addition to the card catalog for theses, there would be a computer listing classified by author, department and subject. (There would also be subject access to theses in the main card catalog. However, since that would not be done in this unit, no hours have been included for it.) Except for routine filing, this would be the responsibility of the archivist.

There would be an orderly maintenance of archives and theses collections. This would include the refiling of materials in special archives boxes and file folders to prevent deterioration, weeding of materials not suitable to the collection, microfilming of materials which are space consuming. The weeding and selection for microfilming would be done by the archivist with routine clerical duties being performed by a student assistant.

There would be systematic accession of archival materials. This would include contact with departments and agencies on campus, close liaison with persons responsible for distribution of publications and with archivsts on other CSUC campuses to determine their collection policies. Accession duties such as date stamping and filing would be done by a student assistant. Public access to archives would be allowed for 20 hours a week.

Thesis advisement would be simplified to include 20 hours a week for basic checking of theses, and 10 hours a week of archivist time would be available for assisting students with complex problems. Delivery of theses after return from bindery would be completed within two weeks of return. Addition of 120 hours per year of student assistant time would allow archivist time to provide an optimum level of service or to provide hours for another professional level service.

PRODUCTION VOLUME 77/78 = Theses: 736 students assisted, 385 theses added.
Archives: 12 bound units, 845 unbound units, 1 microfilm reel.

Task	*Level of Service*		*LIBN*	*LA*	*CLER*	*SA*
			Staffing			
Fine Arts Processing	We add 1,100 art illustrations per year. We select, trim, mount, label, assign subject headings, maintain authority file, etc.	(current)	10	48	0	93
		(minimum)	10	48	0	93
		(optimum)	10	48	0	250

We label about 100+ audio cassettes per year, record music theses from reel-to-reel tape to cassettes, pull 100 music scores for reserve use for class assignments, and add 13 trays of art slides to carousel trays and label each year.

ANALYSIS: Current level is minimum. Given substantial usage (11,200 per year) of art illustrations, it seems undesirable to stop adding to the collection. More art illustrations are needed for optimal service—150-200 student assistant hours per year could handle it.

PRODUCTION VOLUME 77/78 = 1,119 art illustrations added.

Task	*Level of Service*		*LIBN*	*LA*	*CLER*	*SA*
			Staffing			
Microform Processing	66,000 pieces of microform are received per year.[1] These are processed and filed within three days of arrival. 3,800 college catalogs are ordered, processed and discarded each year. We order only the heavily used ones	(current)	288	0	800	100
		(minimum)	288	0	675[2]	50
		(optimum)	288	0	855	170

that are on our microfiche collection and ones from California which are not on fiche. Standing orders keep them coming in as they are available. Searches for missing microforms are performed four times before reordering. An inventory is taken yearly.

ANALYSIS: The current level is minimal for the ordering and processing of college catalogs. It would be possible to search for missing microform only three times before reordering; however, the amount of increase in the cost of replacements in unknown at this time.

Optimum service would require processing and filing of microforms within two days of arrival and a bi-yearly inventory which would likely cut the number of misfiled microform in half.

PRODUCTION VOLUME 77/78 = 67,109 microform units added; 2,056 catalogs added and 1,286 withdrawn.

Notes: [1]For the last two years the rate of increase of new acquisitions had been approximately 7% per year.

[2]The 125 hours saved in microform processing by clerical staff should be applied to administrative support.

Task	*Level of Service*		*Staffing* LIBN	LA	CLER	SA
Reference Inventory and Deselection	This includes pamphlets, newsletters and paperbacks as well as the Reference Collection which makes up the largest part of the task. Inventory of the Reference Collection in both libraries is taken on an annual basis. There is follow-up on books found to be missing, searching for overdues and books reported as missing, bindery volume identification, as well as deselection of "ref" continuations and removal from the collection.	(current)	65	225	47	540
		(minimum)	100	225	47	800
		(optimum)	100	225	50	1000

ANALYSIS: Regular searching for lost materials is not being performed and no annual inventory was done during the 77/78 year. Follow-up searching on the 77 inventory is now being done. Overall, service is below minimum. In order to bring us up to minimum, we would need 250 hours of student assistant time to do a yearly inventory and an additional 40 hours of librarian time for reviewing inventory results. Optimum service would include (1) ready availability of search reports within a week of the search request, and (2) results of the annual inventory would be acted upon for withdraw or reorder within the following semester. The annual collection inventory would best be done in July and August, but due to the uncertainty of the budget during that period of time, this is not possible. Instead, it is delayed until June and undertaken if funds remain at the end of the year. Unfortunately, budget cuts in 77/78 did not allow it to be funded. It should be understood that changes in location cause an added workload on the catalog department and corresponding increase in staff requirements.

PRODUCTION VOLUME for 77/78 = no data kept.

Task	*Level of Service*		*Staffing* LIBN	*LA*	*CLER*	*SA*
Reference File Maintenance	Includes maintenance of holdings of permanent format volumes in the Reference Collection as represented by the Reference shelflist and main entry catalogs and maintenance of the currency of these catalogs by filing new	(current)	195	56	292	271
		(minimum)	195	56	292	271
		(optimum)	Unable to determine need			

and replacement cards, by noting location changes and notifying the cataloging department when appropriate, by updating the reference serials format handling file, and by producing a new reference acquisitions list and other access lists as required. Also includes maintenance of the public file and shelflist of corporate annual reports for 28,000 items (5,000 titles). At present the reference catalog is not current as clerical time for filing has not been available, (an unidentified number of problems remain backlogged). The 77/78 level seems to be a minimum level. At present, the business file (Corp. Annual Reports) is filed up to date.

ANALYSIS: The reference file is currently below acceptable standard due to the backlog in processing added file records. The business file is currently at minimum. Optimally, we would have an on-line interactive reference holdings module with circulation and location data. The simultaneous and timely arrival of new cataloging cards with volumes as they are received would eliminate some filing and sorting steps as well as the typing of temporary cards and the claiming of great numbers of cards and books which arrive three or more months apart. The School of Business has requested expansion of the Corporate Reports to include all New York and America Stock Exchange Companies.

PRODUCTION VOLUME for 77/78 = No data kept.

Task	*Level of Service*		*Staffing* LIBN	*LA*	*CLER*	*SA*
Reference Stack Maintenance	Includes reshelving and refiling in the Oviatt and Sci/Tech Reference areas, at least once a day and more often, if needed, for pamphlet collections, microform, annual report file, reference books, newsletters, and card catalog	(current)	68	61	75	1232
		(minimum)	68	61	75	1232
		(optimum)	68	61	75	1800

area; stacks reading, performed at least once a week; charging material for mends, relocation of materials to reflect programmatic need and growth and development of the collection, as well as major shifts and activities associated with maintenance of location performed as a result of inventory tasks.

ANALYSIS: The growth in the collection promises a steady increase in workload. Currently we are at a minimum level. In the case of corporate annual reports, an investigation into the possible use of microform in relation to staffing requirements seems appropriate. An optimum level of service would provide more hours of trained student shelvers during the peak use periods of the fall and spring semesters and on weekends. This would add 600 student assistant hours and would double the student assistant staff on weekends and from 8 A.M.-12 noon and 8 P.M. -10 P.M. on week days.

PRODUCTION VOLUME for 77/78 = 137,279 items shelved or filed.

Task	*Level of Service*		*Staffing* LIBN	*LA*	*CLER*	*SA*
Oviatt Reference Desk	The desk is staffed with two librarians 9 A.M.-10 P.M. Monday thru Thursday, 9 A.M.-5 P.M. Friday and Saturday, 1 P.M.-5 P.M. Sunday. It is single staffed 8 A.M.-9 A.M. Monday thru Friday and with three librarians during	(current)	6346	0	0	0
		(minimum)	6346	0	0	0
		(optimum)	9226	0	0	0

very heavy periods such as 12 P.M.-1 P.M. The traffic is heavy and the trend is to an increasing number of questions (73/74—77,355; 74/75—77,950; 75/76—81,752; 76/77—82,610; 77/78—85,066). The average is currently 13 questions per hour per librarian. The more questions per hour, the less time available for research assistance. No survey has been made of the number leaving without assistance due to queues. Queues of two to three are common during the 10 A.M.-7 P.M. period. If it reaches four to five, an extra librarian is called in from other duties. If no one is available, queues may reach ten to twelve. Three to four phone calls sometimes are waiting, and if queues at the desk are steady, phone patrons will be asked to call back later.

ANALYSIS: The current level is minimal. Patron complaints are steady but manageable. Phone service could be discontinued but hours on the desk would not be reduced. Rather, better service for patrons at the desk would be possible.

Optimum service would add reference desks on the second, third, and fourth floors staffed with area specialists from 10 A.M.-3 P.M.. Monday thru Friday during fall and spring semesters. The first floor would be maintained as it is currently with the addition of triple staffing on weekends during periods of heaviest usage.

PRODUCTION VOLUME 77/78 = 85,066 questions.

Task	*Level of Service*		*Staffing* LIBN	LA	CLER	S
Sci/Tech Reference Desk	The desk is staffed by a reference librarian 9 A.M.-6 P.M., Monday thru Thursday and 9 A.M.-5 P.M. Friday, by an LAI (Library School Student) 6 P.M.-10 P.M. Monday thru Thursday and 9 A.M.-5 P.M. Saturday, 1 P.M.-10	(current)	2232	1216	0	1
		(minimum)	2232	1216	0	1.
		(optimum)	3512	730 . . . or . .		7.

P.M. Sunday. Traffic has been light, but the trend is to an increas number of questions (1973/74—24,258; 74/75—30,748; 75/76—33,6 76/77—34,716; 77/78—35,191). The light work load at present allows ot work to be done at the desk; e.g., ILL, collection development, filing the Sci/Tech catalog, reviewing new reference services, and other pro sional activities.

ANALYSIS: The current level is minimal. A service cut was made t year, and the desk is no longer staffed from 8 A.M.-9 A.M., M day thru Friday.

Optimum service would provide a reference librarian with a science ba ground 8 A.M.-10 P.M., Monday thru Thursday, 8 A.M.-5 P.M. Friday A.M.-5 P.M. Saturday and 1 P.M.-10 P.M. Sunday. A student assistant library school student would be added during peak hours between A.M.-3 P.M. Monday thru Friday during the regular semester. Also public card catalog would be provided for new titles with possibly a CC catalog for titles already in the collection.

PRODUCTION VOLUME 77/78 = 35,191 questions.

Task	*Level of Service*		*Staffing* LIBN	LA	CLER	S
Microform Desk	A single student assistant is on duty during slow times and two during busy times (15 hrs. per week).[1] Service to patrons is offered 65 hours per week and 12 hours on weekends. Waiting time averages about one minute. Dur-	(current)	20	0	50	40
		(minimum)	20	0	50	41
		(optimum)	20	0	50	46

ing slow times, student assistants photocopy microform for patrons a process materials. Usage is increasing at about 8% per year; and this tre is expected to continue. Some 11,000 photocopies are made for patr and faculty during a year. During busy periods there is a 1½ hour w during slow times there is immediate service. Refiling of materials is d within two hours of return.

ANALYSIS: We are slightly below minimum at this time. We could with double staffing 10 hours per week instead of 8. We must have equ ment assistance at all times to prevent damage to the machines. We co also restrict photocopy service to handicapped only thereby reducing staffing by two or three hours per day. Patron irritation level is an unknown at this time. We might also remove college catalogs from behind the service desk and place it on open shelving. This would save 150-200 hours per year, but lost material would cause patron inconvenience also.

Adding 12 hours of Class III student assistant time on weekends when a CAIIA is not present would be optimum. We could also add a coin-op reader/printer so patrons would wait no more than 5 minutes for a machine.

PRODUCTION VOLUME 77/78 = 15,606 questions; 38,644 items used.

Note:[1] 15 hours of double staffing was based on 77/78 statistics. As of January 1979, the desk has been double staffed approximately eight hours per week.

Task	*Level of Service*		*Staffing* LIBN	LA	CLER	SA
Oviatt Information Desk	This service point is staffed all hours that the library is open and provides the following services: (1) directional assistance to patrons, (2) "screening" for the reference desk, (3) telephone answering, (4) maintenance of "lost and found", (5) checking out instructional audio cassettes, lockers, keys to handicapped room, (6) collecting money from book sale. An average of about 25 questions per hour are answered. Queues are not usual, except during registration and the first two weeks of the semester.	(current)	0	1427	1465	509
		(minimum)	0	200	0	3200
		(optimum)	0	100	3670	0

ANALYSIS: Current service is considered to be minimal. Due to the high volume of activity (81,752 questions in 77/78) it would be undesirable to close this service point at any time the library is open. The South Library has no such information desk, but the traffic is light enough that circulation department personnel and the second floor reference desk can handle it. Optimally, we would double staff the Oviatt Information Desk during registration and the first two weeks of the semester, Monday-Friday, 8 A.M.-5 P.M. The level of staff required here is debatable. Well-trained student assistants might serve as a minimum level of service with supervision and training by a library assistant. However, that number of hours of student assistant time cannot be funded at this time. Conversion of clerical staff to student assistant funds would not be possible as those staff are specially trained and needed for other service points. Ideally, no higher than CAIIA level staff would be provided for all hours.

PRODUCTION VOLUME for 77/78 = 81,752 questions.

Task	*Level of Service*		*Staffing* *LIBN*	*LA*	*CLER*
Data Base Searching	All time expended in response to library user requests for generation of on-line bibliographic retrieval is recorded here. Included are determination of user requirements, user interview, formulation of search strategy, op-	(current)	297	0	0
		(minimum)	2760	0	400
		(optimum)	2760	0	400

eration of the terminal, postsearch interview with user, search cost
user notification, and coordination of the on-line search program. T
service is performed "on demand" and at this time those who are tur
away are those seeking access to data bases not provided by this libr
Students are frequently referred to off-campus data base searching
vices charging a substantially higher user fee. The library currently p
vides no access to either substantive data bases or to computer-assis
instruction programs. The library currently provides no search mo
other than retrospective bibliographic searching, and, other than ser
dictated by National Library of Medicine policies, the library provides
extension of data base search services to off-campus users.

ANALYSIS: We are currently at a less than minimally required leve
service. The addition of an estimated 23 major, frequently requested d
bases would bring us up to minimally acceptable standards. Nam
ABI/Inform, America: History and Life, BIOSIS (Biological Abstrac
CA Condensates and related data bases (Chemical Abstracts), Comp
hensive Dissertations, Disclosure, Energyline, Enviroline, Food Scie
and Technology, GPO Monthly Catalog, Historical Abstracts, Langu
and Language Behavior Abstracts, Magazine Index, Management C
tents, MLA Bibliography, NTIS, PAIS, Pollution Abstracts, SCI-SEARC
SOCSCI SEARCH, Sociological Abstracts, SSIE Current Research, a
U.S. Political Science Documents. This would require an estimated 2,
hours of librarian time and 400 hours of clerical time to support
added services. Provision of access to substantive data bases, training d
bases, and alternative modes of searching are unestimated at this ti
requiring extensive investigation into library systems providing such
cess. To provide even a minimum level of service at this point in ti
seems unlikely so that will also serve as an optimum level for the ti
being. In the future, the profession must find means to train the patro
play a larger role in the process.

PRODUCTION VOLUME for 77/78 = 225 searches.

Task	*Level of Service*		*Staffing* *LIBN*	*LA*	*CLER*
Library Instruction Lecture	This task records time expended in the preparation and delivery of bibliographic lectures and	(current)	882	0	0
		(minimum)	880	0	0
		(optimum)	3300	0	0

general tours. Class lectures are provided at the request of campus instructors. Normally, no instructor is refused. However, the demand is steadily increasing due to the growing complexity of information access.

ANALYSIS: In order to continue responding to all requests for class lectures and to requests for general introductory tours of the libraries, more librarian time must be available for them. The problem of physical space in which to house the lectures is a growing one that will also require attention in the future. Off-campus demand for library tours is considerable and cannot be responded to at all with current staffing levels. Optimally we would have available 3,330 hours for this type of instruction: 1,200 hours for on-campus lectures and tours, and 50 hours to prepare and disseminate information about the service so that those needing it can be aware of it and therefore ask for it. In addition, we would provide 1,000 hours for investigating and providing alternative instruction programs (A/V tapes, cassette modules, etc.) and 1,080 hours for offering three sections of a three-unit library use class each semester (subject to approval by EPC). The reassignment of some hours from consultations, while not providing optimum service, would raise us to a minimally acceptable level.

PRODUCTION VOLUME for 77/78 = 7,846 students served.

Task	*Level of Service*		*Staffing* *LIBN*	*LA*	*CLER*	*SA*
ibrary Inruction onlecture	This task represents time expended in compiling, producing, and revising bibliographies and other handouts for free distribution to library users. This is an effective program in that the number of users reached in rela-	(current)	1228	7	361	101
		(minimum)	1228	0	450	150
		(optimum)	1400	0	450	150

tion to the hours devoted to production of the handouts is quite large. Handouts are produced as reference librarians perceive a need and can afford the time to respond. No formal studies have been done to determine the degree of effectiveness of the handouts or of the degree of impact on reference desk work load. However, informal feedback and comments from the recent faculty survey suggest that they are useful to the user and we believe that they serve to reduce substantially individual requests for assistance at the reference desks.

ANALYSIS: Traditionally, periods of lower library use (semester breaks and summer vacation) have been used for production of these handouts.

However, staff losses due to salary savings obligations have impacted heavily on our ability to produce them. We are currently below minimum in that library users regularly express a need for bibliographies in subject areas currently not covered. The addition of an estimated 200 librarian hours, 100 clerical hours and 50 student assistant hours might allow us to respond to all requests. We consider this to be a minimum level of service, but it may also be the optimum. It should be noted that the production and duplication of bibliographies and handouts impacts heavily on central administration and any increase will require additional student assistant hours there.

PRODUCTION VOLUME for 77/78 = 60,698 handouts distributed.

Task	*Level of Service*		*Staffing* LIBN	LA	CLER	SA
Interlibrary Loans	Full interlibrary loan services are available to faculty and graduate students. Limited service is available to undergraduates through CSUC Interlibrary Borrowing System and The Center for Research Libraries. The service is growing rapidly and is influenced by cooperative agreement and automation as illustrated below:	(current)	485	906	393	2499
		(minimum)	725	906	600	2600
		(optimum)	2000	906	2000	2000

	1971/72	1972/73[a]	1973/74[b]	1974/75	1975/76[c]	1976/77[d]	1977/78[e]
Borrowed	789	1,947	2,092	2,788	3,206	4,296	5,599
Loaned	1,135	1,820	2,380	2,732	4,214	4,685	6,861
Total	1,924	3,767	4,472	5,520	7,420	8,981	12,460

[a]1. Cooperative agreement among CSUC southern campuses (intent to freely share all resources within CSUC libraries).
2. Installation of Dex.

[b]1973—CSUC Union List of Serials.

[c]Introduction of LCCN register.

[d]1976/77—Pilot Program began May 1977. ILL cooperation to CSUC/UC campuses, UC Berkeley, and UCLA.

[e]1. Introduction of nonscience computer searches.
2. Use of UC Berkeley and UCLA. UC Berkeley will lend to undergraduates, UCLA will photocopy for undergraduates, photocopy and loan to graduates and faculty.

Missing pages (mutilations) were ordered until November 1978 (464 requests 1977/78) which took two hours of LAII time per week.

ANALYSIS: Current level is below minimum. Requests are not reviewed by a librarian and most are sent out without being checked an verified. Notification and transmissions by telecopier are handled by students and should be performed by an LA or CAII. Missing pages requests are not processed. Patrons are limited to five requests per week. Data base searching is rapidly expanding. As data base searching increases, interlibrary loan requests go up.

	1975/76	1976/77	1977/78	1978-
No. of searches completed	71	93	225	420

Comments, Issues, and Recommendations Regarding Optimum Services

1. Increase to ten requests per week for minimum service, optimum unlimited requests. (Data base searches have little value if students have no access to articles.)
2. Install an OCLC terminal in the interlibrary loan service area for verification.
3. Requests for books currently in print should be ordered "rush" and given to patron before cataloged.
4. Return "mutilations" and "missing pages" to Acquisitions.
5. If Center for Research Libraries is to be continued, a TWX should be installed for communicating.

If any or all of these recommendations are implemented, additional staff will be needed for increased workload in verification, processing, and bookkeeping to meet minimum standards.

Task	*Level of Service*		*Staffing* LIBN	*LA*	*CLER*	*SA*
General Reference	Originally called "Reference Consultations," defined as advisement and questions (reference, research, directional) answered from the reference librarians' offices rather than the Public Service Points. Theses advise-	(current)	1250	0	0	0
		(minimum)	1250	0	0	0
		(optimum)	3550	0	0	0

ment, which is seasonal (heavy during December and May), was also included. Subject specialists (history, business, English, Pan African Studies, Chicano Studies, education, political science, women's studies, theater arts, Asian Studies, biology, physics, music, U.S. documents, international law, California documents, economics, religious studies, mass communications, sociology, home economics, health science, children's literature) are consulted on long-term projects and difficult research problems.

ANALYSIS: Current level of 1,250 hours, which translates into less than two hours per librarian per week, is minimum. However, complaints are often received because subject specialists and thesis advisors are not av able. (They are assigned to bibliography, lectures, bibliographic data b searching, other service points, meetings, etc.).

This one-on-one assistance is extremely valuable to our students anc essential to our educational program. Since the subject specialist concep an integral part of the department's philosophy of service, many ho have been spent on recruiting and orienting qualified people to perfo this service. Logically, as the specialists gain expertise their consultatic increase; even more certain is, as these specialists deliver more lectures more disciplines their consultations increase in number and complexi

Optimum level (3,550 hours) would double the allocation of present f ulty to four hours per week; and, in addition, would allow us to h additional subject specialists for disciplines not covered.

PRODUCTION VOLUME 77/78 = 4767 (2578 consultations, 736 tl ses, 286 research, 1167 referen

Task	*Level of Service*		*Staffing* LIBN	LA	CLER	S
IML Selection	IML selection involves the review and checking of the annual California state adopted materials, the Los Angeles City Schools authorized textbooks list, and publishers catalogs. Faculty and patron requests are incorporated in the process. Lack of funds prevents the purchase of more th 2% of the L.A. City Schools list and 60-75% of some of the state adopt list. Exhibit copies left by publishers are individually evaluated for ad tion to the collection.	(current)	246	37	0	0
		(minimum)	246	37	0	0
		(optimum)	0	50	0	0

ANALYSIS: In order to avoid duplication and make maximum use the limited budget, this represents the minimum level. A materials budg large enough to purchase 80% of the state adopted materials would a encompass a large percentage (as much as 50% in some areas) of the L Angeles City Schools list. As time goes by, we are finding that in some are the IML has a large percentage of the state adopted materials and that a six-year cyclical basis fewer are needed. It must be remembered th secondary materials are our weak point and are not state-adopted so th the selection process for secondary materials is at least twice as tim consuming as for elementary. Another factor of importance are tho areas, like art, that are not state-adopted and that will require more sel tion time. A fundamental impact would be made on cataloging and pr cessing cost in direct proportion to an increase in the selection budget. budget of $20,000 to $25,000 would satisfactorily satisfy selection nee

PRODUCTION VOLUME 77/78 = 5,360 items added, 4,586 ite withdrawn

Task	*Level of Service*		*Staffing* LIBN	LA	CLER	SA
. Check- and Card ·ing	Holdings are checked for all California State-adopted lists, selected L.A. City Schools authorized lists, some publisher's catalogs, and all patron or faculty requests. Cards are typed for all the lacks that are to be ordered.	(current)	0	51	69	0
		(minimum)	0	51	69	0
		(optimum)	0	200	250	0

Cards are sent within twenty-four hours of typing to the Acquisitions Department for ordering. A pencil copy of each order card is held in the IML in-process file. PRL notices are numerous and are also handled directly by the IML.

ANALYSIS: The current level is minimum and also optimum, if there is no increase in the selection budget. If the budget is increased to allow purchase of 80% of the state adopted and as much as 50% of the L.A. City Schools authorized lists, the impact on the checking would remain about the same, but the card typing would increase by at least half.

PRODUCTION VOLUME 77/78 = Not available.

Task	*Level of Service*		*Staffing* LIBN	LA	CLER	SA
L Catalog-	Original descriptive cataloging is done for all IML materials. This has not always been the case, however, and as a consequence the catalog is full of inconsistencies and problems. We are trying to recatalog the worst of the	(current)	316	682	713	0
		(minimum)	600	1300	1400	0
		(optimum)	316	682	713	0

problem areas and bring these up to current standards. We assign LC-type classification numbers to all books and accession numbers to all other materials, the average time lag is three weeks for new cataloging, and the present backlog of new materials is quite small.

ANALYSIS: We are currently below minimum because of the many items with incomplete cataloging that are already part of the collection, and the large number of exhibit items that are presently being added to the collection. All items should have standard descriptive cataloging and good subject access. The old backlog could probably be eliminated in one year with a full-time cataloger and some clerical time. Ideally, there should be no more than three to four weeks between receipt and cataloged access to new materials. Maintenance could be done with current staffing, assuming that the budget does not increase.

PRODUCTION VOLUME 77/78 = 5,360 items added.

Task	*Level of Service*		*Staffing* LIBN	LA	CLER	SA
IML Processing	The process procedure includes affixing labels, date due slips, attaching spiral binding, constructing boxes for adequate protection of various media and property stamping all materials. The average time lag is one week.	(current)	0	84	177	162
		(minimum)	0	84	177	162
		(optimum)	0	84	177	162

ANALYSIS: The current level is both minimum and optimum. It falls i line with the cataloging process and makes materials available in time to b accessed through the card catalog. An increase in the selection budg would, of course, mean increased expenditures here to maintain th one-week time lag.

PRODUCTION VOLUME 77/78 = 5,360 items added.

Task	*Level of Service*		*Staffing* LIBN	LA	CLER	SA
IML File Maintenance	This task includes filing cards into the card catalog for newly acquired or recataloged material and removing cards for withdrawn or recataloged materials, maintaining the shelflist and authority files. The average time for filing is four weeks after the materials are cataloged.	(current)	107	165	207	37
		(minimum)	107	165	207	37
		(optimum)	60	100	130	25

ANALYSIS: The current level is both minimum and optimum. Ti delays occur when our card production equipment becomes nonfu tional, and this often pushes our catalog maintenance time back ma days or weeks at a time. However, the completion of a project of recatal ing materials that have old, substandard cataloging will decrease t degree the need for constant pulling and refiling of cards. It is difficul estimate the number of materials that need to be recataloged, but gen ally any materials acquired before the library assumed responsibility the IML seem to have substandard cataloging. The elimination of t recataloging backlog would reduce maintenance hours by some 120 ho per year.

PRODUCTION VOLUME 77/78 = Not available

Task	*Level of Service*		*Staffing* LIBN	*LA*	*CLER*	*SA*
L Inven- y and hdrawal	A complete inventory would include the book collection and the media/nonbook collection. Inventory is done in segments such as kits, or games, or records. A regular pattern for inventory has not emerged and has been accom-	(current)	48	142	4	98
		(minimum)	50	200	10	175
		(optimum)	75	300	20	275

plished when, and if, personnel, time and money has allowed. The task involves using the shelflist or accession lists to check holdings. Searches are made for missing items. Orders are generated for those missing items that we wish to replace. The process also involves the withdrawal of items which we do not wish to replace. Weeding also takes place at this time and some materials are relegated to the storage areas as a result of the process.

ANALYSIS: The current level is below minimum. A severe drawback to the entire process is the substandard cataloging procedures employed for many years in the IML. Holdings information was haphazardly recorded, if at all. A complete and thorough inventory, followed by the completion of the recataloging project, would greatly improve future inventories.

In order to bring the level of service to the minimum, an increase of at least twice the existing level must be budgeted. The thorough inventory would also assist in not only identifying missing materials but would also identify those items that are in need of recataloging. After ascension to the minimum level in the inventory area, the whole process could be maintained at the present level which would then be both minimum and optimum.

PRODUCTION VOLUME 77/78 = Not available.

Task	*Level of Service*		*Staffing* LIBN	*LA*	*CLER*	*SA*
IL Circula- n	This task includes manual charging and discharging of materials, preparation of overdue notices, patron assistance at the card catalog, in the stacks and workroom, search/hold procedures, fines payment and processing,	(current)	27	915	0	5629
		(minimum)	27	915	0	5629
		(optimum)	50	1400	0	3500

deposit cards, shelving and shelf reading, telephone assistance to patrons and closing procedures. All activities are performed on a daily basis and there are minimum queues and backlogs.

ANALYSIS: The current level is generally minimal. Circulation services, especially charge, overdues and depositors, could ideally be handled best with an automated system. As many as 2,000 hours could be saved if some of the circulation services could be automated. The current de sitor system also could be firmed up and standardized to allow fo savings of at least 100 hours that are currently devoted to depositor maintenance, overdues, and problems.

As to reference assistance, the current level is below minimum. A ref ence desk staffed at least during peak hours would provide better acc to services and materials. This would require approximately 30 hour week for either a librarian or a library assistant.

Depositors are a special problem. They increase each year and at cert hours of the day make up almost half of the use of the IML. Because th individuals pay a small, refundable fee for the privilege of using the IM materials and facilities, they represent a distinct drain on resources t cannot be adequately funded through regular channels.

PRODUCTION VOLUME 77/78 = 16,644 items used in-house; 35,1 items circulated; 39,293 question

Task	*Level of Service*		*Staffing* LIBN	LA	CLER	S
IML Tours	IML tours are given by the IML staff at the request of the faculty of the School of Education. The purpose is to acquaint the patron with the materials and services available in the IML. IML tours are, in the main, general tours of	(current)	3	44	0	3
		(minimum)	3	44	0	3
		(optimum)	3	44	0	3

the facilities. Some instruction takes place in that the students are taug how to use the IML catalog. The largest portion of time spent in ea lecture is used to familiarize the students with the types and uses of t various materials available. Equipment use instruction is also always give

ANALYSIS: The present level is both minimum and optimum. Prese staff levels are able to respond satisfactorily to all requests for tours. the collection becomes larger and more complex, the tours will propo tionately include the necessary information. This service is not impact by librarian consultations in the IML.

PRODUCTION VOLUME 77/78 = Not available.

Appendix 2

CSUN Library Mission Statement and General Guidelines, 1980

The following mission statement and general guidelines in combination with labor and service analyses will serve as the foundation for the ongoing exercise of developing service specific action statements for goal achievement.

I. Mission Statement

A. The primary mission of the California State University—Northridge Libraries is to serve the library needs of the existing and projected academic programs of the University in accordance with CSUC Trustee-approved Academic Master Plans (7-8)[1]. This complements the mission and philosophy of CSUN to "offer students a broad section of undergraduate and graduate educational programs in which they can develop their intellectual abilities." Students and faculty alike depend on the library resources to supplement classroom and laboratory learning and to support their independent study and research activities (CSUN Mission Statement). Beyond this primary mission, the California State University—Northridge Libraries have a further obligation, that is to, within available resources, cooperate to furnish support for academic programs in other institutions of higher learning and serve as a resource for other users in the region (11). This also complements the university in its mission "to provide leadership, service and knowledge to the community-at-large; and to serve as a center for cultura activity" (CSUN Mission Statement).

B. The development of library objectives is the responsibility o the library staff, in consultation with students, members o the teaching faculty, and administrative officers. (ACRL Stan dards for College Libraries 1.1)

C. The statement of library objectives will be reviewed periodi cally and revised as needed (ACRL Standards for Colleg Libraries 1.2).

GENERAL GUIDELINES

II. The Collection

A. Selection of Materials

1. The following materials will be selected and acquired t support the University community (including nonboo materials such as videotapes, slides, cassettes, prints, an microform).

   a. Core materials to support nearly all the needs undergraduates on campus (4). "Core collection are defined as materials needed to support unde graduate programs (including multiple copies of m terials most in demand). Core collections also encon pass, beyond the requirements for basic instructio those materials required for cultural or general e ucation needs (14).
   b. Graduate materials to support a substantial porti of the needs of graduate students (4). "Gradua collections" respond to the more advanced requi ments of study at the master's level (as dictated the theoretical, technical, or research-oriented ch acter of the local program) (14).
   c. Acquisition of materials adequate in breadth a depth to support faculty populations (8).
   d. A strong collection of reference and bibliograp materials and services to provide fast and effect information service including the location of libr materials that are not available in the library (8

e. Acquisition of a collection of standard works of literature to represent the heritage of civilization (9).

f. A collection of recent and popular works to arouse the inteellectual curiosity of students, to provide for general reading interests, and to stimulate recreational reading(9).

g. A special collection, that is materials as defined by the A.L.A. Glossary to be "of a certain form, on a certain subject, of a certain period, or gathered together for some particular reason, in a library which is more or less general in character." These collections may not always have a direct or proportional relationship to local instructional or research needs. They may be, for example, community-related (local history), graphic (historical maps, fine printing), archival (manuscripts, oral history), or a notable collection which may transcend the current levels of research requirements and is possibly the consequence of a significant gift (14).

h. An archival collection to preserve copies of graphic, audio-visual, and miscellaneous material produced by CSUN, or its constituent parts, as part of a program to preserve a permanent record of the University. (*Administrative Manual*, 2.19.

2. An annual increment to these collections that is, at least, sufficient to keep abreast of new developments in the growth of knowledge and culture should be sought (5).

B. Availability of Materials

1. The library will provide quickly a high percentage of such material needed by its patrons (ACRL Standards for College Libraries 2.1).

2. Library resources will be extended by the following means:

a. Bibliographic control of the system resources
b. Rapid communications among libraries and their users via telephone, telefacsimile, and other electronic devices.

c. Speedy delivery of materials and information fr one library to another via telefacsimile, electrc means, couriers, and public transportation. No charges for interlibrary loan will be assessed one CSUC library to another. Interlibrary loan p cies and procedures among CSUC libraries will p vide equal service to all segments of the CSUC co munity: faculty, full-or part-time; registered stude undergraduate or graduate, full-or part-time; st members; summer session, extension or external gree program students; and other persons as termined by the library director (10).

C. Withdrawal of Materials

1. Deselection and storage of library materials will not oc until such time that the entire collection cannot be hou in the present library facilities.
2. Valuable but less frequently used materials shall be id tified and shelved in on-campus or near-by storage t is less costly than regular library housing, and will retrievable for patron use in a maximum of 48 hours (Weeding document).
3. Inventory reports of collection sizes will be adjustec reflect deletion of obsolete, worn out, lost, or sto materials (9).
4. Annual inventory reports of campus and system-w holdings will distinguish between regular and stor collections (9).

D. Accessibility of Materials

1. In-person borrowing of materials will be extended to segments of the CSUC community as ennumerated the Library Lending Code (10) (*Administrative Man* 2.14).
2. Public access to the collection, to the library staff, anc study facilities will be consistent with reasonable dema both during the normal study week, and during we ends and vacation periods (9).
3. The library is fully committed to being accessible a readily usable by handicapped patrons as specified Section 504 of the Rehabilitation Act of 1973 (*Admi trative Manual* 2.23).

II. Organization of Materials

A. Library collections will be organized by nationally approved conventions and arranged for efficient retrieval at time of need (ACRL Standards for College Libraries 3). In general, the library will follow the classification scheme of the Library of Congress without deviation. Where alternative locations are indicated, the most convenient option consistent with economy will be selected. Reclassification of items will be entertained only in unusual circumstances where deviation is clearly in the best interest of the university (Library Committee, November 16, 1960).

B. There will be a union catalog of the library's holdings that permits identification of items, regardless of format, by author, title, and subject (ACRL Standards for College Libraries 3.1).

C. The catalog will be in a format that can be consulted by a number of people concurrently and at time of need (ACRL Standards for College Libraries 3.1.2).

D. In addition to the catalog, there will also be requisite subordinate files, such as serial records, shelflists, authority files, and indexes to nonmonographic materials (ACRL Standards for College Libraries 3.1.3.).

E. Except for certain categories of material which are for convenience best segregated by form, library materials shall be arranged on the shelves by subject (ACRL Standards for College Libraries 3.2).

F. Active collections will be arranged in open stacks, easily accessible to patrons, except for storage collections, or special collections designated by the library director for their physical condition or high value. Special collections will, nevertheless, be made available to authorized patrons for inhouse use (10).

VI. Staff

A. Staffing will be adequate to provide acceptable levels of service, based on workload measures, and consistent with national, professsional standards (11).

B. Through the study of the library's level of service docume[nt] and related studies, adequate staffing may be determin[ed] for each library function.

C. The library requires staff comprising professsionally train[ed] librarians, support personnel, and technical staff (data pr[o]cessing, etc.) to carry out the stated functions of the librari[es] (11).

D. The marks of a librarian will include a graduate libra[ry] degree from an ALA-accredited program, responsibility f[or] duties of a professional nature, and participation in profe[s]sional library affairs beyond the local campus (ACRL Sta[n]dards for College Libraries 4.2).

E. Advancement for librarians in the CSUC system, as doc[u]mented in the Librarian Personnel Plan (FSA 78-64), is d[e]pendent upon (1) professional competence, (2) profession[al] contributions and achievements, (3) university service, ([4]) professional growth and development, and (5) supervisio[n] and administration-leadership. These requirements mak[e] travel and continuing education essential to academic libra[r]ians, and every attempt should be made for librarians [to] gain access to funds for sabbaticals, educational leaves, an[d] travel opportunities to attend meetings, workshops, sem[i]nars, and to engage in research and/or professional invest[i]gations. (Position Statement on Requirements for Academ[ic] Librarians for Continuing Education and Travel, 8/2/79).

F. The librarians will be organized as a school for personn[el] purposes (CSUN Faculty Senate 1969).

G. There shall be an appropriate balance of effort among l[i]brarians, supportive personnel, and part-time assistants s[o] that every staff member is employed as nearly as possib[le] commensurate with his/her library training experience, an[d] capability (ACRL Standards for College Libraries 4.3.1.).

H. Library policies and procedures concerning staff will be i[n] accord with sound personnel management practice (ACR[L] Standards for College Libraries 4.4).

V. Delivery of Service

A. The library will establish and maintain a range and qualit[y] of services that will promote the academic program of th[e] institution and enourage optimal library use (ACRL Standards for College Libraries 5).

B. Library service will include:

1. Effective and authoritative reference service, including both traditional and computer-based reference service
2. Instruction in the use of the library and its reference tools
3. Assistance to students and faculty in their search for materials and in the preparation of bibliographies
4. Information to the faculty of new publications and new acquisitions
5. Maintenance of a collection of up-to-date, high quality library materials
6. Suitable bibliographic organization of the collection and speedy processing of new materials
7. Fast and convenient circulation of library materials
8. Promotion of the use of the services provided

C. Library materials will be circulated to qualified patrons under equitable policies and for as long periods as possible without jeopardizing their availability to others (ACRL Standards for College Libraries 5.2).

D. The availability of reading materials will be extended wherever possible by the provision of inexpensive means of photocopying (ACRL Standards for College Libraries 5.2.1.).

E. The quality of the collection available locally to patrons will be enhanced through the use of "National Interlibrary Loan Code, 1968" and other cooperative agreements which provide reciprocal access to multi-library resources (ACRL) Standards for College Libraries 5.2.2).

F. Where academic programs are offered away from campus, library services will be provided in accord with ACRL's "Guidelines for Library Services to Extension Students" (ACRL Standards for College Libraries 5.4).

G. Library circulation and acquisitions records will not be made available to any agency of state, federal, or local government except pursuant to such process, order, or subpoena as may be authorized under the authority of, and pursuant to, federal, state, or local law relating to civil, criminal, or administrative discovery procedures or legislative investigatory power (CSUN Faculty Senate) (*Administrative Manual* 2.23).

H. All library personnel will give prompt assistance to handicapped patrons' requests for library service as time and their ability permits, In cases when library service needs are more extensive or specialized, handicapped patrons will be referred to the person, service desk, or office best able to meet their needs (*Administrative Manual* 2.23).

VI. Facilities

A. Provision will be made for adequate and proper facilities tc house materials, for the efficient operation of the library, and for the accommodation of those who wish to use it (6). There will be sufficient space, consistent with experience and national standards, for collections, readers, and staff. There will be special provision for specialized reader stations, e.g. microform, newspaper, map, data terminal, handicapped, etc. (9). In order to carry out this standard, the CSUN Library has proposed a Phase II of the library building.

B. The shape of the library building and the internal distribution of its facilities and services will be determined by functions (ACRL Standards for College Libraries 6.2).

C. Except in unusual circumstances, the university's library collections and services will be administered within a single structure (ACRL Standards for College Libraries 6.3). Presently, due to a lack of space in the main building, the South Library must also be used to house library collections and services. Completion of Phase II of the library will remedy this problem.

D. In order to assure the integrity of the collections, there will be no CSUC branch or departmental libraries staffed or otherwise supported by or through CSUC libraries (9).

VII. Administration

A. Administration of all library functions will be in an efficient and cost-beneficial manner as to maximize the resources and services that are provided (6).

B. The statutory or legal foundation for the library's activities will be recognized in writing (ACRL Standards for College Libraries 7.1).

C. Chancellor's Office cost studies and formulas will inform and guide management decisions.

D. The library director will be a member of the library faculty and will report to the president or vice president of academic affairs (ACRL Standards for College Libraries 7.2).

E. The responsibilities and authority of the library director and procedures for his/her appointment will be defined in writing (ACRL Standards for College Libraries 7.2.1).

F. There will be a standing advisory committee comprising students and members of the teaching faculty which will serve as the main channel of formal communication between the Library and its user community (ACRL Standards for College Libraries 7.3).

G. The library will maintain written policies and procedure manuals covering internal library governance and operational activities (ACRL Standards for College Libraries 7.4).

H. The library will maintain a systematic and continuous program for evaluating its performance and for identifying needed improvements (ACRL Standards for College Libraries 7.4.1).

I. The library will develop statistics not only for purposes of planning and control, but also to aid in the preparation of reports designed to inform its public of its accomplishments and problems (ACRL Standards for College Libraries 7.4.2).

J. The library will develop, seek out, and utilize cooperative programs for purposes of either reducing its operating costs or enhancing its services, so long as such programs create no unreimbursed or unreciprocated costs for other libraries or organizations (ACRL Standards for College Libraries 7.5).

K. The library will be administered in accord with the spirit of the ALA "Library Bill of Rights" (ACRL Standards for College Libraries 7.6).

VIII. Budget

A. Efforts will be made by the library to secure adequate funding to support its materials acquisitions and services. Support for operating expenses will be sufficient to sustain th library mission, to carry out its stated functions, and to pro vide acceptable levels of service (11).

B. The library director will have the responsibility for prepar ing, defending, and administering the Library budget i accord with agreed-upon objectives (ACRL Standards fo College Libraries 8).

C. The amount of the library appropriation will express a rela tionship to the total institutional budget for educational an general purposes (ACRL Standards for College Librarie 8.1).

D. The librarian will have sole authority to apportion funds an initiate expenditures within the library-approved budget, i accord with institutional policy (ACRL Standards for Colleg Libraries 8.2).

E. The library will maintain such internal accounts as are neces sary for approving its invoices for payment, monitoring it encumbrances, and evaluating the flow of its expenditure (ACRL Standards for College Libraries 8.3).

IX. Automation

Utilization of system computer services to assist the Library i some of the functions listed above, e.g. on-line data base searches bibliography preparation; preparing lists of new acquisitions efficient and convenient circulation of library materials; biblio graphic control; gathering and analyzing management data fo efficient and cost-beneficial administration; on-line tutorial pro grams for instruction in the use of the library; providing catalog ing support information; producing technical process material and information; and acquisition and accounting assistance (6-7

NOTE

1. The number in parentheses refers to a page number in the Chancellor's Offic document, "Libraries for Tomorrow's Students." References from sources other than th document are stated after each sentence.

Appendix 3

CSUC Staffing Formula Developed from CSUN Function Cost Analysis Program

William Mason
Associate Dean of Educational Programs and Resources, Chancellor's Office, CSUC

The California State University and Colleges were mandated by the State of California Joint Legislative Budget Committee to report not later than February 1, 1981 recommended changes in library staffing formulas resulting from the implementation of a Library Development Project.

The Library Development Project included three major projects, of which two projects relating to library improvement had been designed and fully implemented on all CSUC campuses at the time of the study. The first, the *Union List of Periodicals*, was a computer-supported publication maintained at the system level which displayed all library periodical holdings and locations throughout the 19 campuses. The second major improvement, automated cataloging support, was implemented by contracting with OCLC (Ohio College Library Center). The installation of computer terminals at all CSUC libraries linked them to a nationwide network of thousands of academic and public libraries to assist in the cataloging and classification of library materials. Another major project focused on the installation of minicomputers, called circulation control transactors, to improve service to patrons by automating routine librar functions such as logging books in and out and placing holds on book on loan. The circulation control transactors provided a readily accessib accounting of the libraries' complete inventory, including the status c each book. At the time of the study in 1979-80, they were installed Sacramento, Los Angeles, Long Beach, San Francisco, San Jose, San Lu Obispo, and San Diego. The remaining 12 campuses are scheduled fc operation by 1981-82. In essence, only two of the three major projects c the Library Development Project were fully implemented at the time c the mandate so the full impact of the project was not reflected in th Functional Analysis Survey.

In order to respond to the mandate by the Joint Legislative Budge Committee, the CSUC did a Functional Analysis Survey of all personn working in 12 libraries for a five-month period from February throug June 1979. A description of this process has been explained in Appendi 4 by Idelle Port.

The identification and definition of tasks within 25 functions and th assignment of these tasks to the cost centers of library administratio library logistical services, and library public services was a prerequisite t establishing budgetary and workload standards. Ninety-four tasks withi the 25 functions were identified and described for use in deriving librar staffing formulas for personnel classifications grouped into: (1) profe sional librarians (academic/administration, academic-related), (2) sta (professional/management, clerical/secretarial, technical/craft, unskilled/sen skilled), and (3) blankets (student assistants and temporary help).

After considering several benchmarks, or proxies, as input variabl for developing an equitable distribution of these resources and for r flecting true need, two benchmarks were selected: (1) budgeted academ year full-time equivalent students (FTES) and (2) number of budgete volumes (VOLM). To measure the direction and strength of a linea relationship between the input variables and reported hours from th Functional Analysis Survey, the Pearson product-moment correlatio formula was utilized. It was statistically demonstrated that there was strong linear relationship between the selected input variables and r ported hours from the Functional Analysis Survey conducted on 1 campuses from February through June 1979. It was therefore assume that the reported findings were representative of the 19 campuses in th CSUC and that the hours for the five-month period were also represen tative of a full year.

The CSUC decided earlier in its deliberations that two sets of staffin formulas should be developed instead of one. The two sets of formul reflected: (1) state-supported positions and (2) state-supported as well subsidized positions. By developing these two sets of budgetary and workload formulas, it was believed that a more comprehensive analysis of library staffing needs in the CSUC could be presented.

Appendix A includes the California State University and Colleges history of library service staffing formulas, definition of the problem and research methodology, selection of cost centers and reported hours, derivation of library services staffing formulas, application of the proposed library services staffing formulas, and the conclusions and recommendations of the study.

DERIVING LIBRARY SERVICES STAFFING FORMULAS IN THE CALIFORNIA STATE UNIVERSITY AND COLLEGES BY THE FUNCTIONAL ANALYSIS APPROACH

I. History of Library Services Staffing Formulas

Library staffing formulas in the California State University and Colleges have undergone three changes since 1965-66. The highlights of these formulas are enumerated in this section.

A. Formulas for 1966/67 through 1971/72

In December 1964, a Chancellor's Office Library Development Committee recommended the following formula, which was approved by the Trustees of the CSUC in 1966, to become effective 1 July 1966.

Public Services:	1 position for each 300 FTE students
Technical Process:	1 position for each 800 volumes added (in 1966-67, the Department of Finance changed this ratio to 1 position for each 850 volumes added)
Administration:	3 positions for campuses with less than 5,000 FTE students 4 positions for campuses with 5,000-10,000 FTE students 5 positions for campuses with more than 10,000 FTE students

B. Formulas for 1972/73 through 1975/76

In January 1971, the Trustees adopted the *Report on the Development of the California State College Libraries: A Study of Book,*

Staffing and Budgeting Problems, November 1970, issued by the Division of Academic Planning of the Chancellor's Office. This report included a staffing formula which took into account many of the variable factors that are present in academic libraries, and especially in a system that included 19 variations on the variables.

Public Services: 1. A basic public service staffing allowance of from 5 to 10 positions varying according to the number of students and faculty:

5.0 positions when projected total FTE student and faculty is less than 1,601

7.0 positions when total is 1,601-6,250

8.0 positions when total is 6,251-10,800

9.0 positions when total is 10,801-15,000

2. Circulation services allowance:

$$P1 = (a/b \times c/d) \pm e$$

where:

a = average weekly hours projected to be charged to all circulation activities by professionals, non-professionals, and student as sistants.

b = 40 hours a week (normal work-week).

c = book, serial and bound periodical circulation for one fiscal year as a percentage of total *countable* volumes held on June 30 of the same fiscal year.

d = systemwide percentage *average* of c; however, should a library's circulation percentage (d), then the number of P1 positions would be determined by dividing average weekly hours charged to circulation by 40 hours, in which case P1 = a/b.

±e = one (1) position for the increase or decrease of each 12,000 volumes charged or 70,000 volumes reshelved of non-charged materials. (NOTE: a/b × c/d provides a basic number of public service area positions. If "a" is projected to change, then P1 would be recalculated. ±e, a workload indicator, provides a growth factor and responds to an increase or decrease in absolute library activity as measured in terms of volumes charged and non-charged books and serials reshelved.)

3. Faculty and student library-demand allowance:
   One position for each 750 FTE faculty and students.

4. Graduate student library-demand allowance:
   One position for each 500 classified graduate students enrolled.

Technical Processes: One position for each 950 volumes budgeted from state funds.

Administration: 2 managerial administrative positions for up to 15 other authorized positions

3......for 16 through 25
4......for 26 through 35
5......for 36 through 50
6......for 51 through 70
7......for 71 through 110
8......for 111 through 160
9......for 160 through 220
10......for more than 220 other authorized library positions

In 1972/73, the first year in which the Board of Trustees' new library development program would have been in effect, the volume entitlements were severely cut on the recommendation of the Department of Finance and the Legislative Analyst's Office. The basic staffing allowance was not approved and the value of "a" of the P1 formula was altered by multiplying the basic allowance for each campus by 40 (hours a week). The number of authorized managerial/administrative positions was changed to:

No. FTE Students	*No. Managerial/Administrative Positions Authorized*
5,000 and under	3.0
5,001 to 10,000	4.0
10,001 to 15,000	5.0
15,001 to 20,000	6.0
over 20,000	7.0

The reduction in volume entitlements affected 100.6 technical processing positions in the system but the CSUC was directed to terminate no permanent staff. In 1972/73, the CSUC adopted the HEGIS budget format which divided public services into Circulation Services and Public Services.

In 1974 and 1975, a review of all formulas was made by a Library Development Committee, representative of the campuses, and appointed by the Chancellor. This Committee proposed a staffing formula based on workload factors and work measurement. However, the report of the Committee was never formally acted on. Thus, the above staffing formulas remained in effect until 1976-77.

C. Formulas from 1976/77 through 1978/79

The "interim" formulas for projecting library staffing and operating expenses were developed by Budget Planning and Administration after consultation with the Division of Library Development and Services and the Library Development Program Committee's subcommittee. This interim approach was to be used until such time as the above Committee accomplished its goal of developing an alternative library formula. The purpose of this interim approach was to systematize and clarify the procedures previously used in generating library budget. It did not purport to be an expression of "appropriate" library support but rather a *maintenance of the level of support incorporated in the 1975/76 Governor's Budget.*

Essentially, the formulas which were developed relate closely to those incorporated in the *Report on the Development of the California State College Libraries: A Study of Book Staffing and Budgeting Problems, November 1970*. They relied on a correlation of work effort in libraries to seven forecastable characteristics (or input variables) of an academic library.

These seven characteristics included: volume acquisitions, elementary textbooks, volumes charged, items shelved, full-time equivalent students, graduate students headcount, and full-time equivalent faculty. Briefly, these library descriptors reflect two characteristics—books and clientele.

The following staffing formula for library administration provides the following:

1. A basic staff allowance of 3.5 positions:

   1.0 Director of the Library
   1.0 Academic-Related Position
   1.5 Clerical Positions
   3.5

2. Additional 1.5 positions at 9,000 college year FTE:

   1.0 Academic-Related Position
   0.5 Clerical Position
   1.5 (or a total of 5.0 positions)

3. Additional 1.5 positions at 20,000 college year FTE:

   1.0 Academic-Related Position
   0.5 Clerical Position
   1.5 (or a total of 6.5 positions)

In the above standard, clerical support is projected at the rate of 1.0 position for the Director of the Library and 0.5 position for each other professional position in this cost center.

CIRCULATION

The circulation staffing formula used the input factors of "Volume Charged" and "Noncharged Items Reshelved." Actual 1973/74 data supplied by each campus was used to develop weighted systemwide ratios of "Volumes Charged/FTE Students," and "Noncharged Items Reshelved/FTE Students."

The two ratios of 28 and 33 respectively were then used in conjunction with the projected student enrollment (FTE) to produce estimates of these workload activity measures.

The circulation formula provided for 1.0 position for every 12,000 volumes charged plus 1.0 position for every 70,000 items reshelved and noncharged.

$$\text{Staffing} = \frac{\text{Volumes Charged}}{12{,}000} + \frac{\text{Noncharged Items Shelved}}{70{,}000}$$

or

$$\text{Staffing} = \frac{\text{A.T. FTE} \times 28}{12{,}000} \quad \frac{\text{A.T. FTE} \times 33}{70{,}000}$$

TECHNICAL PROCESSING

Technical Processing staffing formula remained unchanged at one position for each 950 new volumes acquired.

PUBLIC SERVICE

Clients served is the most significant factor in measuring Public Service workload. The staffing formulas were the same as previously used providing one position for each 750 Academic Year students (FTE), one position for each 500 individual graduate students and one position for each 750 Academic Year faculty positions.

PMP ALLOTMENTS DISTRIBUTION

The percentages applied to the total number of positions generated by the above formulas to yield the PMP allotments of "Academic-Related," "Clerical/Secretarial" and "Blanket Positions" were based on the systemwide average percentages incorporated in the 1975/76 Governor's Budget. They were:

Academic-Related	31%
Clerical/secretarial	46%
Blanket Positions	23%
	100%

D. Formulas for 1978/79

The library staffing formulas operative from 1976/77 through 1978/79 remained unchanged for 1978/79 with but one exception. The technical processing formula was changed from one position for each 950 new volumes acquired to one position for each 1,000 volumes.

E. Formulas for 1979/1980 to the Present

Technical processing formulas were changed again in 1979/80 from one position per 1,000 volumes to one position for each 1,060 volumes. Otherwise, the 1976/77 through 1978/79 library staffing formulas remained intact. In summary, since the CSUC Board of Trustees approved the library automation project, the library technical processing cost center formula has been reduced from 1.0 full-time equivalent position for each 850 volumes appropriated to 1.0 FTE positions for each 1,060 volumes, or a reduction of 25 percent.

II. Problem Definition and Methodology

A. The Problem

Library staffing formulas, particularly for technical processing positions, in The California State University and Colleges have come into question by budget review agencies as well as the Legislature since the development and implementation of the Library Development Project. *The Supplementary Report to the Committee on Conference Relating to the 1980/81 Budget Bill* reflecting agreed language on statements of intent, limitations, or requested studies included Item 379:

> It is recommended that CSUC shall report to the legislative budget committees (1) not later than November 1, 1980 regarding recommended changes in the allocation of library technical processing positions and (2) not later than February 1, 1981 regarding recommended changes in library staffing formulas resulting from implementation of the Library Development Project.

Two major projects of the Library Development Project relating to library improvement have been designed and fully implemented on all CSUC campuses. The first, the *Union List of Periodicals*, is a computer-supported publication maintained at the system level which displays all library periodical holdings and locations throughout the 19 campuses. The second major improvement, automated cataloging support, was implemented by contracting with OCLC (Ohio College Library Center). The installation of computer terminals at all CSUC libraries links them to a nationwide network of thousands of academic and public libraries to assist in the cataloging and classification of library materials.

Another major project focuses on the installation of minicomputers, called circulation control transactors, which will improve service to patrons by automating many routine library functions such as logging books in and out and placing holds on books on loan. The circulation control transactors will provide a readily accessible accounting of the libraries' complete inventory, including the status of each book. Circulation control transactors are currently installed at Sacramento, Los Angeles, Long Beach, San Francisco, San Jose, San Luis Obispo, and San Diego. Six additional campuses are scheduled for operation in 1980/1981 (Chico, Fresno, Fullerton, Hayward, Northridge, and Pomona), while the remaining six campuses are scheduled for 1981/82. In essence, only two of the three major projects of the Library Development Project are presently implemented so the full impact of the project cannot be determined at this time.

While the review agencies and the Legislature are asking for recommended changes in library staffing formulas, the CSUC is indeed aware that the libraries have already been subject to reductions in technical processing positions since 1972/73. Specifically, librarians know that the technical processing formulas have been reduced by 25 percent, which has resulted in a cumulative loss since 1972/73 of 602.8 technical processing positions or $8,201,237. Yet, the CSUC librarians are still subject to the persistent problem that the Legislature presumably does not understand that the State of California has had a return on its investment from the Library Development Project.

The primary problem related to library automation in the CSUC is the presence of these different perceptions related to the return on investment from the Library Development Project.

B. Assumptions

ertain assumptions were made prior to making the analyses and even-
al recommendations as a result of the investigation. These assumptions
e as follows:

1. Personal services includes all positions generated by existing staffing formulas as well as positions that were administratively established in Library Administration, Circulation, Technical Processing, and Public Service.
2. A task analysis of these personnel on twelve campuses, including small, medium, and large-sized campuses, for a five-month period from February through June 1979 represents the tasks performed on all campuses within The California State University and Colleges for a given year.
3. Library staffing includes two types: (1) State-supported positions, and (2) subsidized positions. State-supported positions are used to determine *budgetary* formulas to include in the *Budget Formulas and Standards Manual* while both State-supported and subsidized positions constitute the basis for determining library *workload* formulas.
4. The study does not include recommended changes in library staffing formulas *solely* resulting from implementation of the Library Development Project because the project is still in various stages of implementation.
5. The CSUC Functional Analysis Survey is limited only to actual campus *budgetary* and *workload* standards across each cost center by personnel classification. The survey does not respond to the determination of acceptable *service* standards for the libraries in The California State University and Colleges.
6. The study measures only *current*, not projected, activities conducted in the libraries. If new activities are undertaken, special Program Change Proposals for funding would be required independent of the proposed formulas in this study; e.g., adjusting catalog card headings to conform to new rules contained in *Anglo-American Cataloging Rules, Second Edition*, data base search services, etc.,

C. Functional Analysis Approach

A functional analysis of libraries is the recording of all time, including sick leave and vacation as well as coffee breaks, by personnel in the library in increments of fifteen minutes.

Time is classified into tasks which are then combined into functions. The California State University and Colleges conducted a Functional Analysis Survey and established a Functional Analysis Study Liaison Group to: (1) develop function and task lists to be used by the libraries participating in the study, (2) develop list of production units for those tasks identified, (3) identify categories of employees from whom data will be collected, (4) establish liaison persons on each participating campus, (5) develop and distribute two forms which would be used for collecting data, and (6) review the data from the participating libraries.

Twelve campuses participated in the Functional Analysis Survey from February through June 1979. Forms were submitted at the end of each calendar month to the Chancellor's Office, the data were keypunched, the computer edited the data, and, when they were both complete and correct, processed and summarized the data in monthly reports.

Appendix A shows a classification of 25 functions divided into 94 tasks for the CSUC while Appendix B identifies and defines these same 94 tasks into cost centers. More detailed descriptions of these tasks and data manipulations are given in subsequent sections.

D. Functional and Task Schema for Library Services

A prerequisite to establishing budgetary, workload, or servic standards is the identification of a comprehensive functiona schema of library services. Appendix A shows a classificatio structure of 25 functions as follows: administration, librar personnel, administrative support, library personnel training professional tasks, special assistance and consultation, author ized time off, systems analysis, computer programming, main tenance, deselection, selection, ordering, receiving, accoun ing, cataloging, physical processing, inventory processes, majo or public file maintenance, general circulation, reference an information services, instruction in library use, interlibrar loan and special projects.

Within these functions, 94 tasks have been identified an described for use in a California State University and Co leges library functional analysis study to be described late Appendix A also gives the definition of each task within i appropriate function.

E. Assignment of Tasks to Cost Centers

The identification and definition of tasks within functions are only the initial step toward the development of staffing formulas. The assignment of tasks to cost centers is the next step. Present cost centers for library services are administration, circulation, technical processing, and public service. Each cost center has different staffing formulas with its own unique input variables.

While assigning the 94 tasks to the existing cost centers, it was decided that two temporary cost centers were needed for analytical purposes. Therefore, a library support services and an unassigned cost center were identified so selected task hours could be accumulated for further mathematical manipulation. The assignment of tasks to these six cost centers is noted in Appendix B.

As explained more fully later, library support services task hours were prorated across circulation, technical processing, and public services. The unassigned hours identified in Task 003 (Department Administration), Task 021 (Administration; Departmental), and Task 056 (Authorized Time Off) were likewise prorated. Hours performed in Task 003 and 021 were prorated across library support, circulation, technical processing, and public service while Task 056 was prorated across these four cost centers as well as administration.

F. Personnel Classification Schema

Existing budgetary formulas in the *Budget Formulas and Standards Manual* include provisions for academic-related, clerical/secretarial, and blanket positions for library cost centers. Personnel classifications and titles as outlined in the *Budget Data Classification Structure* that are appropriate for the library cost centers are included in Appendix C.

In order to conduct a functional analysis survey and then be able to develop staffing formulas, personnel classifications were grouped into (1) professional librarians (academic/administration, academic-related), (2) staff (professional/management, clerical/secretarial, technical/craft, unskilled/semi-skilled) and (3) blankets (student assistants and temporary help).

G. Benchmarks

1. Selective Characteristics for Benchmarks

There are many situations in which some very complex problems arise as soon as benchmarks have been identified. The most critical among these are: (1) availabil and comparability of data, (2) timeliness of data, (3) cho of time periods, (4) acceptability by reviewing agenci and (5) simplicity and understandability of data.

It is hardly necessary to emphasize that benchmarks ca not be used unless the required data are available. T question of comparability can also be quite troubleson particularly when the data are obtained from differe sources. It is alleged that campus librarians collect a count data that are not always comparable from one ca pus to another. It does not matter whether this criticisn valid, but it serves to indicate that it can be very diffic to make sure that the data are actually comparable.

Probably one of the most critical characteristics of a benc mark for budgetary purposes is the timeliness of the da The budgetary process has such limited timelines that d changes and budget updates must be accomplished with a matter of hours. Time does not exist for making su veys, hard counts, or measurement of data. It is an age computerization, of numerous changes to input variab and of expectation of quick turnaround of new, correct budget output.

In general, the period that the data must represent is t budget year. Unfortunately, most benchmark data a not available for the budget year in question because definition, the budget year is in the future. Estimates mu then be used for such futuristic data.

Benchmark data must also be simple and easily unde stood. Otherwise, the data will be suspect and confusi to the users. Such data have the tendency to be questic able and subject to considerable rhetoric.
If benchmark data are not acceptable to reviewing bod as being expressive of true need, they cannot be use Acceptability is one of the most critical characteristics f a benchmark to possess.

2. Benchmarks for Determining Need

Developing an equitable distribution of resources event ally becomes a search for possible benchmarks that refle true need as well as utilizing these benchmarks in some manner to develop budgetary formulas. Some of these benchmarks are directly expressive of resource need while others serve as approximations of resource need.

The CSUC considered several benchmarks as input variables for staffing formulas. Some of these were:

a. Actual academic year full-time equivalent students (FT05 + FT08)
b. Budgeted academic year full-time equivalent students (FT05 + FT08)
c. Actual college year full-time equivalent students (FT09)
d. Budgeted college year full-time equivalent students (FT09)
e. Number of budgeted volumes (VOLM)
f. Number of recorded circulation of circulating, reference, and bound periodicals collections (including renewals)
g. Number of interlibrary loan items provided to and received from other libraries
h. Total reference transactions per typical week
i. Number of points of egress
j. Number of library operating hours
k. Number of public service stations
l. Number of graduate students
m. Number of FTES at the graduate level of instruction
n. Number of full-time equivalent faculty

3. Selection of Benchmarks

After considerable investigation, the following benchmarks were used to reflect need for library services positions in The California State University and Colleges:

a. Budgeted academic year full-time equivalent students (FTES)
b. Number of budgeted volumes (VOLM)

They meet all the aforementioned characteristics required for benchmarks. An interesting and convenient phenomenon about these variables is that they are also correlated to other benchmarks that were mentioned earlier but we rejected because they did not possess some of the selecte characteristics for budgetary purposes.

A word of caution must be given on the use of a benc mark as a synonym for a performance measure. A benc mark, or input variable, is really nothing more than a acceptable measure of relationship to a resource variabl An input variable should not be interpreted to mean ot erwise. For instance, full-time equivalent students is a input variable for the prediction of public service pe sonnel positions. Let us assume that 224,450 FTES wou generate 853.6 library positions for public service. Th should not be interpreted to mean that each full-tim equivalent library position will serve 263 full-time equiva lent students. Instead, the interpretation should be th the input variable is an acceptable measure of relatio ship for predicting the number of positions in the publ service cost center. Unfortunately, the use of an inpu variable as a performance measure is a common misu of input variables, particularly by reviewing agencies.

The tendency to misuse input variables as performanc measures would be eliminated if such input variables a sun spots were used instead of FTES as an input variabl in the above illustration. No one would suggest then th a full-time position in public service would produce 26 sun spots. Similarly, it should not be stated that a fu time position in public service would serve 263 full-tim equivalent students.

III. Selection of Cost Centers and Reported Hours

A. Selection of Cost Centers

The CSUC took under advisement the continuance of th existing cost centers: (1) library administration, (2) librar circulation, (3) library technical processing, and (4) publ services. After a careful review of the situation, it was recog nized that not only were the titles inappropriate but also th differentiation of circulation and public services was not wa ranted. Therefore, three cost centers were established as fo lows: (1) library administration, (2) library public service and (3) library logistical services.

The major reason for this action is that the titles of the exis ing cost centers are not descriptive of their respective task

In fact, they are misleading. A reader's review of the tasks assigned to cost centers (Appendix B) should readily support this conclusion. For instance, the title of technical processing suggests to a lay person that the personnel in this cost center are only processing volumes. A look at the tasks included under this cost center reveals that there are many tasks other than processing orders and cataloging new acquisitions.

Logistical services appears to be a more description and all-encompassing title for the tasks included in the cost center. For instance, library accounting, preparation of claims schedules, general inventory, retrospective conversions, deselection, and general selection are some of the tasks that are supportive but not directly related to the processing of volumes.

Similarly, differentiating circulation from public services is artificial and suggests further to a lay person that circulation is not a public service. Therefore, the Committee recommends that these cost centers be combined and the title of public service be retained. Since circulation and public services have the same input variable of budgeted full-time equivalent students, maintaining separate cost centers is cosmetic and not a real differentiation for budgetary purposes. Furthermore, a stronger linear relationship exists between the two variables of budgeted FTES and reported hours when the cost centers are combined.

B. Distribution of Reported Hours to Recommended Cost Centers

Tables 1 through 3 indicate the number of hours reported by the 12 campuses for the months of February through June 1979 in the designated cost centers. Each table shows a breakdown of the hours reported by professional librarians, staff, and students. Hours performed in Tasks 003, 021, and 056 have been prorated and are included in the designated cost centers.

State-supported hours include all reported hours that have been presumed to be paid by the State of California from expenditures available from the 1978-79 Final Budget. Only twenty percent of the reported student work/study hours have been included in state-supported hours because the federal government subsidizes 80% of the payment for these services.

Total hours are defined as all reported hours, regardless of the sources of funds. The major differences between state-supported and total hours are the subsidized portion of work/study, unpaid library interns, volunteers, WIN/COD, CETA, PWA, etc., hours.

In summary, 990,064 state-supported hours and 114,959 subsidized hours, or a total of 1,105,023 hours, were reported in the Functional Analysis Study by the 12 participating campuses for the months of February through June 1979.

C. Relationships of Benchmarks to Reported Hours

If a benchmark, or input variable, is to be used in the development of a formula to determine the number of library services positions, the input variable should have an acceptable measure of relationship to the resource variable. To measure the direction and strength of a linear relationship between the input variables and reported hours from the functional analysis survey, the Pearson product-moment correlation formula was utilized.

Table 1. Distribution of Reported Hours in Administration

	State-Supported Hours				*Total Hours*		
Campus	*Academic Support*	*Staff*	*Blankets*	*Total*	*Academic Support*	*Staff*	*Blankets*
A	2,192	3,805	408	6,405	2,206	3,805	626
B	4,088	909	7	5,004	4,302	945	13
C	2,093	3,749	537	6,379	2,093	3,749	552
D	1,224	1,765	54	3,043	1,224	1,765	55
E	2,451	1,341	131	3,923	2,451	1,532	141
F	4,228	2,352	943	7,523	4,228	2,352	1,601
G	3,442	1,328	350	5,120	3,465	1,328	466
H	2,882	3,654	704	7,240	2,882	3,748	719
I	4,393	2,950	1,467	8,810	4,393	2,955	1,636
J	1,537	1,056	21	2,614	1,537	1,057	54
K	2,708	2,839	745	6,292	2,708	2,926	1,222
L	1,065	276	251	1,592	1,065	313	261
Total	32,303	26,024	5,618	63,945	32,554	26,475	7,346

Table 2. Distribution of Reported Hours in Public Service

	State-Supported Hours				*Total Hours*			
s	*Academic Support*	*Staff*	*Blankets*	*Total*	*Academic Support*	*Staff*	*Blankets*	*Total*
	18,701	23,521	37,229	79,451	20,172	24,454	40,865	85,491
	10,106	13,116	14,250	37,472	10,523	14,415	28,118	53,056
	11,394	19,226	36,844	67,464	11,415	19,226	39,554	70,195
	2,891	8,386	3,544	14,821	2,891	8,387	3,889	15,167
	9,227	11,949	15,561	36,737	9,227	12,508	18,148	39,883
	11,650	14,388	27,778	53,816	11,634	15,775	36,624	64,033
	4,382	4,190	9,420	17,992	4,707	4,174	10,686	19,567
	11,986	14,149	24,078	50,213	11,986	15,097	28,327	55,410
	16,402	16,011	21,647	54,060	16,349	21,335	27,631	65,315
	4,803	9,988	10,048	24,839	4,803	10,188	13,811	28,802
	14,434	18,326	21,939	54,699	14,396	18,482	24,369	57,247
	4,016	3,240	5,132	12,388	4,016	3,229	5,605	12,850
	119,992	156,490	227,470	503,952	122,119	167,270	277,627	567,016

Table 3. Distribution of Reported Hours in Logistical Services

State-Supported Hours				*Total Hours*			
Academic Support	*Staff*	*Blankets*	*Total*	*Academic Support*	*Staff*	*Blankets*	*Total*
10,224	30,261	17,785	58,270	11,082	31,035	20,629	62,746
7,230	17,992	2,702	27,924	7,719	24,703	6,279	38,701
10,819	28,949	10,303	50,071	10,798	28,949	11,475	51,222
2,651	11,173	1,837	15,661	2,651	11,172	2,355	16,178
12,754	20,688	4,605	38,047	12,754	21,611	5,018	39,383
11,748	29,967	15,334	57,049	11,866	30,949	22,605	65,420
3,604	10,006	6,260	19,870	4,595	10,284	6,845	21,724
9,602	22,912	14,536	47,050	9,602	25,750	17,500	52,852
11,119	24,139	6,349	41,607	11,824	28,437	8,539	48,800
3,281	11,609	3,811	18,701	3,281	13,056	4,352	20,689
4,960	23,220	9,848	38,028	5,343	23,616	11,230	40,189
1,622	5,300	2,967	9,889	1,622	8,860	3,246	13,728
89,614	236,216	96,337	422,167	93,137	258,422	120,073	471,632

The Pearson product-moment correlation provides useful sures to test the linear relationship between two variab and x that is independent of their respective scales of surement. Four such measures were utilized in this sta formula study: (1) coefficient of correlation, r, (2) t-test coefficient of determination, r^2, and (4) limits of predictic y for a given value of x.

If the value of the coefficient of correlation, r, is close to we can assume there is little or no linear relationship betw the two varibles. If the value of r approaches +1.0 or − we can assume there is a strong linear relationship.

The sample correlation coefficient r is an estimator of a p lation correlation coefficient, which would be obtained if coefficient of correlation were calculated using all the pc in the population. A common test statistic for testing the hypothesis

$$H_o{:}\rho(\text{rho}) = 0$$

against the alternative hypothesis

$$H_a{:}\rho(\text{rho}) \neq 0$$

for the reported hours and budgeted full-time equiva students is

$$t = \frac{r\sqrt{n-2}}{\sqrt{1-r^2}}$$

and, if we choose a significance level of .01, we will rejec when t is more than 3.169 or t is less than -3.169. Testing null hypothesis for hours worked by academic-related sonnel in the public service cost center by use of the stude t statistic reveals

$$t = \frac{.92\sqrt{12-2}}{\sqrt{1-.85}} = \frac{(.92)(3.16)}{.38} = \frac{2.9072}{.38} = 7.65$$

Observing that the test statistic exceeds the critical value 3.169, we reject the null hypothesis and conclude with a pr ability of .99 that there is evidence to indicate that the b geted full-time equivalent students provide information the prediction of academic-related personnel hours in public service cost center.

We can also determine how good predictions based on a least squares equation are taking the case of predicting a single *y* value corresponding to a given value of *x*. Also, we can assert with a probability of 1-alpha that the individual value we will actually obtain will be between the limits of Ŷ-A and Ŷ + A, called the limits of prediction.

$$\hat{Y} = a + bx$$

and

$$A = t\alpha/2 \cdot S_e \sqrt{\frac{n+1}{n} + \frac{(x-\bar{x})^2}{\Sigma x^2 - n\bar{x}^2}}$$

Substituting the following values derived from the relationship of state-supported logistical services hours and budgeted academic year full-time equivalent students,

$$\begin{aligned} a &= 1065.08 \\ b &= .69356 \\ t_{.001} &= 3.169 \\ S_e &= 1.65951 \\ n &= 12 \\ x &= 230{,}330 \\ \bar{X} &= 12{,}882 \\ \Sigma x^2 &= 2{,}552{,}145{,}400 \end{aligned}$$

we calculate a value of 179,984 hours for Ŷ and a value of 49 for A. Thus, we can assert with a probability of 0.99 that the individual hours utilized with a budgeted FTES of 230,330 in the CSUC will be contained in the interval of 179,935 and 180,033 hours.

The coefficient of correlation, the t-test coefficient of determination, and limits of prediction for each variable *y* and *x* were reviewed and considered by the Committee in its deliberations in recommending appropriate input variables and cost centers.

If the Pearson's *r* is squared, we get another statistic denoted by r^2 and called the coefficient of determination. Actually r^2 is a more easily interpreted measure of relationship when we are concerned with the strength of relationship because it is a measure of the proportion of variance in one variable "explained" by the other. For example, an r^2 measure of .85 tells us that 85% of the variance in reported hours worked by academic-related personnel in the public service cost cent explained by the number of budgeted full-time equival students.

Table 4 shows the r, r^2, and significance of r for each of correlations between the designated variables of y and x also indicates the measures describing the linear relationsh of the appropriate benchmarks, or input variables, to state-supported reported hours for each personnel classif tion grouping within the respective three cost centers.

Hours performed in Task 003 (Department Administrati and Task 021 (Administration; Departmental) were prora across logistical services and public services while Task (Authorized Time Off) was prorated across these two c centers as well as administration.

D. Converting Reported Hours to Library Staffing Formul

Now that input variables and cost centers have been ide fied, reported hours from the Functional Analysis Sur must be converted so staffing formulas for The Califor State University and Colleges can be developed.

To measure the direction and strength of a *linear* relations between the input variables and reported hours from Functional Analysis Survey, the Pearson product-moment c

Table 4. Functional Relationships of Benchmarks to State-Support Resources Utilizing Three Cost Centers

Cost Center	*Variable X*	*Variable Y*	*r*	r^2	*Significan of r*
Administration	BFTES	Total hours	.86	.74	.00016
Administration	BFTES	Academic-related hours	.54	.29	.03611
Administration	BFTES	Staff hours	.78	.62	.00120
Administration	BFTES	Blanket hours	.68	.47	.00712
Logistical Services	BVOL	Total hours	.94	.88	.00001
Logistical Services	BVOL	Academic-related hours	.85	.72	.00024
Logistical Services	BVOL	Staff hours	.95	.90	.00001
Logistical Services	BVOL	Blanket hours	.75	.56	.00259
Public Services	BFTES	Total hours	.95	.90	.00001
Public Services	BFTES	Academic-related hours	.96	.93	.00001
Public Services	BFTES	Staff hours	.90	.82	.00003
Public Services	BFTES	Blanket hours	.89	.79	.00005

relation formula was utilized. It was statistically demonstrated earlier that there was a strong *linear* relationship between the selected input variables and reported hours from the Functional Analysis Survey conducted on 12 campuses from February through June 1979. It was assumed that the reported findings were representative of the 19 campuses in the CSUC and that the hours for the five-months period were also representative of a full year. Therefore, the reported hours were multiplied by 2.4 to express them on an annual basis.

California State University, Dominguez Hills continued the Functional Analysis Survey through December 1979. The Director of the Library indicated that the findings for this longer period were substantially the same for the campus as were the results of the five-month study conducted by the other CSUC campuses. Thus, the assumption was supported by experience at California State University, Dominguez Hills.

The mathematical equation of a straight line is

$$Y = a + bx$$

where *a* is the *y*-intercept and *b* is the slope of a line. Both *a* and *b* have unique values.

These unique values were expressed in terms of annual hours for each library cost center by personnel classification. Assuming that each person holding a full-time equivalent position is employed for 2,080 hours (52 weeks × 40 hours) per year, these unique values can be converted to full-time equivalent positions by dividing each of the a and b values by 2,080. Thus, staffing formulas can then be expressed in terms of full-time equivalent positions (Y).

It was previously recommended that the three cost centers be library administration, logistical services, and public services with budgeted academic year full-time equivalent students as the input variable for library administration and public services and budgeted volumes as the input variable for logistical services.

Deriving Staffing Formulas

The CSUC decided early in its deliberations that two sets of staffing formulas should be developed instead of only one. The two sets of formulas should reflect: (1) state-supported positions an (2) state-supported as well as subsidized positions. By developin these two sets of formulas, it was believed that a more compr hensive analysis of staffing positions in The California State Un versity and Colleges could be presented.

A. State-supported Budget Formulas

Staffing formulas for state-supported positions comprise th first set. The earlier calculations revealed a functional rel tionship between reported hours and budgeted academic ye full-time equivalent students in the administration cost ce ter. Although a regression equation was used for deriving th number of positions for the library administration cost ce ter, the CSUC used an equivalent formula based on a ran of full-time equivalent students. Application of the regressi equation produced 110.7 positions while the suggested fo mulas generated 106.5 positions.

Table 5 shows the formulas for administrative services. T present formulas have been retained, with the exception adding an academic-related position on all campuses. T change in this formula is primarily attributable to the increas

Table 5. Comparative Analysis of Library Staffing Formulas

Cost Centers and Classifications	*State-Supported Formulas*	*Workload Formulas*
Administrative Services		
Administration	Y_a = 1 per campus	
Academic-Related	$Y_1 = 2.0$ when $0 \leq FT09 \leq 8{,}999$	
	$Y_1 = 3.0$ when $9000 \leq FT09 \leq 19{,}999$	
	$Y_1 = 4.0$ when $FT09 \geq 20{,}000$	
Staff	$Y_2 = 1.5$ when $0 \leq FT09 \leq 8{,}999$	
	$Y_2 = 2.0$ when $9000 \leq FT09 \leq 19{,}999$	
	$Y_2 = 2.5$ when $FT09 \leq 20{,}000$	
Logistical Services		
Academic-Related	$Y_1 = -2.88 + .000485x$	$Y_1 = -2.90 + .0004999$
Staff	$Y_2 = -4.24 + .001136x$	$Y_2 = -2.28 + .0011437$
Blankets	$Y_3 = -4.42 + .000577x$	$Y_3 = -6.05 + .0007416$
Public Services		
Academic-Related	$Y_1 = 1.23 + .0008x$	$Y_1 = 1.13 + .000824x$
Staff	$Y_2 = 3.79 + .000874x$	$Y_2 = 3.07 + .0010104x$
Blankets	$Y_3 = 0.91 + .001627x$	$Y_3 = 2.58 + .0018719x$

management functions of planning, organizing, actuating and controlling related to library automation, personnel administration, and other recent advances in library administration.

The formulas for state-supported positions in logistical services are:

$$Y_1 = -2.88 + .000485x$$
$$Y_2 = -4.24 + .001136x$$
$$Y_3 = -4.42 + .000577x$$

Where Y_1 equals academic-related positions, Y_2 equals staff positions, Y_3 equals blanket positions, and x equals budgeted volumes per campus.

Formulas for public services are:

$$Y_1 = 1.23 + .0008x$$
$$Y_2 = 3.79 + .000874x$$
$$Y_3 = 0.91 + .001627x$$

Where Y_1 equals academic-related positions, Y_2 equals staff positions, Y_3 equals blanket positions, and x equals budgeted academic year full-time equivalent students per campus.

B. Workload Formulas for Library Staffing

The foregoing formulas for budgeting state-supported library positions were derived from the Functional Analysis Survey on 12 campuses from February through June 1979. Only the hours for state-supported positions were utilized in the development of these recommended formulas. This is understandable because the revised formulas are for budgeting library positions funded only by the state.

However, as mentioned earlier in this study, state-supported positions are used to determine only *budgetary* formulas for inclusion in the *Budget Formulas and Standards Manual*, not *workload* formulas. To determine total library *workload* staffing formulas, not only state-supported hours but also subsidized hours must be utilized. The Functional Analysis Survey did include the collection of such data for subsidized positions funded from non-state funds so formulas can be derived that reflect present workload standards.

Regardless of the source of funds, the level of library workload is a function of the number of hours worked. The study included a total of 1,105,023 hours, of which 990,064 hours were state-supported and the remaining 114,959 hours were subsidized hours. Important conclusions can be drawn from the utilization of these subsidized hours in libraries: (1) som 10.4 percent of the present workload in the libraries wa funded through subsidization from non-state sources and already an integral part of the total workload, and (2) th elimination of subsidized hours would have an adverse in pact on the operation of the libraries if the loss of these func were not replaced by state funds.

Recognizing that subsidization is not always eternal, the CSU concluded that staffing formulas should be developed n only for state-supported budgets but also for measuring tot workload requirements. Workload formulas that reflect th existing library workload, regardless of the sources of fund should be expressed so library staffing requirements can b better understood by the CSUC as well as state review agencie

Because subsidized hours in administration were only 2,4 hours, there was no point in making a change to the previo formulas developed for state-supported budgets. Thus, fo mulas hold for administrative workload.

Workload formulas for logistical services are as follows:

$$Y_1 = -2.90 + .0004999x$$
$$Y_2 = --2.28 + .0011437x$$
$$Y_3 = -6.05 + .0007416x$$

Public services workload formulas are:

$$Y_1 = 1.13 + .000824x$$
$$Y_2 = 3.07 + .0010104x$$
$$Y_3 = 2.58 + .0018719x$$

In each set of these workload formulas, Y_1 represents academ related positions, Y_2 is staff positions, and Y_3 stands for bla ket positions. The *x* value is budgeted volumes for logisti services and budgeted FTES for public services.

V. Application of Library Staffing Formulas

A. State-Supported Budget Formulas

This section is devoted to the application of the foregoi staffing formulas among The California State University a Colleges. Budgeted fuli-time equivalent students and volun for 1980-81 were used as the *x* values for public services a logistical services, respectively.

Tables 6 through 9 show the number of positions genera by the application of the formulas for state-supported p

Table 6. Academic-Related Positions Generated by State-Supported Budget Formulas

Campus	*AY FTES*	*Budgeted Volumes*	*Administrative Services*	*Logistical Services*	*Public Services*	*Total*
Iayward	7,450	19,961	3.0	6.9	7.2	17.1
'omona	11,750	24,976	4.0	9.3	10.6	23.9
an Luis Obispo	14,200	27,820	4.0	10.7	12.6	27.3
:hico	12,000	25,116	4.0	9.4	10.8	24.2
'resno	12,000	25,662	4.0	9.7	10.8	24.5
Iumboldt	6,530	18,082	3.0	6.0	6.5	15.5
akersfield	2,220	12,649	3.0	3.4	3.0	9.4
.ong Beach	21,050	37,799	5.0	15.5	18.1	38.6
.os Angeles	14,300	29,280	4.0	11.4	12.7	28.1
'ullerton	14,700	29,267	4.0	11.4	13.0	28.4
)ominguez Hills	4,800	16,203	3.0	5.1	5.1	13.2
acramento	16,000	32,048	4.0	12.7	14.0	30.7
an Bernadino	2,950	13,652	3.0	3.9	3.6	10.5
an Diego	23,450	41,367	5.0	17.2	20.0	42.2
Iorthridge	19,000	34,981	4.0	14.1	16.4	34.5
an Francisco	17,400	34,041	4.0	13.7	15.2	32.9
an Jose	18,000	34,257	4.0	13.8	15.6	33.4
onoma	4,100	15,073	3.0	4.6	4.5	12.1
tanislaus	2,550	12,966	3.0	3.6	3.3	9.9
Totals	224,450	485,200	71.0	182.4	203.0	456.4

tions. The formulas produce 456.4 academic-related positions, 774.5 staff positions, and 578.4 blanket positions for a grand total of 1,809.3 positions.

B. Workload Formulas for Library Staffing

Tables 10 through 12 indicate the number of positions generated by the application of the workload formulas. Table 13 shows that 464.7 academic-related, 831.7 staff, and 714.3 blanket positions for a grand total of 2,010.7 would be produced by the workload formulas.

These tables indicate that the present budget formulas would produce 1,639.6 library positions in 1980-81 while state-supported budget formulas would generate 1,809.3 positions, a difference of 169.7 positions. Workload formulas produce 2,010.7 positions, or a difference of 371.1 additional positions.

In summary, each set of formulas increased the number of positions significantly beyond those generated by the present

Table 7. Staff Positions
Generated by State-Supported Budget Formulas

Campus	*AY FTES*	*Budgeted Volumes*	*Administrative Services*	*Logistical Services*	*Public Services*	*Total*
Hayward	7,450	19,961	1.5	18.4	10.3	30.2
Pomona	11,750	24,976	2.0	24.1	14.1	40.2
San Luis Obispo	14,200	27,820	2.0	27.4	16.2	45.6
Chico	12,000	25,116	2.0	24.3	14.3	40.6
Fresno	12,000	25,662	2.0	24.9	14.3	41.2
Humboldt	6,530	18,082	1.5	16.3	9.5	27.3
Bakersfield	2,220	12,649	1.5	10.1	5.7	17.3
Long Beach	21,050	37,799	2.5	38.7	22.2	63.4
Los Angeles	14,300	29,280	2.0	29.0	16.3	47.3
Fullerton	14,700	29,267	2.0	29.0	16.6	47.6
Dominguez Hills	4,800	16,203	1.5	14.2	8.0	23.7
Sacramento	16,000	32,048	2.0	32.2	17.8	52.0
San Bernadino	2,950	13,652	1.5	11.3	6.4	19.2
San Diego	23,450	41,367	2.5	42.8	24.3	69.6
Northridge	19,000	34,981	2.0	35.5	20.4	57.9
San Francisco	17,400	34,041	2.0	34.4	19.0	55.4
San Jose	18,000	34,257	2.0	34.7	19.5	56.2
Sonoma	4,100	15,073	1.5	12.9	7.4	21.8
Stanislaus	2,550	12,966	1.5	10.5	6.0	18.0
Totals	224,450	485,200	35.5	470.7	268.3	774.5

formulas in the *Budget Formulas and Standards Manual.* These positions are needed to provide the number of hours presently utilized in the CSUC libraries. It may appear paradoxical that the campus libraries presently utilize a significantly higher number of positions and hours than are budgeted. However, a knowledgeable observer knows that this is made possible by converting funds from academic-related positions to student assistant and temporary help funds. Findings from the Functional Analysis Survey support this contention.

VI. New, or Expanding, Tasks in the 1980s

Basically, two sets of library staffing formulas have been derived by use of the Functional Analysis Survey. As stated previously, the Functional Analysis Survey is an effective management tool for determining staffing formulas at an existing level of service. Such an approach is not, however, appropriate for determining an adequate and equitable academic library service for the future because the approach does not allow for the measurement of new tasks to be performed.

The CSUC did anticipate some new and expanded tasks that will emerge during the 1980s. Probably one of the more demanding tasks for resources will be when The California State University and Colleges commences using the new rules of author entry published in the *Anglo American Cataloging Rules, Second Edition.* These major changes in nationally accepted cataloging rules are estimated by the Library of Congress to affect approximately 11% of all author entries in card catalogs. On the basis of studies made at two academic libraries, one small and one large, it is further estimated that 1.0 clerical positions will be required for every 16,000 titles added annually. The effect of these rules and the special staffing required by the implementation of new rules will extend over a period of approximately five years.

Additional services become necessary as a result of library policy or technological advances. For example, the provision of data base

Table 8. Blanket Positions
Generated by State-Supported Budget Formulas

Campus	*AY FTES*	*Budgeted Volumes*	*Logistical Services*	*Public Services*	*Total*
Hayward	7,450	19,961	7.1	13.0	20.1
Pomona	11,750	24,976	10.0	20.0	30.0
San Luis Obispo	14,200	27,820	11.6	24.0	35.6
Chico	12,000	25,116	10.1	20.4	30.5
Fresno	12,000	25,662	10.4	20.4	30.8
Humboldt	6,530	18,082	6.0	11.5	17.5
Bakersfield	2,220	12,649	2.9	4.5	7.4
Long Beach	21,050	37,799	17.4	35.2	52.6
Los Angeles	14,300	29,280	12.5	24.2	36.7
Fullerton	14,700	29,267	12.5	24.8	37.3
Dominguez Hills	4,800	16,203	4.9	8.7	13.6
Sacramento	16,000	32,048	14.1	26.9	41.0
San Bernadino	2,950	13,652	3.5	5.7	9.2
San Diego	23,450	41,367	19.5	39.1	58.6
Northridge	19,000	34,981	15.8	31.8	47.6
San Francisco	17,400	34,041	15.2	29.2	44.4
San Jose	18,000	34,257	15.2	30.2	45.4
Sonoma	4,100	15,073	4.3	7.6	11.9
Stanislaus	2,550	12,966	3.1	5.1	8.2
Totals	224,450	485,200	196.1	382.3	578.4

Table 9. Number of Positions Generated by State-Supported Budge
Formulas by Position Classification

Campus	*AY FTES*	*Budgeted Volumes*	*Academic Related*	*Staff*	*Blanket*	*Total*
Hayward	7,450	19,961	17.1	30.2	20.1	67.4
Pomona	11,750	24,976	23.9	40.2	30.0	94.1
San Luis Obispo	14,200	27,820	27.3	45.6	35.6	108.5
Chico	12,000	25,116	24.2	40.6	30.5	95.3
Fresno	12,000	25,662	24.5	41.2	30.8	96.5
Humboldt	6,530	18,082	15.5	27.3	17.5	60.3
Bakersfield	2,220	12,649	9.4	17.3	7.4	34.1
Long Beach	21,050	37,799	38.6	63.4	52.6	154.6
Los Angeles	14,300	29,280	28.1	47.3	36.7	112.1
Fullerton	14,700	29,267	28.4	47.6	37.3	113.3
Dominguez Hills	4,800	16,203	13.2	23.7	13.6	50.5
Sacramento	16,000	32,048	30.7	52.0	41.0	124.7
San Bernadino	2,950	13,652	10.5	19.2	9.2	38.9
San Diego	23,450	41,367	42.2	69.6	58.6	170.4
Northridge	19,000	34,981	34.5	57.9	47.6	140.0
San Francisco	17,400	34,041	32.9	55.4	44.4	132.7
San Jose	18,000	34,257	33.4	56.2	45.4	135.0
Sonoma	4,100	15,073	12.1	21.8	11.9	45.8
Stanislaus	2,550	12,966	9.9	18.0	8.2	36.1
Totals	224,450	475,200	456.4	774.5	578.4	1,809.3

search services is a new capability in libraries. Most of the librarie in The California State University and Colleges are providin these services to patrons, but no budgetary recognition has ye been made for staffing. The benefit to patrons of data base searcl services is widely accepted. It requires considerably more profes sional time to direct the patron with this service than it would t direct the patron to printed sources where the patron could ob tain the information by manual means and at a great expenditur of the patron's time.

Another example of expanding service is the library instructio program that academic libraries are undertaking. Again, this ser vice has not historically been considered in the development o staffing formulas.

Expanding programs for deselection of unused library books periodicals and other forms of library materials are emerging o the campuses. As these deselection programs become more full developed and implemented, additional resources will be require to adequately perform this service.

Table 10. Academic-Related Positions Generated by Workload Budget Formulas

Campus	*1980-81 Budgeted FTES*	*1980-81 Budgeted Volumes*	*Administrative Services*	*Logistical Services*	*Public Services*	*Total Positions*
Hayward	7,450	19,961	3.0	7.3	7.1	17.4
Pomona	11,750	24,976	4.0	10.8	9.6	24.4
San Luis Obispo	14,200	27,820	4.0	12.8	11.0	27.8
Chico	12,000	25,116	4.0	11.0	9.7	24.7
Fresno	12,000	25,662	4.0	11.0	9.9	24.9
Humboldt	6,530	18,082	3.0	6.5	6.1	15.6
Bakersfield	2,220	12,649	3.0	3.0	3.4	9.4
Long Beach	21,050	37,799	5.0	18.5	16.0	39.5
Los Angeles	14,300	29,280	4.0	12.9	11.7	28.6
Fullerton	14,700	29,267	4.0	13.2	11.7	28.9
Dominguez Hills	4,800	16,203	3.0	5.1	5.2	13.3
Sacramento	16,000	32,048	4.0	14.3	13.1	31.4
San Bernardino	2,950	13,652	3.0	3.6	3.9	10.5
San Diego	23,450	41,367	5.0	20.4	17.8	43.2
Northridge	19,000	34,981	4.0	16.8	14.6	35.4
San Francisco	17,400	34,041	4.0	15.5	14.1	33.6
San Jose	18,000	34,257	4.0	16.0	14.2	34.2
Sonoma	4,100	15,073	3.0	4.5	4.6	12.1
Stanislaus	2,550	12,966	3.0	3.2	3.6	9.8
Totals	224,450	485,200	71.0	206.4	187.3	464.7

Uncertainties have not permitted a thorough analysis of the services projected in the 1980s by the nineteen campuses in The California State University and Colleges. Therefore, the development of revised library staffing formulas to provide resources for new or expanded tasks during the 1980s must wait until further studies are conducted. Then, the CSUC would expect to submit Program Change Proposals to accommodate these revisions in resource requirements.

VII. Conclusions and Recommendations

The California State University and Colleges has reached its conclusions regarding changes in staffing formulas for library services and makes the following recommendations:

Table 11. Staff Positions Generated by Workload Budget Formulas

Campus	*1980-81 Budgeted FTES*	*1980-81 Budgeted Volumes*	*Administrative Services*	*Logistical Services*	*Public Services*	*Total Positions*
Hayward	7,450	19,961	1.5	20.5	10.6	32.6
Pomona	11,750	24,976	2.0	26.3	14.9	43.2
San Luis Obispo	14,200	27,820	2.0	29.5	17.4	48.9
Chico	12,000	25,116	2.0	26.4	15.2	43.6
Fresno	12,000	25,662	2.0	27.1	15.2	44.3
Humboldt	6,530	18,082	1.5	18.4	9.7	29.6
Bakersfield	2,220	12,649	1.5	12.2	5.3	19.0
Long Beach	21,050	37,799	2.5	40.9	24.3	67.7
Los Angeles	14,300	29,280	2.0	31.2	17.5	50.7
Fullerton	14,700	29,267	2.0	31.2	17.9	51.1
Dominguez Hills	4,800	16,203	1.5	16.2	7.9	25.6
Sacramento	16,000	32,048	2.0	34.4	19.2	55.6
San Bernardino	2,950	13,652	1.5	13.3	6.0	20.8
San Diego	23,450	41,367	2.5	45.0	26.8	74.3
Northridge	19,000	34,981	2.0	37.7	22.3	62.0
San Francisco	17,400	34,041	2.0	36.6	20.6	59.2
San Jose	18,000	34,257	2.0	36.9	21.3	60.2
Sonoma	4,100	15,073	1.5	15.0	7.2	23.7
Stanislaus	2,550	12,966	1.5	12.5	5.6	19.6
Totals	224,450	485,200	35.5	511.3	284.9	831.7

1. Present personnel classifications specified in the *CSUC Budget Formulas and Standards Manual* are too limited for The California State University and Colleges today. The CSUC recommends budgetary recognition of three broad personnel classification groupings that include designated PMP allotments outlined in the *Budget Data Classification Structure*:

    a. Professional librarians to include academic administration and academic-related personnel classifications.

    b. Staff to include professional/management, clerical/secretarial, technical/craft, and unskilled/semi-skilled personnel classifications.

    c. Blankets to include student assistants and temporary help

2. The California State University and Colleges recommends tha the current program elements of library administration, cir culation, technical processing, and public services be di

continued and replaced by one program element of library services.

3. Within the one program element of library services, three cost centers including administration, public services, and logistical services would be established for analytical and budget formula purposes. The California State University and Colleges recommends that full-time equivalent students be used as the input variable for determining the number of positions in administrative services and public services while budgeted volumes be used as the input variable for generating positions for logistical services. These input variables are acceptable measures of relationship to resource variables and are not under any circumstances to be used as synonyms for performance measures.
4. The Functional Analysis Survey provided a snapshop view of reported hours from February through June 1979 for each

Table 12. Blanket Positions Generated by Workload Budget Formulas

Campus	*1980-81 Budgeted FTES*	*1980-81 Budgeted Volumes*	*Logistical Services*	*Public Services*	*Total Positions*
Hayward	7,450	19,961	8.8	16.5	25.3
Pomona	11,750	24,976	12.5	24.6	37.1
San Luis Obispo	14,200	27,820	14.6	29.2	43.8
Chico	12,000	25,116	12.6	25.0	37.6
Fresno	12,000	25,662	13.0	25.0	38.0
Humboldt	6,530	18,082	7.4	14.8	22.2
Bakersfield	2,220	12,649	3.3	6.7	10.0
Long Beach	21,050	37,799	22.0	42.0	64.0
Los Angeles	14,300	29,280	15.7	29.3	45.0
Fullerton	14,700	29,267	15.6	30.1	45.7
Dominguez Hills	4,800	16,203	6.0	11.6	17.6
acramento	16,000	32,048	17.7	32.5	50.2
an Bernardino	2,950	13,652	4.1	8.1	12.2
an Diego	23,450	41,367	24.6	46.5	71.1
Northridge	19,000	34,981	19.9	38.1	58.0
an Francisco	17,400	34,041	19.2	35.2	54.4
an Jose	18,000	34,257	19.4	36.3	55.7
onoma	4,100	15,073	5.1	10.3	15.4
tanislaus	2,550	12,966	3.6	7.4	11.0
Totals	224,450	485,200	245.1	469.2	714.3

Table 13. Number of Positions Generated by Workload Budget Formulas by Position Classification

Campus	*1980-81 Budgeted FTES*	*1980-81 Budgeted Volumes*	*Academic Related Positions*	*Staff Positions*	*Blanket Positions*	*Total Positions*
Hayward	7,450	19,961	17.4	32.6	25.3	75.3
Pomona	11,750	24,976	24.4	43.2	37.1	104.7
San Luis Obispo	14,200	27,820	27.8	48.9	43.8	120.5
Chico	12,000	25,116	24.7	43.6	37.6	105.9
Fresno	12,000	25,662	24.9	44.3	38.0	107.2
Humboldt	6,530	18,082	15.6	29.6	22.2	67.4
Bakersfield	2,220	12,649	9.4	19.0	10.0	38.4
Long Beach	21,050	37,799	39.5	67.7	64.0	171.2
Los Angeles	14,300	29,280	28.6	50.7	45.0	124.3
Fullerton	14,700	29,267	28.9	51.1	45.7	125.7
Dominguez Hills	4,800	16,203	13.3	25.6	17.6	56.5
Sacramento	16,000	32,048	31.4	55.6	50.2	137.2
San Bernardino	2,950	13,652	10.5	20.8	12.2	43.5
San Diego	23,450	41,367	43.2	74.3	71.1	188.6
Northridge	19,000	34,981	35.4	62.0	58.0	155.4
San Francisco	17,400	34,041	33.6	59.2	54.4	147.2
San Jose	18,000	34,257	34.2	60.2	55.7	150.1
Sonoma	4,100	15,073	12.1	23.7	15.4	51.2
Stanislaus	2,550	12,966	9.8	19.6	11.0	40.4
Totals	224,450	485,200	464.7	831.7	714.3	2,010.7

task within the designated cost centers on twelve California State University and Colleges campuses. It did not provide a picture of conditions prior to or after the implementation of the Library Development Project and could not have reflected appropriate staffing modifications that will eventually result from the full implementation and operation of all automation sub-programs. Consequently, The California State University and Colleges does not recommend the immediate implementation for budgetary purposes the library staffing formula derived from the data reported in the Functional Analysis Survey.

5. The CSUC acknowledges that a change in staffing formula involving a redistribution of library staffing is warranted but to make such changes at this time is premature until library automation sub-programs are fully implemented and operational. This study demonstrated that current staffing formulas generate approximately the same dollar amount as the

library staffing formulas that were derived from data reported in the Functional Analysis Survey. In other words, the current library staffing formulas are adequate to meet the needs of the CSUC libraries as reflected by the Functional Analysis Survey. Therefore, it is recommended that The California State University and Colleges continue using the current staffing formulas for budgetary purposes only and then utilize its delegated fiscal flexibility to modify internally the distribution and classification of library positions among the campuses with these budgeted amounts.

6. The functional analysis approach for determining staffing formulas at an existing level of service is an effective management tool. Such an approach is not, by definition, appropriate for determining an adequate and equitable level of academic library service for the future. However, the comparison of the findings from functional analysis studies over a period of time does provide a picture of change in staffing practices. Therefore, The California State University and Colleges recommends that another Functional Analysis Survey be conducted on all campuses from July 1983 through June 1984 when the automation sub-programs will will be fully implemented. Such a study will determine the structural shift of library personnel requirements between the periods from February through June 1979 to July 1983 through June 1984.
7. New activities require temporary or permanent staffing. For instance, catalog support services in United States libraries will commence using the new rules of entry published in the *AngloAmerican Cataloging Rules, Second Edition,* in January 1981. It is estimated that approximately 22 percent of all author entries in card catalogs will require changing to conform to the entries for new material added to the catalogs and that special staffing will be required for a period of, probably, five years. The California State University and Colleges recommends that special Program Change Proposals for such short-term projects be submitted for funding rather than waiting for the revision of the current library staffing formulas.
8. Some 10.4 percent of the total hours reported in the Functional Analysis Survey were subsidized by non-state funds. The elimination of these subsidized hours would materially affect the level of service performed by the CSUC libraries. The California State University and Colleges recommends that the funding review agencies in the State of California become

aware of the importance of these subsidized library positions. If such external funding is eliminated, these review agencies must understand that the level of library services would likewise be lowered. Thus, The California State University and Colleges further recommends that the current library staffing formulas be revised to avoid the reduction in the level of library services if subsidization from non-state sources were discontinued.

Appendix 4

Statewide Application of California State University—Northridge Function Cost Analysis Program

Idelle Port

From February-June, 1979, all personnel in twelve California State University and Colleges (CSUC) campus libraries kept track of time spent on tasks, using a modified version of the approach developed and used at CSU Northridge described in *Cost Analysis of Library Functions: A Total System Approach.*[1] The study was an investigation of all activities performed in these libraries for the purpose of recommending library staffing formulas related to the actual activities occurring in these libraries. It was assumed that these libraries of campuses ranging in size from 2,000 to over 20,000 FTE students were representative of the nineteen CSUC libraries and that the five-months data could be extrapolated to twelve-months activities by multiplying by 12/5. Both assumptions were validated in that the staff utilization within a function (i.e. group of tasks), by classification of personnel and as a percentage of total staff time, did not vary greatly from campus to campus. Tasks within the functions fluctuate from month to month and library to library, but the broader functions remained relatively constant. With the exception of positions held open either to meet mandated salary savings or converted to cover operating expenses, the five months' staffing data closely represented

5/12 of that year's budgeted library positions, so far as dollar amount. However, it was apparent that some librarian positions were used to fund a greater number of staff or student assistant positions. Also campuses with access to work-study student assistants, for which the campus pays 20% of wages (the Federal Government pays the remaining 80%) stretched their funds by employing work-study student assistants as much as possible.

The modifications made to the original CSU Northridge data collection format were made in several meetings with the entire liaison group (one representative per library) to satisfy the group perception of tasks. Several new tasks were defined and in some cases existing tasks were split into multiple tasks.

Changes were needed to accommodate the varying organizational structures in twelve libraries so that time for a given task could be reported by any organizational unit performing the task, regardless of how the unit was named or which organizational unit did it. With few exceptions (e.g. some libraries process serials separately from periodicals, and there isn't complete agreement on the distinction in definition between serials and periodicals), the modifications allowed the libraries to report all time spent in these libraries in a uniform way. There was one task (#451) that was used for a campus-designated special project (usually a one-time limited project) other than the defined tasks. The attached list defines the tasks, grouped into the functions of Library Administration, Circulation, Technical Services, Reader Service, and a category of Department Administration, Department Administrative Support, and Authorized Time-Off.

Although data on output of tasks (i.e. production units) were collected, they did not result in consistent, usable unit times in terms of industrial engineering-style work measurement, and are not included here. Instead, when the time data were used to develop staffing formulas, overall proxy measures such as FTE students and budgeted volumes were used in regression analysis, as described in *Deriving Library Services Staffing Formulas in the California State University and Colleges by the Functional Analysis Approach*, by the Library Functional Analysis and Staffing Formula Survey Committee, 1981 (see Appendix 3).

Microfiche of the cumulative five-month time data for the twelve CSUC libraries (labeled A-L for anonymity) are included in the pocket located inside the back cover of this book.

Although prior to the data collection some libraries expected the libraries on small, medium-sized, and large campuses to show differing patterns of staff utilization, this conjecture was not supported by the data. Similarly, some expected to detect differences between urban and rural campuses, which also was not supported by the data. Except for greater or lesser use of work-study students and some relatively minor services offered at some libraries but not others (e.g. thesis counseling), the distribution of time across all twelve libraries is remarkably similar.

However, one important factor is not revealed by the data on how time was spent—the level of service provided patrons. Such things as how quickly from the time of ordering that a book appears on the library shelves or what percentage of times the patron finds a title requested was not investigated. The time data were reported at an unknown level of service, but one which was assumed to be reasonably or minimally adequate when in some way averaged across all twelve libraries. Perhaps the best management use of this type of time data would be linking it to the level of service. This would be accomplished by sampling or checking such measures as how quickly from the time of ordering a book appears on the library shelves, estimating the change in staffing needed to produce the desired level of service, and then checking the level of service sometime after the staffing adjustments have been made. This procedure would provide library management with a way of continuously adjusting staffing and service together with quantified measures of both.

CALIFORNIA STATE UNIVERSITY AND COLLEGES TASK DEFINITIONS

Library Administration

001 *Library administration, general.* Planning and reviewing library operations. Directing activities of subordinates by the Director, Associate Director, and Assistant Directors. Planning for buildings, space, physical facilities in general. Budget planning and review for library materials, personnel, O.E., and equipment. Interaction related to the above between department chairpersons and the three levels of library managers; also among the library managers themselves. Developing management tools. Directing administration and office staff.

002 *Library administration, advisory committees.* Activities related to 001 carried on by permanent or ad hoc committees. Executive Board, Librarians' Advisory Committee for Planning, Library Council, Library Faculty (for non-personnel matters). Other committees; Student Rep Board, standing committees.

004 *Campus administration.* Faculty Senate Committees; PP & R, EPC, Graduate Studies, Educational Resource Committee. Campus advisory

committees and task forces; CCAB, fair employment practices, Dean's Council. Statewide Faculty Senate. Advising campus organizations.

005 *Assigned library representation.* (Reserved for use by the Library Director of those specifically directed by him to perform this task.) Library representation at special functions.

006 *Exhibits.* Planning and negotiating for exhibits and materials, preparation for displaying, installing materials and removing them. Lecturing on exhibits or arranging for associated presentations. Bulletin board preparation and maintenance.

007 *Chancellor's Office administration.* Chancellor's Office committees: Library Development Advisory Committee, Functional Analysis Study. Responding to Chancellor's Office technical and administrative proposals and positions.

008 *Regional Cooperation Groups.* Regional cooperation groups (e.g., "mutual use" groups and ILL groups). Include Friends of the Library, community and public relations groups.

016 *Faculty promotion, tenure, and review.* All work associated with the Library Personnel Committee. All departmental activities associated with librarians' promotion, tenure, and review. Written evaluations, interviews, librarian grievance procedures (having to do with promotion, tenure, and review).

017 *Faculty and staff personnel (including student assistants), general.* Faculty recruiting, job (pre-employment) interviews, hiring. All staff recruitment, review, and grievances. Faculty grievances not primarily related to promotion, tenure, and review. Faculty and staff career counseling, education counseling. Include student assistants.

022 *Administration; library and all others.* All clerical and typing activities in support of Tasks 001, 002, 004, 005, 006, 007, 008, 016, and 017. Include photocopying.

023 *Support of professional associations and research.* All clerical and typing activities in support of professional associations and research.

027 *Opening, sorting and distributing all classes of U.S. and campus mail.* All mail previously sorted on campus for the appropriate organizational unit or by library material type.

031 *Required training.* All training initiated by the library; not optional for the personnel involved. Includes both trainee and trainer. Do not put on-the-job training under the particular task, but include it here.

032 Optional training. Job-related training initiated by the employee, particularly such things as apprenticeship training. Includes both trainer and trainee. If released time is involved to attend classes that is definitely charged to this task. Library time (on the 4C schedule) should be charged if it is entirely or mostly job-related. 4C time that is primarily for self-improvement should not be charged. Non-library time should not be reported. 4C time for something like a second master's or a doctoral degree may be charged. Librarians should not confuse optional training with professional development. Training is more formally structured and likely to be in a school context. Workshops that are optional and sponsored by CSUC or the campus or library are charged here. Workshops by professional organizations are charged to Professional Development. Include here supervisors' seminars for library assistants and management workshops for librarians.

041 Professional development. Reading and studying professional and technical literature to keep up with one's professional field. Attending, as a listener, meetings of professional societies and lectures they sponsor. Participating in workshops sponsored by professional organizations.

042 Professional associations. Work as an officer or committee member.

043 Research. Preparation of papers, speeches, demonstrations for presentations at professional meetings or for publication in professional literature. Design and conduct of actual research projects including background reading. Writing a professional book, and related activities performed by the author. All research on library time must be job related otherwise it should not be reported.

051 Special assistance and consultation. Any activity not regularly scheduled and not part of one's job description—and of relatively short duration—that benefits people other than those in one's own immediate work group.

066 Systems analysis. All discussion, review, critique, design of automation systems or automation system proposals originating primarily within the library. Work on library automation task forces; e.g., CLSI, OCLC, is charged to library administration, advisory committee, Task 002. Critique of Chancellor's Office documents is charged to Task 007, Chancellor's Office administration. Include here analysis, design, and review of library procedures if they use the methods of systems analysis, e.g., the "green flyer" study of technical processing time.

076 New programming. Designing, flow charting, coding, testing, debug-ging and documenting computer programs that are new to the library Conferring with computer center personnel on debugging problems and relevant hardware and software developments affecting new library programs.

077 Reprogramming. Modification of existing library programs in re-sponse to changing library needs—use only for reprogramming initiated by the library; changes required by the Computer Center should be reported under Program Maintenance.

078 Program maintenance. Program modifications resulting either from discovering bugs after the system has been in operation, or as a result of changes at the Computer Center, such as installation of new models of the operating system, or as a result of new computers or equipment being installed. Do not use for library initiated changes.

081 Building maintenance and security. Obtaining and performing any physical maintenance work. Opening and closing buildings. All key con-trol work.

082 Revenue producing machines. Obtaining and performing physical maintenance, re-supply, cash handling.

084 Non-revenue producing machines. Obtaining and performing any physical repairs performed by library staff or re-supply of equipment not already covered, e.g., microform readers, audio and video equip-ment, projectors.

153 Payroll. Processing student assistant time sheets, raise lists, raise approvals or denials. Preparation and distribution of payroll summary and budget memos. Posting and calculating monies left in work study entitlements. Includes staff payroll.

154 Equipment and operating expenses. Timing encumbrances, charges and freight for O.E. and equipment accounting. Reconciling with Auto-mated Accounting Ledger and Accounting Department. Include order-ing, receiving and inventorying all supplies other than library material (e.g., pencils and paper clips) for the library as a whole. For supplies to the department show under Task 021.

312 Photocopy service. Staff processing of library patron photocopy (paper or microform).

451 Campus designated special project.

Technical Services

101 Deselection: Weeding. Developing procedures for data collection. Maintaining records of serial and periodical holdings for deselection. Activities associated with conducting usage surveys.

102 Deselection to storage (e.g., compact storage). Selection and movement. Production unit: count volumes.

103 Withdrawing. Batching, searching, and verifying entries; pulling cards from the various catalogs; updating main shelflist and machine shelflist records for books missing or destroyed. Production units: count volumes; count items if not volumes.

104 Withdrawing records via on-line data base (e.g., OCLC). Production unit: count volumes.

111 General selection. Select monographs, serials, periodicals and non-book materials. Any work to accomplish this task not accounted for elsewhere. Requesting backfile material for new titles. E.g., (Reference Selection: Select current paperbacks. Select pamphlets and newsletters. Select reference books, card certain requests, do preliminary checking: solve cataloging and recataloging problems involving reference material; solve reference inventory problems and shifts in location. Review phone book collection; type order request cards.)E.g., (Instructional Materials Lab Selection: Selection of instructional materials, curriculum guides and replacement items. Review of such items prior to cataloging.). E.g., (Special Collections selection: Select material for special collections; deal with out-of-print and rare book dealers and collectors; confer with potential donors of collections or individual items. Decide on housing of material selected for or given to the library.). Production units: count titles selected.

112 Approval selection. Select current in-print materials from approval shipments and blanket orders; modify profile, examine new approval programs and vendors. Review approval shipments. Production units: count titles selected.

113 Gifts selection. Selection and review time for making decisions governing retention or disposal of gift items. Production units: count titles selected.

118 Pre-order checking and verification. Establishing entry under which material is to be ordered; supplying all necessary bibliographic data needed for both ordering and cataloging (includes locating LC copy for cataloging). Establishing price and availability of material. Preliminary checking done from blurbs, catalogs (publishers' and o.p. dealers' and media distributors'), suggestions (on order request cards), bibliographies, multimedia indexes, gift books, journals. Checking library holding. Typing of order request card. Carding for material selected directly by bibliographers from vendor displays and visits, from the computer-produced list of items upon which multiple holds have been placed and from inventory cards. Surveys of library holdings against bibliographies: recording call number of items library has and indicating lacks. Returning of checked material to bibliographer for action. Production unit: count titles checked.

119 Pre-order checking and verification: OCLC. (The same as 118 except with use of OCLC terminal and OCLC data base.) Production units: count titles checked.

131 Ordering; library materials. Preparation of orders; verification of program discipline code and fund, grouping of titles, assignment of order number and vendor, preparing cover card. Order typing, revising order, signing and distribution. Preparation of confirming orders. Establishing of source. Fund and program discipline code assignment, order compilation and typing. Maintenance and update of order section files. Include approval ordering time here. Solicitation of free publications. Initiation of claims. Checking renewal lists. Production units: count approval titles as well as regularly ordered titles.

141 Receiving; general. Unpacking library materials; matching invoices with material; matching orders with invoices and material. Returning defective materials; returning material sent in error; originating credit memos where required. Corresponding with vendors as necessary. Maintaining query programs, processing cancellations, reviewing statements. Verifying that library has ordered the material being received. Distributing all material to proper work area for further processing as required. (Does not apply to supplies and equipment.) Sorting, shelving and distribution. Production units: count volumes received, other print-items, microform-reels, microfiche or microcards, nonprint items.

142 Receiving; gifts. Phone contact with potential donors; determination of library needs for material. Scheduling pick-up or delivery. Counting items on arrival. Acknowledgement. Shelving for review, distribution. Sending material for student sale, disposing of unusable items, sending of material to be retained into the regular bibliographic checking process. Sorting, shelving, and distribution. Production units: cou volumes received, other print items, microform-reels, microfiche or microcards, nonprint items.

144 *Receiving approval.* Unpacking, sorting, shelving and dating of approval shipments. Assignment of subject program discipline codes for accounting. Distribution of shipments after review. Return of rejected material. Shelving and maintenance of approval inventory. Tearing, separating and filing of slips; preparation of groups for direct expenditure payment. Form selection: separation, checking, and distribution of slips. Sorting, shelving, and distribution. Production units: count volumes received, other print items, microform-reels, microfiche or microcards, nonprint items.

145 *Periodical processing, check-in.* Maintaining periodical record, checking in issues, filing periodical record cards, typing new check-in cards. Maintaining periodical shelflist. Setting up and maintaining internal records. Verifying that library has ordered the material being received. Maintaining vendor correspondence. Production units: count loose issues-paper, microform-reels, microfiche or microcards.

46 *Serial processing, check-in.* Maintaining the internal serial record. Checking-in added volume reading file for claiming, maintaining vendor correspondence, checking statements. Posting holdings to internal serial records. Maintaining looseleaf services. Include college catalogs and phonebooks. Verifying that library has ordered the material being received. Production units: count serial issues-paper, microform—reels, microfiche or microcards.

47 *Government documents processing.* Checking in issues, maintaining UDOC shelflist, setting up and maintaining internal records. If you catalog government documents, report that time under cataloging. If you shelve government documents along with books so that end processing is required, report the end processing time for government documents in Task 204. Production units: count number of items-paper, microform-reels, microfiche or microcards.

51 *Library accounting system (whether manual or otherwise).* Preparation of invoices, direct expenditures, encumbrance orders, cancellations, corrections, credit memos, refunds, use tax, etc., for keypunching. Batching orders, invoices, etc. for keypunching. Keypunching; revising, sorting, and processing preliminary to submission of a run; submission of runs; checking and correction of error where required. Distribution of reports. Monthly balancing. Maintenance of files relating to HEW grant

spending. Scratching of tapes as required. HEGIS coding: coding each title on invoice by HEGIS code and making a breakdown of costs including postage and handling for each HEGIS code included on the invoice. Coding computer worksheets for HEGIS coding.

152 Preparation of claims schedules (FISCAL). Preparation of claims for payment. Assembly and typing of claim. Filing of encumbrance orders and confirming orders. Liquidation of encumbrances; closing out of completed orders. Processing pre-paid orders. Placing vouchers on claim Processing of petty cash. Checking statements and related correspondence. Preparing monthly balancing.

160 Bibliographic checking. Post-receipt of library materials. Manual not OCLC. For OCLC bibliographic checking report in Task 165.

161 Adaptive cataloging. Cataloging of material from LC copy: books periodicals, serials, added editions, analyzed series, microfilm and microfiche; number changes and incomplete call numbers for new materials. Desk file maintenance and typing as required by above activities Production unit: count titles.

162 Original cataloging. Establishing entry, added entries, cross references, series information and subject headings as necessary for works fo which no Library of Congress copy is available. Descriptive cataloging subject cataloging, classification. All material. Desk file maintenance an typing as required by the above activities. Production unit: count titles

163 Recataloging. Reclassifying or otherwise modifying the records an item already part of the library collection: changing entry, closin entry, changing classification, changing holdings information. Card co rection work. All materials. Production unit: count titles.

164 Add holdings—manual. All activities necessary to change previous produced library holding records to reflect addition of added copies volumes. (Do not include periodicals, continuations, or serials unless yo add holdings to the shelflist.) Production unit: count volumes or copie

165 OCLC copy cataloging/checking. Searching OCLC data base for ca aloging copy. On-line cataloging of titles with acceptable OCLC catalo ing. Printing out records with cataloging in need of extensive modificatio Researching OCLC data base for titles not found on firm search. A material. Production units: count titles cataloged, titles searched an printed, and titles searched but not found.

166 OCLC adaptive cataloging. Adaptive cataloging involving modi cation of OCLC print-out of LC and other acceptable contributed co to be input to OCLC under task #171. All material. Includes preparing nput forms of old LC copy not already in the OCLC data base. Inputing the data from the form is reported in task #171. Production unit: ount titles.

67 *OCLC original cataloging; new.* Establishing entry, added entries, ross references, series information, and subject headings as necessary or works for which no OCLC data is available. Submitting this data on vorkforms for OCLC terminal input using appropriate tags, indicators, nd subfield codes. All materials. Production unit: count titles.

68 *OCLC original cataloging; revised.* Reviewing and correcting as necssary the established entry, added entries, cross references, series inormation, subject headings, descriptive cataloging, fixed fields, tags, ndicators, and subfield codes on substandard OCLC cooperative cataoging. Production unit: count titles.

69 *OCLC recataloging.* Reclassifying or otherwise modifying the reords of an item already part of the library collections: changing entry, hanging classification, changing holdings information, closing entry, einstating entry, and submitting this data on workforms for OCLC erminal input. All materials. Production unit: count titles.

70 *Card preparation.* Typing call numbers on catalog copy, typing nasters for original cataloging, adding contents notes, making Xerox orrections to bring catalog copy into correspondence with material, nounting for Xerox, Xerox-reproduction of master into card sets, matchng, typing headings, typing cross references, etc. Edit for typing errors.

71 *OCLC inputting.* Keyboarding records into OCLC from prepared oding sheets, corrected printouts, or other "final" copy.

72 *Add holdings—OCLC.* All activities necessary using OCLC to change reviously produced library holding record to reflect addition of adding opies or volumes. Production unit: count volumes or copies.

01 *In-house binding.* Insertion of paperbound material into pam covers; onstruction of board covers for off-size paperbound material; Togic inding; all other binding. Production units: count items treated.

02 *Bindery preparation and returns.* Preparation of books and periodial and serial issues for binding. Pulling of unbound issues from stacks, ollating, typing up bindery slips, revising, tying and packing for shiping. Typing of packing list. Notifying missing issues section. Setting up nits to be bound in house. Checking returned bindery shipment. Keep-

ing totals of remaining bindery budget. Maintaining records to gui encumbrance of binding funds. Production units: count items treate

203 Mending. Repairing library materials sent from the collection in damaged condition or initially cataloged in a damaged condition. Trim ming, gluing, taping, stitching, etc. Preservation of materials. Sorti and redistributing to proper unit. Production units: count items treate

204 End processing (all materials). Sorting and processing books ar nonbooks, typing and affixing labels, property stamping, affixing pock and date due slip, keypunch book card, proof, tattle-taping, sorting f distribution, hinging in material if necessary. Each organizational ur that performs physical processing beyond receiving and check-in tas reported in Function 14, reports it here. Count item as it is added to th collection as defined by format in the CSUC Annual Statistics. Gover ment documents have been counted in Task 147, unless they are cat loged and shelved with the book collection—in that case count them volumes. Production units: volumes, other print items, microform reel microfiche and microcard items, nonprint items.

220 General inventory.

242 Public periodical record creation and maintenance. All activities ass ciated with creating and maintaining the public records after catalogin or changing records after recataloging. Production unit: count transaction

244 Public serial records creation and maintenance. All activities assoc ated with creating and maintaining public records after cataloging, changing records after recataloging. Production unit: count transaction

250 Catalog maintenance. Creating and maintaining major library car catalogs (to be distinguished from personal desk files or working contr files.) Filing into and revising in catalogs such as the Shelflist, the Offici Catalog, the Author/Title and Subject Catalogs, the Music Score Phon record Catalog, and Music Score Shelflist, the Record Shelflist, the Mus Official, and the Proof Files. Replacing worn or missing labels, guid cards, and catalog cards, expanding catalogs as required, etc. Productio unit: count cards filed.

251 Machine shelflist maintenance. Keypunching card sets from slip submitting computer runs to Computer Center, production of curre acquisitions list, editing printouts, shelflist tape updating, job accoun ing, decollating, binding, production of the Science/Technology boo catalog, maintaining records of library tapes in the Computer Cent library, production and updating of Science Subject Guide, and othe lata processing activities. Production unit: count number of cards ›unched.

?52 *Authority file maintenance.* All activities associated with maintaining ınd updating the Subject Authority File, Series Treatment File, and Name Authority File found in the Official and Music Official. Preparing ıuthority cards for subjects, series, personal and corporate names, and ıniform titles with see and see references and information cards; typing :ards and filing into the files. Production unit: count cards filed.

?57 *Union lists.* Coding for Union List of Periodicals/Serials. Any other ınion list. Production unit: count transactions.

450 Retrospective conversion. OCLC or other. Production units: count :itles.

Circulation

271 *Circulation control and desk.* Charging-out library materials, answering questions, issuing library cards, and returning library cards (lost or left) to owners. Filing records of issued library cards. Discharging books, checking for holds. Automated System Work including preparation and submission of computer input, retrieval of computer output; error correction (processing of snags, etc.), and Computer Center liaison. Production units: count items charged.

272 *Fines and billing.* Processing bills and notices for books returned late or on-loan and overdue. Billing for damaged items. Encumbering student records. Processing lost book reports and contested bills. Receiving and accounting for payment of bills. Searching for overdue books, periodicals, and contested overdue items. Reserve Book Room processing for overdue and returned late items. Searching prior to fines or billing.

273 *Exit control.* Staffing exit points and checking material as patron exits.

274 *Stack maintenance, general.* Shelving items used in the library (books, bound periodicals). Shifting materials in the stacks (includes measurement, relabeling). Include shelving new books. Shelving circulated books in stacks. Production units: maintain separate counts of all volumes and loose items shelved.

275 Stack reading, general. Reading assignment performed in the stack Monthly random reading assignments. Developing, revising and impl menting automated stack reading programs.

276 Reserve book room, operation. Charging, discharging, and proces ing holds (i.e., reserve requests). Adding to and withdrawing from r serve, ordering or copying items for reserve, and use, maintainin inventory, shelving, stack reading of RBR items, reserve searching. Pr duction units: count charges.

277 Search holds. Handling search request at charge desk for boo and periodicals. Searching for material for patrons. Recalling books. Co ducting periodic faculty and staff recalls. Searching for materials r ported missing. Production units: count searches.

351 Interlibrary loan. Borrowing: Verifying sources and locations. Ty ing and sending out requests. Unwrapping, checking, notifying patro shelving for pick-up, charging out Receiving or retrieving when du Notifying patron. Production units: count requests sent.

352 Interlibary loan. Lending: Receiving requests, verifying availabilit locating and retrieving, searching, processing for mailing, wrapping an sending. Sending overdue notices. Discharging and clearing record Production units: count requests received.

Reader Service

310 Reference desk. All time spent regularly assigned to reference des regardless of the activities performed during the assignment perio Production units: count directional questions, under five minutes refe ence questions, over five minutes reference questions.

311 General reference. All other reference work. Reference not pe formed at a reference desk, e.g., follow-up reference, consultative refe ence service in offices. Production units: count directional question under five minutes reference questions, over five minutes referenc questions.

314 Information desk. All time spent at the information desk regardles of tasks performed. Production units: count directional questions, unde five minutes reference questions, over five minutes reference questions

316 Thesis consultations. Include senior projects.

318 Automated data base searches. Determining patron requirement formulating search, operating terminal, evaluating user response, kee

ing statistics, ankd obtaining publicity. Production units: count number of search requests initiated, number of data base accesses (i.e., one request may equal three data base accesses).

319 Slide Collection Desk. Providing directional reference, and search assistance. Providing assistance in the use of the collection. Production units: count directional questions, under five minutes reference questions, over five minutes reference questions.

320 Microform Desk. Providing directional reference, and search assistance. Providing assistance in the use of the collection. Productin units: count directional questions, under five minutes reference questions, over five minutes reference questions.

331 Informal instruction by library staff. Preparing bibliographic lectures and tours for classes, delivering lectures in classes, conducting general tours. Production units: number of lectures, number of tours.

333 Manual or machine-produced bibliographies, lecture handouts, patron instructions. Compile, produce, revise bibliographies and handouts for general distribution. Produce other training aids. Providing any instruction not covered by 331.

334 Formal instruction by library staff. Offered for credit in school catalog. Preparation and instruction. Office hours. Only report time funded by the library.

Department Administration, Departmental Administrative Support, and Authorized Time-Off

003 Department administration. Generally the same as 001 Library Administation but essentially confined to the department. Any departmentally constituted committees, groups, or meetings concerning the department as a whole, particularly its policies, budgets, and staffing. Specific task-oriented groups should charge to the specific task involved.

021 Administration; departmental. All clerical and typing activities in support of Task 003. Include departmental photocopying. Include ordering, receiving and distributing supplies from campus or library stores. Report departmental statistics record-keeping here.

056 Authorized time-off. Nonproduction activities for which the state pays: vacation, sick time, compensating time-off, holidays, coffee breaks, nonproduction meetings (staff association), departmental parties, jury duty. People working in more than one department (fractional appoint-

ments) will charge all such time to their major department rather tha
prorating. Docked time is not reported anywhere.

NOTE

1. Betty Jo Mitchell, Norman E. Tanis, and Jack Jaffe, *Cost Analysis of Library Functions;* *Total System Approach* (Connecticut: JAI Press, 1978).

Appendix 5

CSUN Librarians' Advisory Committee for Planning: Report on Library Function Cost Analysis Program

This report is a response by the Librarians's Advisory Committee for Planning (LACP) to the request to consider the Function Cost Analysis (FCA) programs in the Library at California State University, Northridge. Following the summary of recommendations a summary of findings is presented, and the recommendations are then explained in the body of the report.

SUMMARY OF RECOMMENDATIONS

1. A suitably modified FCA program should be retained for a trial period of one year.
2. Duplicate statistics should be investigated at the department level.
3. A mechanism to provide necessary input for continuing refinement of FCA should be established.
4. Limitations of task measurement should be addressed at the department level after extensive departmental consultation.
5. Each department should re-conceptualize the activities performed by librarians within that department.

FINDINGS

A. *Collection of Statistics.* In its interviews with librarians the LACP heard the following points about the FCA program:

1. Some librarians question the need for comprehensive collection of statistics.
2. Others recognize the need to collect some kind of statistics, but want to know exactly which ones are actually needed.
3. Many librarians believe that a function cost program can be implemented by an alternate method of gathering statistics, such as by estimation or sampling.
4. Some statistics collected by the FCA program duplicate statistics kept in another way, e.g., hours spent at service points.
5. No one favors a permanent work-measurement system.
6. Librarians who oppose the FCA program would be willing to resume reporting their activities on a daily basis if the FCA program can be re-conceptualized.

B. *Cost-Benefit.*

1. It is an expensive program.
2. It requires valuable time to operate.
3. Its benefits are doubtful.

C. *Communication.* Inadequate communication exists between the individuals who fill out the FCA forms and those who use the FCA reports. Problems apparent to LACP are:

1. Significant morale problems.
2. Uncertainty about the purpose of FCA: is it a departmental management tool, a library management tool, or an aid to develop a system-wide staffing formula, or a combination of these?
3. Contradictions between actual work performed and the task definitions. Two examples are: a) how is time to be recorded when two activities are performed within the same time period, and b) should certain tasks be assigned to one department only, even though they apply to several departments.

D. *Limitations of Task Measurement.*

1. Some people think tasks should be made more specific; others think they should be broadened.
2. Task measurement reporting is not accurate.
3. Task measurement does not measure the quality of the work.

4. FCA is inflexible to change.
5. Some work activities are not reflected in FCA.

RECOMMENDATIONS

After consultation with the library faculty, administrators, and the library systems analyst, the Committee offers the following comments and recommendations.

A. *Collection of Statistics.*

FCA is a response to the trend for accountability that is placed upon the library. The library is accountable to the library staff, the Library A-V Committee, the campus community, the CSUC system, the legislature, the Department of Finance, the Governor, and, ultimately, to the taxpayers.

Although the Committee recognizes that other methodologies for data gathering, such as sampling or estimates, may be valid, it believes that an on-going program of daily data gathering is essential for maximum results.

The Committee therefore recommends the retention of a suitably modified FCA program, as suggested in this report, for a trial period of one year.

The Committee also recommends that, if duplicate statistics are being kept, the problems be investigated at the departmental level.

B. *Cost-Benefit.*

The Committee recommends that the benefits of this program be examined at the end of the one-year trial period.

C. *Communication.*

The Committee recognizes that the FCA program can be useful as a library management tool, departmental management tool, and as an aid in developing a staffing formula.

The Committee also recognizes imperfections in FCA, such as improper task definition. Since members of library departments perform the daily activities being measured, FCA imperfections should be corrected at the departmental level. Input from individuals and department heads should be encouraged to ensure that FCA reflects actual work activity.

The Committee therefore recommends the establishment of a mechanism to provide the necessary input for continuing refinement of FCA. Its purpose should be to foster good communication and coordination among the various levels of the library: individual, department, and administration. The mechanism we suggest is:

1. One specific individual should be clearly identified as the coordinator of the FCA program. He/she would have the following charges:

    a. To consult with departments and administrators on all written suggestions.
    b. To respond to questions and suggestions and to reply in writing to all suggestions forwarded to him/her by department heads.
    c. To implement agreed upon changes and refinements to FCA after consultation.

    The Committee recommends that the library systems analyst be considered for the role of coordinator.

2. Individuals who wish to request changes in FCA should consult with their department heads.
3. Any recommendations for change from a department should be sent in writing to the coordinator by the department head.
4. There should be adequate consultation at the departmental level before any recommended changes or suggestions are forwarded to the coordinator.

D. *Limitations of Task Measurement.*

The chief limitations noted by the Committee are: 1) measuring quality, 2) quantifying librarian activities, and 3) correlating work performed with task measured. Regarding the first limitation, it should be understood that FCA cannot be used a tool for measuring quality. The Committee recommends that the latter two problem areas be addressed at the department level after extensive departmental consultation.

Specifically, we recommend that each department re-conceptualize the activities that are performed by librarians within that department, and analyze them in terms of the department's main function or purpose. Some activities will be restricted primarily to one department, such as those in the reference department which relate directly to library instruction. Others are common to all departments, such as administrative duties like hiring personnel or attending meetings.

One possible schema for analyzing departmental activities could consist of four broad categories, each of which would contain all activities related to that particular aspect of departmental operations. These categories could be: 1) Primary purpose of the department; 2) Maintenance of professional skills; 3) General maintenance; and (4) Administrative activities. As an example, since the main purpose of the Reference Department is instruction, all activities relating primarily to instruction could be grouped together within a category called "Instructional Activities." Tasks related to research, professional reading, workshops and so on would fall under "Maintenance of Professional Skills." "General Maintenance" could consist of housekeeping activities such as reading the daily mail. And "Administrative Activities" would include departmental meetings, personnel work, and so on.

It is the hope of the Committee that the recommendations contained in this report will be accepted and that a sincere attempt will be made by all concerned to alter the function cost analysis program to make it more representative of the actual work done in the library, not only by librarians, but by all staff members and student assistants. We have done our best to weigh all the facts, and we believe that the FCA program has the potential to provide factual support that will benefit the library in future years.

Appendix 6

Bibliography: PPBS in Libraries

Allen, Kenneth S. *Current and Emerging Budgeting Techniques in Academic Libraries, Including a Critique of the Model Budget Analysis Program of the State of Washington.* (Bethesda, Md., ERIC Document Reproduction Service ED 071 726.)

Applequist, Claes-Goran and Zandren, S. *The Development of a Planning, Programming and Budgeting System.* Technical Report presented at the Evaluation Conference on Institutional Management in Higher Education. Paris, November 2-5, 1971.

Association of Research Libraries. *Review of Budgeting Techniques in Academic and Research Libraries.* (ARL Management Supplement volume one, number two.) Washington, D.C., Office of University Library Management Studies, April, 1973. (Bethesda, Md., ERIC Document Reproduction Service ED 087 387.)

Axford, H. W. "An Approach to Performance Budgeting at the Florida Atlantic University Library," *College and Research Libraries,* 32 (March, 1971) 87-104.

Baldwin, Daniel R. "Managerial Competence and Librarians," *Pennsylvania Library Association Bulletin,* 26 (January, 1971) 17-25.

Bommer, Michael R. W. *The Development of a Management System for Effective Decision Making and Planning in a University Library.* Supplemental to Final Report. Doctoral dissertation, December, 1972. Pennsylvania University, Philadelphia, Wharton School of Finance and Commerce. (Bethesda, Md., ERIC Document Reproduction Service ED 071 727.)

Bromberg, Erik. *Simplified PPBS for the Librarian.* Prepared for the Dollar Decision Pre-Conference Institute sponsored by the Library Administration Division of the American Library Association, Dallas, Texas June, 1971. *Protean,* 2 (Spring, 1972) 9-18. (Bethesda, Md., ERIC Document Reproduction Service ED 047 751.)

Bryk, Oliver. "Application of PPB on State and Local Levels." Paper presented at an Institute of Program Planning and Budgeting Systems for Libraries at Wayne State University, Detroit, Michigan Department of Library Science, Spring, 1968. (Bethesda, Md., ERIC Document Reproduction Service ED 045 127.)

Buckman, Thomas R. "Planning—Programming—Budgeting Systems In University, National, and Large Public Libraries in the United States," *Libri,* 22 (1972) 256-270.

Burness, Carl G. "Defining Library Objectives." Paper presented at an Institute on Program Planning and Budgeting Systems for Libraries at Wayne State University, Detroit, Michigan, Department of Library Science, Spring, 1968. (Bethesda, Md., ERIC Document Reproduction Service ED 045 116.)

Byers, Barbara B. "PPB—An Aid to Decision-Making." *Special Librarie Association, Toronto Chapter, Bulletin,* 31 (1971) 12-19.

Ching-Chih Chen (ed.) *Quantitative Measurement and Dynamic Library Service.* Pheonix, Arizona: Oryz Press, 1978.

Colley, D.I. "Planning, Programming, Budgeting System (PPBS)," *Library World* (London), 72 (February, 1971) 237-38.

Cook, D.L. "What You Always Wanted to Know About PPBS—and Have Not Been Hesitating to Ask." *Protean,* 2 (Spring, 1972) 21-26.

De Genaro, Guy J. *A Planning-Programming-Budgeting System (PPBS) in Academic Libraries: Development of Objectives and Effectiveness Measures* Ph.D dissertation. University of Florida, 1971.

De Genaro, Richard. "Library Administration and New Management Systems," *Library Journal,* 103 (Dec. 15, 1978) 2477-82.

Detroit Public Library. Municipal Reference Library. "Programming Planning, Budgeting Systems; a Selected List of Recent References." *MRL Bulletin,* January, 1969.

Ellis, A. E. "Influence of PPB on Budgeting." Paper presented at an Institute on Program Planning and Budgeting Systems for Libraries at Wayne State University, Detroit, Michigan, Department of Library Science, Spring, 1968. (Bethesda Md., ERIC Document Reproduction Service ED 045 123.)

Evans, G. Edward. *Management Techniques for Libraries.* New York: Academic Press, 1976.

Fazar, Willard. *Application of PPB to Certain Federal Programs.* Paper presented at an Institute on Program Planning and Budgeting Systems for Libraries at Wayne State University, Detroit, Michigan, Department of Library Science, Spring, 1968. (Bethesda, Md., ERIC Document Reproduction Service ED 045 117.)

———. *The Importance of PPB to Libraries.* Paper presented at an Institution on Program Planning and Budgeting Systems for Libraries at Wayne State University, Detroit, Michigan, Department of Library Science, Spring, 1968. (Bethesda Md., ERIC Document Reproduction Service ED 045 114.)

———. "Program Planning Budgeting Theory: Improved Library Effectiveness by use of the Planning-Programming-Budgeting System," *Special Libraries,* 60 (September, 1969) 423-33.

Gelfand, Morris, A. "Budget Preparation and Presentation: Creating a Favorable Climate for Budget Approval." *American Libraries,* 3 (May, 1972) 496-500.

Goldbert, Robert L. *A Systems Approach to Library Program Development.* Metuchen, New Jersey: Scarecrow Press, 1976.

Gordon, G. G. "Challenge of PPBS." *California Teacher's Association Journal,* 66 (January, 1970) 30-1. (Also in Ward, P. L. and Beacon, R. Comp. *School Media Center: A Book of Readings.* Metuchen, New Jersey: Scarecrow Press, 1973, pp. 82-84.)

Green, J. "Automated Responsibility Reporting for Libraries: a Program Budgeting and Reporting System Recently Installed in the Oklahoma Department of Libraries." *Oklahoma Librarian,* 20 (January, 1970) 18-21.

Grossbard, Stephen I. "PPBS for State and Local Officials." *North Dakota Library Notes,* April, 1975.

Hamburg, Morris, *et al. Library Planning and Decision-Making Systems.* University of Pennsylvania. Cambridge, Massachusetts: The MIT Press, 1974.

———. *A Systems Analysis of the Library and Information Science Statistical Data System: The Preliminary Study. Interim Report.* Pennsylvania University, Philadelphia, 1969. (Bethesda, Md., ERIC Document Reproduction Service ED 035 421).

Hannigan, Jane A. "PPBS and School Media Programs." *American Libraries,* 3 (December, 1972) 1182-84.

Hatch, Lucile, and Forsythe, Ralph A. "Upgrading Performance Through PPBS in School Media Centers." *Library Trends,* 23 (April, 1975) 617-30.

Hawaii. State Library. *PPB Bibliography.* TAC Publication No. 70-2325. Honolulu: Office of Library Service, 1971.

Hoadley, I. B. (ed.). "Budgeting and Finances in Libraries." *Protean,* 2 (Spring, 1972).

Hoadley, I. B. "The Protean Speaks." *Protean,* 2 (Spring, 1972) 4-8.

Hoffman, W. "Data Processing Applied to Library Budgets." Paper presented at an Institute on Program Planning and Budgeting Systems for Libraries at Wayne State University, Detroit, Michigan, Department of Library Science, Spring, 1968. (Bethesda, Md., ERIC Document Reproduction Service ED 045 122.)

Holland, E. D. "Initials PPBS Stand for Planning, Programming, Budgeting System." *California School Libraries,* 41 (May, 1970) 143-44.

Howard, Edward N. "Toward PPBS in the Public Library." *American Libraries,* 2 (April, 1971) 386-93.

Howard, Lore. "A Better Look at Budgets." *School Library Journal,* 18 (March, 1971) 93-94.

Hunter, Neil. *Library Management: A Management Decision Bibliography* West Yorkshire, England: MCB (Management Decision) Limited 1974.

Jenkins, Harold R. "The ABC's of PPB: An Explanation of Hov Planning—Programming—Budgeting Can Be Used to Improve th

Management of Libraries." *Library Journal*, 96 (October, 1971) 3089-93.

Keller, Harry. *Development and History of the Concept of PPB*. Paper presented at an Institute on Program Planning and Budgeting Systems for Libraries at Wayne State University, Detroit, Michigan, Department of Library Science, Spring, 1968. (Bethesda, Md., ERIC Document Reproduction Service ED 045 113.)

Keller, John E. "Program Budgeting and Cost Benefit Analysis in Libraries," *College and Research Libraries*, 30 (March, 1969) 156-60.

Koening, M. E. D. "Budgets and Budgeting." *Special Libraries*, 68 (July-August, 1977) 228-40.

Lee, Sul H. (ed.). *Library Budgeting: Critical Challenges for the Future.* Ann Arbor, Michigan: The Pierian Press, 1977.

———. *Planning—Programming—Budgeting System* (PPBS). (Library Management Series, No. 1.) Ypsilante, Michigan: The Pierian Press, 1973.

Leimkuhler, F. F. and Billingsley, A. "Library and Information Center Management" in *Annual Review of Information Science and Technology*, vol. 7, Washington: American Society for Information Science, (1972) 499-533.

Lembo, D. L. "Approaches to Accountability," *School Libraries*, 21, (Fall, 1971) 15-19.

Little, R. D. "Budgeting for Instructional Resources in the Individual School Building," *Wisconsin Library Bulletin, 67 (Summer, 1971) 327-31.*

Lushington, N. "What's Going on Here" *Connecticut Libraries*, 14 (Fall, 1972), 3-6.

McCauley, Elfreida B. "Budgeting for School Media Services: A Procedural Guide to PPBS and an Exploration of Valid Sources of Funding for School Media Programs," *School Media Quarterly*, 4 (Winter, 1976) 126-34.

Magaro, J. D. "PPBS: a Means Toward Accountability," *Audio-Visual Instruction*, 20 (December, 1975) 10-12.

Mason, D. "PPBS: Application to an Industrial Information and Librar Service," *Journal of Librarianship*, 4 (April, 1972) 91-105.

———. "Programmed Budgeting and Cost Effectiveness," *Aslib Proceed ings*, 25 (March, 1973) 100-10.

Mason, Thomas R. "Program Planning for Research Libraries in a Uni versity Setting," Paper presented to the Association of Research Li braries, Washington, D.C., January 26, 1969. (Bethesda, Md., ERIC Document Reproduction Service ED 027 845.)

Meyers, Judith K. and Barber, Raymond W. "McNamara, Media an You," *Library Journal*, 96 (March 15, 1971) 1079-81; and *School Li brary Journal*, 18 (March, 1971) 91-93.

Michael, Mary Ellen and Young, Arthur P. *Planning and Evaluating Li brary System Services in Illinois*. Illinois University, Urbana, Librar Research Center, August, 1974. (Bethesda, Md., ERIC Documen Reproduction Service ED 095 916.)

Milliman, Jerome W. and Pfister, Richard L. *Economic Aspects of Librar Service in Indiana*. Indiana Library Studies, Report No. 7, Indian State Library, 1970.

Morey, George E. *Identification of Common Library Goals, Objectives an Activities Relative to a Planning, Programming, Budgeting System*. Thesi (EdS), Western Michigan University, 1970. (Bethesda, Md., ERIC Document Reproduction Service ED 048 976.)

Morris, J. "PPBS: A Way to Prove Your Program," *Hoosier School Librar ies*, 14 (April, 1975) 32-33.

Morse, Philip M. *Library Effectiveness: A System Approach*. Cambridge: MIT Press, 1968.

Noyce, J. *Planning, Programming, Budgeting Systems in Libraries: An Anno tated List of References*. Brighton, England: Smoothie Publications 1972.

Noyce, J. L. Comp. *Planning, Programming, Budgeting Systems and Man agement by Objectives in Libraries; an Annotated List of References*. 3d ed Brighton, England: Smoothie Publications, 1974.

Palmer, D. "Measuring Library Output," Paper presented at an Institute on Program Planning and Budgeting Systems for Libraries at Wayne

State University, Detroit, Michigan, Department of Library Science, Spring, 1968. (Bethesda, Md., ERIC Document Reproduction Service Ed 045 118.)

Piele, Philip K. *Planning-Programming-Budgeting Systems.* (Educational Management Review Series, Number 2.) Oregon University, Eugene. ERIC Clearing House on Educational Management. January, 1972. (Bethesda, Md., ERIC Document Reproduction Service ED 058 622.)

Raffel, Jeffrey A. and Shishko, Robert. *Systematic Analysis of University Libraries: An Application of Cost-Benefit Analysis to the M.I.T. Libraries.* Cambridge: MIT, 1969.

Riggs, Donald E. *Centralized Technical Processing and PPBS: A Literature Review.* Bluefield State College, West Virginia; Concord College, Athens, West Virginia, 1975. (Bethesda, Md., ERIC Document Reproduction Service ED 108 688.)

Rogers, Rutherford D. and Weber, David C. *University Library Administration.* New York: H. W. Wilson Co., 1971.

Santa Barbara Elementary and High School District, California. *P.P.B.S. and the Library: Goals, Objectives, Program.* Report of the Librarians' workshop, 1971. (Bethesda, Md., ERIC Document Reproduction Service ED 050 776.)

Schaller, Lyle E. "Make Your Budget Work for You! PPBS and Other Budget Techniques," *Mayor and Manager,* (February, 1969) 17-21.

Schofield, J. L. "PPBS and Some Related Management Systems In Great Britain," *Libri,* 23 (1973) 75-79.

Schultz, Jon S. "Program Budgeting and Work Measurement for Law Libraries," *Law Library Journal,* 63 (August, 1970) 353-62.

Sellers, D. Y. "Basic Planning and Budgeting Concepts for Special Libraries," *Special Libraries,* 64 (Fall, 1973) 70-75.

Shields, Gerald R. and Burke, J. Gordon (eds.). *Budgeting for Accountability in Libraries: A Selection of Readings.* Metuchen, New Jersey: Scarecrow Press, 1974.

Smith, J. C. Planning Library Facilities and Services Within Budgetary Constraints," *Southeastern Librarian,* 21 (Summer, 1971) 118-22.

Somers, G. A. "Planning—Programming—Budgeting Systems: Panacea or Pandora's Box?" *Wisconsin Library Bulletin*, 69 (January, 1973) 13-14.

Spencer, M. "Projecting Program Costs Over an Adequate Time Horizon," Paper presented at an Institute on Program Planning and Budgeting Systems for Libraries at Wayne State University, Detroit, Michigan, Department of Library Science, Spring, 1968. (Bethesda, Md., ERIC Document Reproduction Service ED 045 119).

Stitleman, Leonard. "Cost Utility Analysis Applied to Library Budgeting." Paper presented at an Institute on Program Planning and Budgeting Systems for Libraries at Wayne State University, Detroit, Michigan, Department of Library Science, Spring, 1968. (Bethesda, Md., ERIC Document Reproduction Service ED 045 126.)

Sturtz, Charles. "The Difference Between Conventional Budgeting and PPB." Paper presented at an Institute on Program Planning and Budgeting Systems for Libraries at Wayne State University, Detroit, Michigan, Department of Library Science, Spring, 1968. (Bethesda, Md., ERIC Document Reproduction Service Ed 045 115.)

Summers, William. "A Change in Budgetary Thinking," *American Libraries*, 2 (December, 1971) 1174-80.

Surrey and Sussex Libraries in Cooperation. *Planning—Programming—Budgeting Systems: A Bibliography*. SASLIC, 1971.

Thomas, Pauline. *Technion Library Systems Study*. Armonk, New York: International Business Machines Corp., 1976.

Tudor, Dean. *Planning—Programming—Budgeting Systems*. (Exchange Bibliography #121.) Monticello, Illinois: Council of Planning Librarians, 1970.

———. *Planning—Programming—Budgeting Systems*. (Exchange Bibliography #183. A Supplement to Exchange Bibliography #121.) Monticello, Illinois: Council of Planning Librarians, 1971.

———. *Planning—Programming—Budgeting Systems*. (Exchange Bibliography #289.) Monticello, Illinois: Council of Planning Librarians, 1972.

———. "Special Library Budget," (bibliography), *Special Libraries*, 63 (November, 1972) 517-27.

J.S. Department of Health, Education and Welfare, Education Office. *Statewide Long-Range Planning for Libraries.* Report of Conference, September 19-22, 1965, Chicago, Illinois, sponsored by Library Services Branch; edited by Herbert A. Carl. Washington, D.C., 1966.

/iebrock, Ingo. "PPB—An Aid to Decision-Making." In *Special Libraries Association, Toronto Chapter, Bulletin*, 31 (1971) 5-11.

Vashington State Library. *Performance Budgeting Bibliography Including Planning—Programming—Budgeting*. Olympia, Washington: State Library, 1969.

Veaver, Barbara F. *Programming Planning is the Name of the Game. Final Report, First Year Project CLASP*. Worcester, Mass.: Central Massachusetts Regional Library System, 1975. (Bethesda, Md., ERIC Document Reproduction Service ED 116 686.)

Vedgeworth, R. "Budgeting for School Media Centers," *School Libraries*, 20 (Spring, 1971) 29-36.

Vilkinson, J. P. "Dollar Decisions: LAD Preconference Institute of the 1971 ALA Dallas Conference," *IPLO Quarterly, 13* (October, 1971) 98-102.

'oung, Harold C. *Exploratory Study of Planning, Programming, Budgeting Systems (PPBS) in University Libraries Having Membership in the Association of Research Libraries*. Unpublished Ph.D. dissertation, University of Michigan, 1974. Also with title: *Planning, Programming, Budgeting Systems in Academic Libraries; an Exploratory Study of PPBS in University Libraries Having Membership in the Association of Research Libraries.* Gale Research, 1976.

'oung, Helen. "Performance and Program Budgeting: An Annotated Bibliography," *ALA Bulletin*, 61 (January, 1967) 63-67.

Appendix 7

Index

Appendix 8

Labor Analysis for 12 CSUC Libraries, 5 Months (see Microfiche in Pocket on Back Cover

The attached microfiche contain, in the pocket inside the back cover, 5 months of data from 12 libraries in the CSUC system representing all personnel hours for those libraries during the period March-June, 1979.